A
CENTENNIAL HISTORY

of

ALLEGHANY COUNTY

VIRGINIA

By OREN F. MORTON, B. LIT.

ORIGINALLY PUBLISHED
Dayton, Virginia
J. K. RUEBUSH COMPANY
1923

Please direct all correspondence and orders to:

www.southernhistoricalpress.com
or
SOUTHERN HISTORICAL PRESS, Inc.
PO BOX 1267
375 West Broad Street
Greenville, SC   29601
southernhistoricalpress@gmail.com

Originally published: Dayton, VA 1923
ISBN #0-89308-926-5
All rights Reserved.
Printed in the United States of America

CONTENTS

APPENDIX

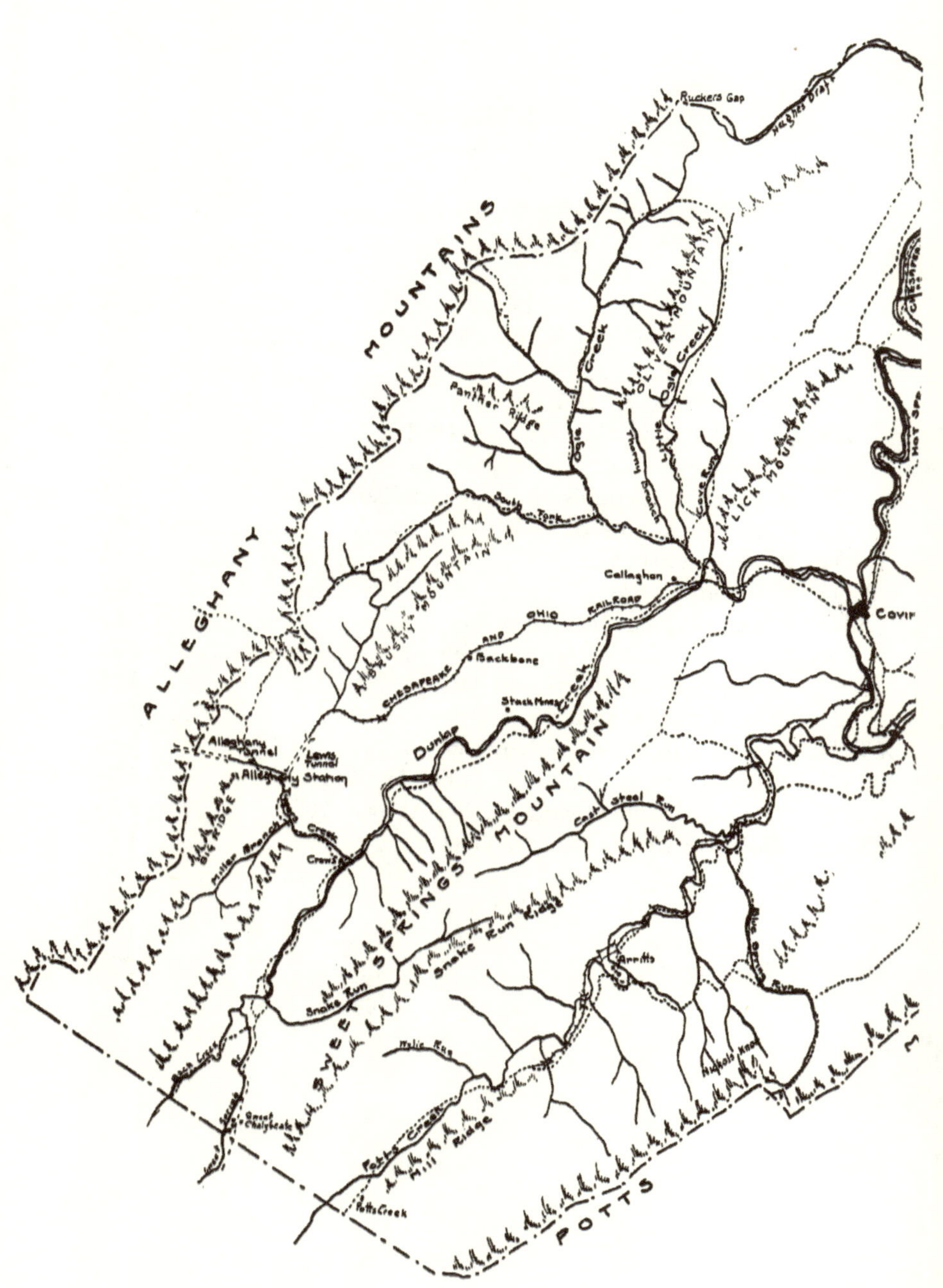

MOUNTAINS
ALLEGHANY
Ruckers Gap
Hughes Draft
OLIVER MOUNTAIN
Owl Creek
Little
Panther Ridge
Ogle Creek
Cove Run
LICK MOUNTAIN
Hot Sp.
South Fork
Callaghan
Covin
OHIO
RAILROAD
AND
Backbone
CHESAPEAKE
ROUGHY MOUNTAIN
Stack Mines Creek
Stack Mines
Dunlap
Alleghany Tunnel
Lewis Tunnel
Alleghany Station
Cook Steel Run
BIG RIDGE
Creek
Miller Branch
Crows
SWEET SPRINGS MOUNTAIN
Snake Run Ridge
Arritts
Run
Snake Run
Holm Run
Nicholls Knob
Green Creek
Sweet Chalybeate
Potts Creek
Hill Ridge
Potts Creek
POTTS

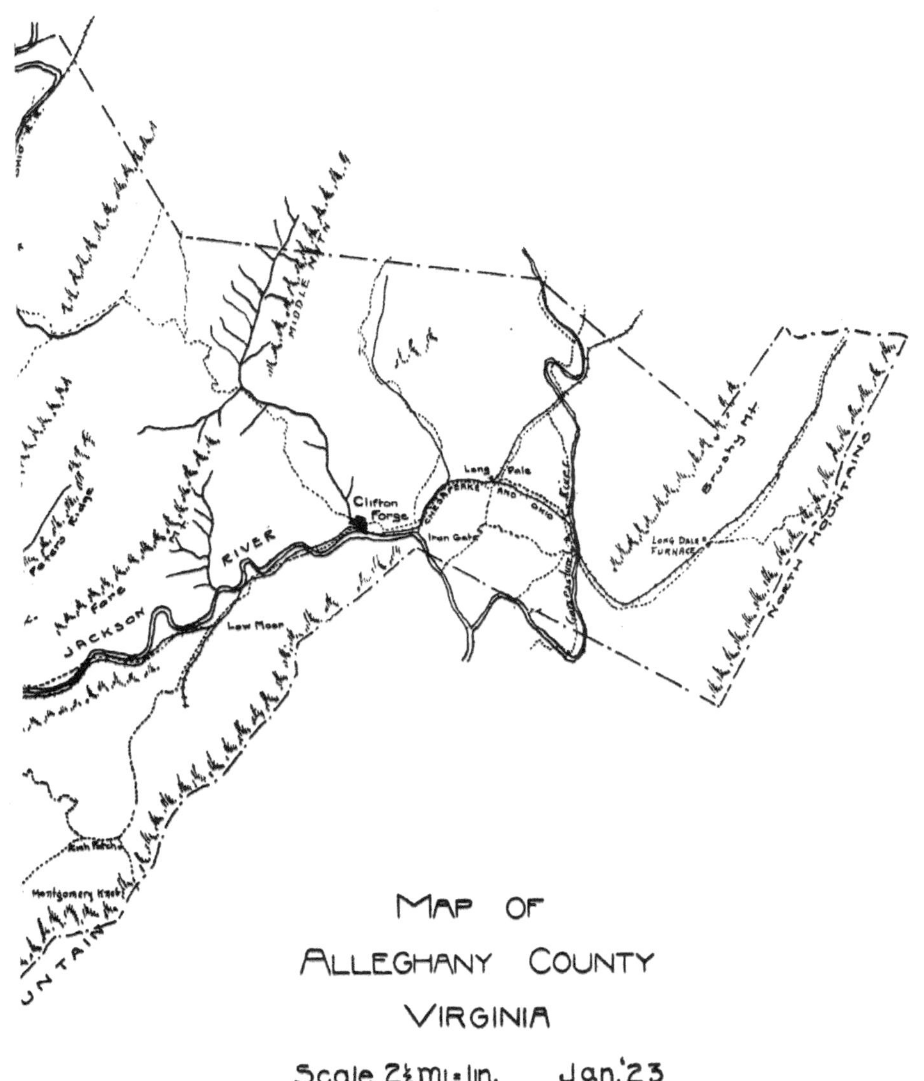

Map of
Alleghany County
Virginia
Scale 2½ mi = 1 in.   Jan. '23

A CENTENNIAL HISTORY OF ALLEGHANY COUNTY

I

THE GEOGRAPHY OF ALLEGHANY

OUT OF nearly three thousand counties in the American Union, the only ones bearing the name of its best known mountain system are in Virginia, Pennsylvania, and New York. The first of these three lies in the midst of the Appalachian ridges. In outline it is irregular. From the northeast corner to the southwestern, Alleghany county extends forty-three miles. The extreme breadth is eighteen miles. The area is 458 square miles, or 293,120 acres. The bordering counties in Virginia are Bath, Botetourt, Craig, and Rockbridge. Those in West Virginia are Greenbrier and Monroe. From the county seat it is 205 miles by rail to the capital of Virginia, 164 miles to the capital of West Virginia, and 221 miles to the capital of the United States.

The magisterial districts are Boiling Spring in the south, Covington in the northwest, and Clifton in the northeast. The city of Clifton Forge is politically independent of Alleghany county, but is geographically a part of Clifton district.

The western limit of the county is the Alleghany Front, the central ridge of the Appalachian system. It is a natural boundary, since it divides the waters flowing into the Atlantic from those feeding the Mississippi River. In the extreme east is North Mountain, the western limit to the Valley of Virginia. As far north as the vicinity of Covington, the uplift between Dunlap and Potts creeks is called Peter's Mountain. Potts Mountain separates the upper valley of Potts Creek from Craig county. The other ridges within the county or on the eastern border bear a variety of local names.

The lowest altitude—almost precisely 1,000 feet—occurs on Jackson's River at Iron Gate. The valley levels vary from 1,000 feet to more than 2,000. Clifton Forge is 1,047 feet above sea level, and Covington is 1,225 feet. Lick Mountain, just west of

Covington, rises to a height of 2,980 feet. The greatest elevations are Adcock's Knob in North Mountain, 3,573 feet, Hickory Knob in the Alleghany Front, 3,381 feet high, and an unnamed prominence, four miles north of Hickory Knob, with an altitude of 3,451 feet.

The entire county is watered by the James, known as Jackson's River above its junction with the Cowpasture. Within Alleghany county this stream has a course of thirty-four miles. After holding for a long distance the same general direction as the Alleghany Front, Jackson's River makes a sharp bend, two miles below Covington, and flows northeastwardly to the Iron Gate, where it turns to the southeast. At Covington it is joined by Dunlap Creek, and at the point of its great bend by Potts Creek. These two affluents are large enough to be known as rivers. They are parallel streams and flow to the northeast. Two miles below Iron Gate, Jackson's River meets the Cowpasture, which has a very crooked course of ten miles in the east of Alleghany county. It is almost as long and large as its companion, but its only important tributaries in this county are Padd's and Simpson's creeks. Other tributaries of Jackson's River are Falling Springs Run, Smith Creek, and Wilson's Creek.

Nearly always the streams of Alleghany county are rapid. Except for the influence of industrial operations, they are as generally clear. Springs, sometimes of freestone water and sometimes of limestone, are numerous. But in the limestone belts, much of the rainfall sinks into underground channels, reappearing in powerful springs at the base level of the valleys. A spring at Low Moor is said to have a flow of 500 gallons a minute.

The sandstones, limestones, and shales belong to some of the oldest formations known to American geology. They are too old to contain coal, petroleum, or natural gas, yet they include iron ores, porcelain, and brick clays, blue and magnesian limestones, cement rock, pyrites, marl, commercial slate, and even a deposit that resembles marble.

This county is very mountainous, and not one-fourth of its surface is even fairly adapted to tillage. Foremost in fertility but least is extent is the dark, rich loam of the very limited river and creek bottoms. The benches and more level tracts of upland are thinner and often stony, and where a limestone base is not present they are less fertile. Good soil sometimes occurs on the higher slopes, but in general the proper use of the mountain surface is as pasture ground or forest reserve.

The mountain ranges by which Alleghany is inclosed protect this county from the great atmospheric disturbances that use the immense basin of the Mississippi as a playground. They also shield it from the east winds that are so unpleasant on the Atlantic coast. Therefore the local climate is not one of extremes. It is of mountain quality with respect to a pleasant, tonic air. Yet it cannot be defined as a cold climate, since the river bottoms lie at a lower level than portions of the Shenandoah Valley. The temperatures at Clifton Forge and Covington are about the same as at Staunton, where the mean is thirty-five degrees for the winter, seventy-five for the summer, and fifty-five for the year. Alleghany is a healthful region, although the industrial operations impart a somewhat unpleasant quality to the morning fogs along Jackson's River.

When this county was a wilderness, there was much more animal life than there is now. The buffalo and the elk were gone when the Declaration of American Independence was written. The wolf, once a great scourge to the young livestock, held his ground until within the recollection of people now living. The puma, or panther, a larger but less troublesome beast of prey, is also locally extinct. The wildcat, the fox, and an occasional black bear still linger, and now and then an eagle disports himself in the sky. Neither have the deer utterly vanished. Small mammals are the raccoon, the opossum, the ground hog, the muskrat, the mink, the cottontail, the gray squirrel, the chipmunk, and the bat. Turkeys, pheasants, quail, and other game birds have declined in numbers. Buzzards and hawks are perhaps as numerous as ever, but the small migratory birds that visit us during the warm season are not so plentiful as a keeping down of the insect life requires. Rattlesnakes and copperheads are few, except in the localities they habitually haunt. In the streams which remain clear are fish in some variety.

As is everywhere the case among the Alleghanies, nature covers every hill and valley with forest when left to herself. Small pines grow on thin land and in the dry, thirsty soil of the slate ridges, but the trees which usually predominate are those that shed their leaves on the approach of winter. A varied undergrowth of small trees, shrubs, and vines is more in evidence now than when white settlement began. Among the wild fruits are the pawpaw, the grape, the blackberry, the huckleberry, the raspberry, the strawberry, and the teaberry, or wintergreen.

The best grass is found in the bottoms and on the limestone uplands. These soils, especially the bottoms, are likewise best adapted to tillage; and it is here that the largest fields of corn and grain are to be seen.

The scenic beauty of Appalachian America is well known to the observant tourist. The landscape is never monotonous, because there is a change with each new point of observation. When the woodlands of this county are in summer foliage, the contour of the many ridges assumes a most pleasing appearance.

II

IN THE DAY OF THE PATHFINDER

Fort Henry, built where the city of Petersburg now stands, lay in 1671 on the inland line of white settlement in Virginia. The commandant knew there was money in trading with the Indians, and the exploring party he sent out in that year penetrated to the falls of New River. But for almost fifty years later, our knowledge of the country west of the Blue Ridge is almost limited to the journal kept by the party just mentioned, and to a narrative of disputed trustworthiness written about the same time by John Lederer, a German visitor. From the east the Blue Ridge looks rather rugged and lofty, and was thought almost impossible to cross. The country on the west was believed to be a good place to let alone.

In 1716 Alexander Spottswood, governor of Virginia, headed a party of exploration. He set out from Williamsburg, then the capital of the colony. After leaving Fredericksburg there was no road. The Blue Ridge was almost certainly crossed by way of Swift Run Gap, and near where Elkton now stands the west bank of the South Branch of the Shenandoah was reached. The governor and his gay companions now uncorked the large variety of liquors they had brought with them. Probably not enough firewater remained for another big drunk, and the aristocrats of the party seem to have had enough of the wilderness. Further exploration was left to the rangers attached to the expedition.

But the Valley of Virginia was now officially discovered, for it had been penetrated by men in authority. "New Virginia," as the land beyond the mountains was first called, was explored with some rapidity, and was found to be an attractive region. It was stocked with game, the lowlands were a prairie, and no Indians were seen except hunting parties. Yet very few of the early settlers came from east of the Blue Ridge. The Tidewater was a land of tobacco plantations. Every estate lay on or near some river that was always navigable for sea-going vessels. The planter did not like the idea of moving 150 miles beyond the heads of navigation. Immigration from England had grown small, and the broad belt between the Blue Ridge and navigable water was slow to fill up.

Within a dozen years after the visit by Spottswood there was a very considerable movement into the Valley of Virginia. The larger share of the settlers came from the north of Ireland. A smaller share came from Switzerland and other regions along the upper course of the river Rhine. Nearly all these people landed at Philadelphia, then the largest city of the colonies.

A little more than a century earlier, the Irish province of Ulster was almost emptied of its native population by the English. The choicest lands were confiscated, and were then colonized from the other side of the Irish Sea. The larger portion of the newcomers were from the southwest of Scotland, but there were many from the north of England. In this immigration were some French Protestants and a few Welch. No inconsiderable number of the native Irish became identified with the new people by reason of their acceptance of the Presbyterian faith. The mixture became known to history as the Scotch-Irish stock. It was a plain, hardy, industrious element, and Ulster became prosperous.

Yet there was a nagging persecution, partly religious and partly industrial, of the Scotch-Irish people. The immigrants were Presbyterians and the native Irish were Catholics. The former as well as the latter felt the heavy hand of a government which placed under heavy disabilities those who did not adhere to the Church of England. The Presbyterian ministers were not permitted to perform the marriage ceremony, and there were times when their congregations could not safely meet in public. The industrial persecution was because the thrift and industry of the Ulster people made them competitors of the English. One result was the ruin of their linen industry. The persecution did not wholly cease till 1782, and then only because of the success of the American Revolution.

To get away from this harsh and inconsiderate treatment, the people of Ulster flocked to America by thousands. But in the settled southeast corner of Pennsylvania there was little room for the strangers and little real welcome. They moved inland, until they were beyond the first range of mountains, and by doing so they pushed westward the American frontier. They took kindly to the mountains, because they came from a country of hills. They took naturally to pioneering, because they were used to a simple life. They were overcomers by nature, and in Appalachian America they proceeded to subdue the forest, the beasts of prey, the Indians, the French, and the British.

The Blue Ridge is nearer the seaboard in Pennsylvania than in Virginia. The Valley of Virginia is but a continuation of the broad Cumberland Valley. Nature, aided by Indian paths used for centuries, had thus provided an easy line of travel to the South. Advertisements extolling New Virginia caused many of the immigrants from Europe to pour into the uninhabited region. These people thus reached Virginia by a side entrance, and without coming into direct touch with the English element forming almost wholly the white population of Tidewater. Thus it is easy to understand why there has always been a very perceptible difference between the two sections of Virginia separated by the Blue Ridge. Nevertheless, the laws and institutions of the colony began at once to exert an assimilating influence.

Only eleven years after Spottswood's revel on the bank of South River, five planters of Tidewater petitioned the Governor and his Council to be granted 50,000 acres on "the head branches of James River to the west and northwestward of the Cowpasture." It seems somewhat curious to read of an attempt to colonize the valley of the James above Iron Gate five years before there was any settlement at Staunton or within thirty miles of that point. However, the Ulstermen did not know what to think of wild land that was not covered with forest. The grassy plains of the Shenandoah were not so attractive to them as we might suppose. They preferred bottom land along a creek. Here they were sure of water, and the hills on either side were certain to supply wood. The petition of the five planters does not seem to have been acted upon. They had engaged other men to do the exploring.

In the summer of 1732 John Lewis settled a mile north from where Staunton soon arose. He was a man of means and leadership, and was accompanied by some thirty of his Ulster friends. The tide in this direction became rapid. Within twelve years several hundred families of the Scotch-Irish were scattered over the present counties of Augusta, Rockingham, and Rockbridge, and others were pressing toward Roanoke and the Holston.

For two years after Lewis and his companions came to Lewis Creek they were living in a "no man's land." Until 1720 no organized county included any part of the region behind the Blue

Ridge. Spottsylvania was then established, but of the Valley of Virginia it took in only that small strip lying wholly east of South River and between lines meeting it a little below Port Republic and a little above Front Royal. In 1734 Spottsylvania was reduced to its present dimensions, the remaining and much larger portion receiving the name of Orange. Yet the Act of Assembly creating Orange county made it cover the entire region west of the Blue Ridge, so far as it lay within the boundaries claimed by Virginia. In 1738 the summit of the Blue Ridge was made the western line of Orange. The vast remainder of its territory was now erected into the counties of Frederick and Augusta, the line dividing them running from the Fairfax Stone at the southern extremity of the western end of Maryland to the source of the stream rising in the northwest corner of Greene county. The present boundary between Rockingham and Shenandoah is a part of this line. But until there should be a larger population west of the mountains, the new counties were styled the districts of Frederick and Augusta, and were left under the jurisdiction of Orange. It was not until the last month of 1745 that separate county government was organized in Augusta. The new county contained about 4,000 people scattered over a wide area.

The first curtailment of Augusta took place in 1769, when Botetourt came into existence. The line between the old county and the new ran through the middle of the present county of Rockbridge. From the source of Kerr's Creek it ran northwestwardly to the Ohio River, crossing Warm Springs valley in Bath in the vicinity of Dunn's Gap. Rockbridge, Rockingham, and Greenbrier were set apart in 1777, Bath in 1790, and Monroe in 1799.

From the beginning of settlement until the end of 1769, what is now Alleghany county lay in Augusta. During the next twenty years it lay wholly in Botetourt. From 1790 until 1822 the greater part lay in Bath. From 1802 to 1822 the northern line of Monroe crossed the basin of Dunlap Creek eight miles below the present line. That portion of the Alleghany area not lying in Bath or in Monroe continued to be a part of Botetourt.

By "Alleghany area" is meant the region inclosed by the boundary of Alleghany county, and just as though that boundary were in existence at the time of white settlement.

III

EARLY LAND PATENTS

THE HEADRIGHT LAW of Virginia in the colonial period rested on the same principle as the present homestead law of the national government. If the immigrant was of age and could prove he had paid the cost of his passage from Europe, he was entitled to fifty acres of the public domain. He was entitled to fifty acres more for each adult male member of his household. To perfect his title, he was expected to settle on the land, to improve at least six per cent. of the acreage, and to pay each year a quitrent of ten shillings ($1.67) on each fifty acres. Fifty acres was also the amount of public land which might be taken up by a private soldier of the Indian wars, if he availed himself of a certain proclamation issued in 1763.

There was another way of disposing of the public domain. The royal governor, with the concurrence of his Council, might grant a block of land to an individual, or to a group of men acting as a company. There was supposed to be a limit to the price per acre which the grantee might charge to buyers. Deeds were issued in the name of the grantee, but in theory the object of this method was to settle a definite number of families on the grant within a stated time. In practice there was created a non-resident proprietorship, enabling influential citizens to corner huge blocks of the most desirable land, and to exact from the people settling thereon sums of money altogether out of proportion to the services rendered. The minimum price limit was often violated. Furthermore, the colonial government was very lenient toward its favorites in enforcing forfeiture where there was a failure to comply with the conditions named in the order of council.

The headright method was equitable. It assumed that the settler was capable of choosing land for himself. Its tendency was to fill Virginia with a substantial class of citizens. The other method thrust a needless intermediary between the public land and the settler, and compelled the latter to pay tribute to this intermediary. It was also monopolistic, because it practically withdrew the choice land from free settlement. The homeseeker had to pay the price demanded or plunge farther into the wilderness. In many an instance he made the latter choice, and in consequence a thin fringe of settlement was pushed forward too rapidly for convenience or safety.

In Alleghany the headright law had scarcely a chance to cut any figure. As for the corn right, or tomahawk right, which we sometimes read of, it did not acquire a recognized status until 1766, and it had little bearing on the settlement of this county.

The following paragraph occurs in a petition presented to the Virginia Legislature by some citizens of Botetourt in 1779. The Alleghany area was then included in Botetourt. There is no doubt that the petition voiced a very prevalent feeling:

"A few artful monopolizers, possessed of immense sums of money, which they have accumulated by taking advantage of the necessities of individuals, have it in their power to engross the greatest part of the public lands on this side of the Ohio, whilst the brave soldier is limited to a small portion, and the virtuous citizen is implicitly debarred from getting any at all."

An order of council, dated October 29, 1743, placed 30,000 acres of public land in the control of James and Henry Robinson, James Wood, and Thomas and Andrew Lewis. The Robinsons were aristocratic planters of Tidewater Virginia. Colonel Wood was the surveyor of Frederick county and a prominent land monopolist. These names occur among the grantees because it was very important to secure the aid of influential men who stood in with those in places of authority, and could therefore put the project "across." Thomas and Andrew Lewis, then twenty-five and twenty-three years old, respectively, were sons of Colonel John Lewis, the leader in the settlement of Augusta. They seem to have been the only active members of the syndicate, and they did the surveying.

The order of council authorized the Lewis brothers and their partners to survey the 30,000 acres in an indefinite number of tracts, all lying in the basin of the James above the mouth of the Cowpasture. The territory drained by the waters passing the confluence covers the whole of Alleghany, nearly all of Bath, half of Highland, and a small part of Monroe. Of the ninety-one separate tracts surveyed by the Lewises in 1745-46 only about fifteen lie in Alleghany. With the others we are not concerned in the present volume.

These original surveys average about 300 acres. Without exception they are choice tracts of river bottom. Little prime land in the entire basin is not included in the patents based upon them. Consequently the holdings under the Lewis order of council constitute the key to the early history of the upper basin of the James. The men taking up these parcels were persons of enterprise and resource. They were capable of carrying on a plantation rather than a farm. The various holdings may indeed be classed as plantations, and in nearly or quite every instance the proprietors became the owners of slaves and the masters of indentured servants. As a matter of course these early comers were relatively well-to-do. They were influential, socially and politically, and their names frequently appear among the men holding civil office or commanding the militia.

The further progress of private ownership in this district may be read in the patents for the remaining fragments of river-bottom and the more desirable tracts of upland. Much of the later patenting went to the enlargement of the original estates. And since the subsequent surveys were not always made into new farms, their history is of far less interest than that of the primary surveys.

We have mentioned that the surveying of the ninety-one tracts took place in 1745-46. The county surveyor did not return to the upper James until four years had elapsed. In 1750 and 1751 he surveyed thirty-seven more tracts, which aggregate not quite 2,000 acres. Those of above 100 acres number only four. Twelve were taken by settlers already here. Some others were seemingly taken by junior members of the pioneer families. During the next four years, which interval brings us to the outbreak of the French and Indian war, the new surveys are still fewer. This marked falling off in the amount of land surveyed tells a very plain story. Nearly all the best lands were taken at the outset. The later surveys, so far as associated with the names of later comers, appear to indicate men of less stability and more limited means.

It is not to be assumed that any stated acreage, as put down in the surveyor's book, is a close approximation to the actual amount. The Lewises knew how to survey, but the wilderness was broad and an acre meant little unless it were a deficient acre. If the size of a piece were understated, more tracts could be squeezed into the grant. So the length of a course was sometimes paced off or guessed at. An open line was occasionally drawn, although in violation of the instructions given to surveyors. It is significant that in nearly or quite every case the true area, as determined by subsequent survey, overruns the area first reported, sometimes to a very considerable extent. The loose way in which the courses were often run appears in the frequency with which the phrase, "containing by estimation," is found in the deeds based on the primary surveys.

In the surveys not held until a purchaser should appear, the surveyor entered this form: "Now in possession of ——— ———." This does not necessarily imply that the person named was already living on the land, or indeed that he ever lived on it. Some of the claimants lived in the settlements east of Shenandoah Mountain. They took additional land in the newer settlements for the purpose of speculation or to provide for their sons.

When did the very earliest settlers come into the Alleghany area? It is possible to give a very close answer. Alexander Dunlap located near the site of Goshen about 1742. We are told he was the earliest settler on the Great Calfpasture, and that no one had yet located any farther west. A few men had cabins on the Cowpasture in 1745. These settlers came in 1744, possibly in 1743. Joseph Carpenter came with Peter Wright from New York in the spring of 1746. We have no knowledge of any earlier permanent settlers on the lower course of Jackson's River. A number of homeseekers came in 1746, or very shortly afterward, and when the Indian war of 1754 broke out, there was quite a settlement on Jackson's River within the Alleghany area and on the lower course of Dunlap Creek.

Meanwhile several families seem to have settled on the Cowpasture below Griffith's Knob, but our knowledge of their locations is very unsatisfactory. Indeed, so early as 1741, John Grome had patented 400 acres at the mouth of this river. But Grome was a non-resident, being an influential planter of Tuckahoe Virginia. In the suit of James Simpson against Margaret Campbell, 1756, a number of persons are named as inhabitants of the lower Cowpasture, and some of them undoubtedly belong to the Alleghany area. The names are as follows: Hugh and William Martin; William, Agnes, and Samuel McMurry; Edward Edwards; William, Mary, and Robert Gillespie; Patrick Carrigan; James Beard; James Scott; Margaret Coherin; Thomas Simpson; James Arbuckle and Margaret his wife; and Thomas Fitzpatrick.

It is significant that the muster rolls of the Augusta militia for 1742 do not include the names that soon afterward appear in the long valleys above Iron Gate. The first official recognition of any settlers in this region was in February, 1745, when the court of Orange appointed James Mayse a constable for the lower Cowpasture and the neighboring districts. The same court, May 23, 1745, instructed John Lewis to list "all the Inhabitants of the Cow and Calf Pastures and the Settlers back of the same."

Peter Wright's survey of 286 acres covered the bottom on which the principal part of Covington is built. In 1792 he divided the land between his sons, John and William. Not many years afterward the Wrights went West. We are told that one of them sold his land to George Sibley for $500 in cash, a wagon and two horses, and a barrel of whiskey, using the wagon and team to move to the vicinity of Indianapolis. The Peter Wright of 1782 was seemingly the most wealthy man in the valley.

The long survey of 782 acres taken by Joseph Carpenter began very near the railroad bridge at the south border of Covington, and extended down the river so as to include the bend beginning near the mouth of Potts Creek. The Carpenter holdings also took in the fine bottom on the south side of the railroad at Mallow Station. In 1764 the pioneer divided 464 acres equally between his sons, Joseph, Jr., and Solomon, each paying a consideration of ten pounds. But in 1773 Solomon sold 160 acres to his brother-in-law, John Mann, for 130 pounds. A year earlier this piece had been purchased at public sale by William Hughart for ninety pounds ($300). John Mann had already bought 230 acres in 1762 for seventy pounds. Jeremiah Seeley, another son-in-law, took a survey of 100 acres at the mouth of Dry Run in 1754. But Seeley left the neighborhood during the Indian war and the land was patented by Peter Wright.

A Lewis survey of 270 acres at the mouth of Dunlap Creek was taken by Arthur (Alexander?) Dunlap, but patented by William Jackson, and in 1772 sold to Richard Morris for 100 pounds. A neighboring tract of 100 acres was patented by William Dunlap in 1750. In the same year Adam Dickenson patented 875 acres lying around Callaghan Station. Another Lewis survey on Dunlap Creek was patented by his son, John Dickenson, but passed to Andrew and Thomas Lewis. It was not until 1760 that anyone settled at the head of this stream.

The Lewis surveys on Jackson's River above the site of Covington and below the vicinity of the line of Bath county aggregate about 2,000 acres. The original owners were Robert Armstrong, Robert Crockett, David Davis, James Ewing, William Jameson, James Montgomery, and George Wilson. With the exception of Armstrong and possibly Montgomery, these men had their homes on the Calfpasture or elsewhere. Armstrong lived in the bend just below the Bath line. The Armstrong holdings became extensive and the family prosperous. James Montgomery appears to be the man of that name who was killed by Indians.

Of the two surveys by Crockett, one was at the mouth of Cedar Creek, the other above the mouth of Falling Spring Run. The former was acquired by James Fitzpatrick in 1762. The latter passed into the hands of the Hamiltons and Kincaids. The Davis land was on the east side of the river at the mouth of Falling Spring Run. It passed to William Mann in 1761, and was sold by him to John Robinson in 1784 for only $200. The Ewing survey was patented by Archibald Armstrong. The Jameson land cornered on Ewing's. It was purchased in 1765 by Archibald Armstrong, Sr., and sold by him in 1767 to Robert Armstrong, Sr. The Montgomery tract was patented in 1750 by Charles Walker. The Wilson land was finally bought in 1791 by Moses Mann, who paid 250 pounds for it.

In 1769 Colonel William Preston, a non-resident, took out five patents on Potts Creek, these amounting to 995 acres.

The following particulars are from some of the early deeds recorded in Botetourt.

Dennis Callaghan bought of Hugh McDonald and Mary, his wife, seventy acres on Ugly, surveyed 1773. Price, 100 pounds.

Michael Cairns from Bedford bought of Jeremiah Seeley and Hannah, his wife, for 350 pounds, fourteen acres of the homestead adjoining Robert Shanklin, 1771. The high price is because of depreciated paper money.

Jeremiah Carpenter of Greenbrier, for 300 pounds, bought of Moses Mann, son of John, deceased, and Fanny, wife of Moses, 160 acres, 1779.

Thomas Carpenter bought of William P. Martin of Halifax county 115 acres on Potts Creek, 1787, for 100 pounds.

In 1787, John Craig gave power of attorney to Moses Mann to sell his half interest in a place on Brush Creek, a branch of Dunlap. The other half interest belonged to Joseph Hunter, a tory.

John Dickenson of Augusta bought of Jeremiah and Hannah Seeley, 1772, 200 acres on Falling Spring Run for 100 pounds.

James Elliott bought of William Mann and Jean his wife, 1773, for fifty-five pounds, forty-nine acres on Jackson's River below the mouth of Back Creek.

David Glassburn bought of Thomas Carpenter, 1784, fifty acres on Jackson's River for 100 pounds.

William Griffith bought of James Milligan and Elizabeth his wife, 1776, for 103 pounds, forty-four acres on the Cowpasture, patented 1767.

Aron Hughes bought of William Gillespie and Mary his wife, 1780, for 10,000 pounds (depreciated money), 320 acres on the Cowpasture.

Andrew Kincade bought of William Hamilton of Greenbrier, 1780, for 400 pounds, 283 acres on Jackson's River.

William Kincade bought of Andrew Kincade and Mary his wife, 1785, for 200 pounds, 110 acres on Jackson's River.

William Larence bought of James Robison and Elizabeth his wife, 1775, ninety-five acres on west side Camp Mountain for ninety-five pounds.

Michael Mallow bought of Zopher Carpenter and Mary his wife and David Glassburn and Elizabeth his wife, 1789, 130 acres on north side Jackson's River for 275 pounds.

William Mann bought of Jacob Persinger and Catherine his wife, 1772, for twenty-four pounds, 115 acres on Indian Draft of James River.

Moses Mann bought of James Boggs and Margaret his wife, of Greenbrier, 1784, for 100 pounds, a tract on Jackson's River adjoining Richard Morris and Andrew Kinkead. The acreage is not stated.

John McCalister bought of James Robinson, 1775, for fifty-five pounds, 117 acres on Dunlap.

Edward McMullin bought of Andrew Lewis, 1772, 325 acres on Dunlap for thirty pounds ($100).

John Neel bought of Edward McMullin and Sarah his wife, 1780, fifty-two acres on Dunlap for forty pounds.

Jacob Persinger bought of William McMurray, 1770, twenty acres on McMurray's Creek, a branch of the Cowpasture. Consideration unnamed.

Jacob Persinger bought of William Thompson, executor of James Patton, 1771, for twenty-five pounds, forty-four acres on Willson's Creek of James River.

Jacob Persinger, Sr., sold land on Nelson's (Wilson's?) Creek, a branch of James, 1775, to John Hansberger.

Jacob Persinger, Jr., bought of James Williams of Montgomery county, 1777, 110 acres on Potts Creek for thirty-five pounds.

James Robinson bought of Alexander Dunlap and Agnes his wife, of Clover Lick, Augusta county, 1773, for fifty pounds, 100 acres at mouth of Dunlap.

John Robinson bought of Moses Mann and Fanny his wife, 1784, 230 acres on Jackson's River for sixty pounds.

John Scott bought of Edward and Sarah McMullin, 1786, thirty-six acres on Jackson's River above Archibald Armstrong and below Robert McClintock for sixty-five pounds.

William Scott bought of Jonathan and Mary Taylor, 1783, a parcel on Potts for 150 pounds.

Jonathan Smith bought of William Whooley and Barbara his wife, 1782, ninety-three acres on Potts for 1,400 pounds.

George Stout bought of William Gillespie and Mary his wife, 1780, fifty acres on Jackson's River for 1,000 pounds.

We next mention the land patents in the Alleghany area granted prior to 1770. Name of patentee, position, acreage, and date of patent are given in consecutive order.

Abercromby, Robert—East side Jackson's River at mouth Falling Spring—320—1760.

Armstrong, Archibald—Jackson's River—254—1760.

Armstrong, Robert—Jackson's River—270—1760.

Beard, James—NW side lower Pasture river—24—1763.

Carpenter, Joseph—Jackson's River—782—1750.

Carpenter, Zopher—NW side Jackson's River—135—1763.

Clendennin, Thomas—Jackson's River—68—1757.

Dickenson, Adam—Meadow (Dunlap) Creek—875—1750.

Dickenson, John—great meadows on Meadow Creek—490—1760.

Dickenson, John—Peters (Dunlap) Creek—16—1763.

Dickenson, John—Peter's Creek—33—1763.

Dunlap, William—mouth of Meadow Creek of Jackson's River—100—1750.

Hughart, Thomas—SE side Jackson's River—65—1760.

Jameson, John—Jackson's River—280—1760.

Mann, William—Jackson's River below Back Creek—49—1765.

McCallister, James—Jackson's River—100—1760.

McCutchen, William—mouth of Cedar—169—1760?

McMurry, William—McMurry Creek of Cowpasture—20—1761.

Montgomery, James—NW side Jackson's River—54—1757.

Morris, Richard—Jackson's River below Armstrong—93—1769.

Patton, James—branch of Peter's Creek—190—1750.

Preston, William—Potts Creek—250—1769.

Preston, William—Potts below Laurel Gap—150—1769.

Preston, William—Potts—200—1769.

Preston, William—Potts at Walnut Bottom—300—1769.

Preston, William—Potts—95—1769.

Scott, James—S side Jackson's River—24—1765.

Scott, James—SE side Cowpasture—18—1765.

Scott, James—both sides Cowpasture—490—1751.

Simpson, James—SE side Cowpasture—300—1761.

Walker, Charles—Jackson's River—220—1750.

Wright, Peter—Jackson's River—286—1750.

Wright, Peter—W side Jackson's River—64—1761.

Wright, Peter—Potts Creek—100—1767.

Some later patents are these:

William Hunter—Dunlap—60—1781.

Samuel Dew—Potts Creek (Michael Aritt land)—2274—1789.

James McAllister—Dunlap—200—1793.

Christopher McPherson—Potts—(?)—1793.

Eve Johnson—Potts (George Wolf land)—60—1793.

Samuel Logner—Dunlap—60—1793.

John Johnson—Karnes Run (formerly Whooley's Run)—1,000—1795.

Jacob Persinger—Rich Patch—924—1798.

IV

LIFE IN THE PIONEER DAYS

IN NEARLY every instance, the place of birth of the parents of the pioneer or the pioneer himself was on the other side of the ocean. The landing was at Philadelphia, and occasionally there was a sojourn of some years in Pennsylvania. The route to "New Virginia" led through the towns of Lancaster and Frederick, across the Potomac at Shepard's Ferry, and up the Shenandoah Valley to Staunton. This side the Potomac it followed what was sometimes called the "Indian road" and sometimes the "Pennsylvania road." This trail rather closely followed the course of the present Valley Turnpike, and was adopted as a county thoroughfare by the court of Orange in 1745. From Staunton the newcomers continued as best they could over rough paths to the Cowpasture and Jackson's rivers.

Men are slow to adopt a radical change in their manner of living. The pioneer sought to feed, clothe, and house himself as he had done in his native land. Europe was an old country but much less densely peopled than it is now. It fed itself and there was no lack of building material. To the newcomer the frontier looked as though it had never been peopled at all. It was very much as though he had simply moved into an uninhabited annex to his home-land. His standard of living was plain and he proceeded to make himself at home. However, the American environment compelled some departure from the old ways. For example, the immigrants had been living in stone dwellings. It was now more convenient to build a log cabin. Indian corn was a new food and fodder plant, yet was accepted at once. The potato, however, was not well known in Scotland before 1760.

The climate was found to be more sunny than that of the European home, and the summer season considerably warmer. The soil was of virgin fertility. Yet the seaports of America were 200 miles away, and the few towns on the route to them were mere villages. On the frontier nearly every man was a producer and not a consumer. There was little market for farm produce, and he had to live within his own resources as far as possible. Some of the immigrants brought a considerable stock of hard cash. But in the wilderness itself there was no money and few commodities that would bring money. Certain manufactured goods, as well as salt and ammunition, were necessities. All these things had to be brought from the seacoast and were expensive. Yet after the settlement had once been made living was easier in the new home than in the old. The supply of fish and game was more ample and varied. And, after all, what great difference did it make if there were wolves and wild men in the American wilderness? There were wolves in Ulster and it was necessary to pay a bounty on their heads. And when the native Irish rose in rebellion even women and children were put to death, just the same as by American Indians.

It is an error to assume that deerskin hunting shirts and coonskin caps were universally worn, or that the home of the settler was scarcely any improvement over the Indian hut. The dress suit of the person who by the usage of the time was styled a gentleman or a yoeman was more elaborate than in our day. The colors were brighter and more diversified. A man's suit might be green, bright red, or plum color. William Jackson, for whom Jackson's River is named, lived on the verge of settlement, and yet he wore a wig and a stock and buckle. Robert Armstrong was a hunter, but wore silver buckles. James Byrnside, who was reared near Griffith Knob, was charged $10 for three beaver hats, and it would have taken two of his best cows to pay for them. The statue of Andrew Lewis at Richmond presents that general in hunting shirt and leggings. Such was not his ordinary apparel, for he is known to have been particular in the matter of dress. His brother Charles, who lived on the Cowpasture, was equally particular, and his brown suit, inventoried at $50, was worth much more than an average horse.

Yet it is true that some of the immigrants almost literally took to the woods. Slumbering instincts, inherited from remote ancestors, began at once to assert themselves. Such men neglected the soil and made hunting a business. The skins they did not need for clothing could be sent to the sea-ports. The bounty on the destructive wolf put some additional coin into their pockets. In fact, nearly every pioneer seems to have yielded in some degree to this "call of the wild."

The person acquiring 100 or more acres in the Augusta colony was usually a yoeman, his class constituting the backbone of British society. The gentleman, according to the aristocratic meaning of the word, was a person whose ancestors had never been serfs. He had a coat of arms and had the privilege of wearing a sword. There were very few of this class in Augusta, although prominent men were given the title by courtesy. Yet there was less democracy then than now. In deeds and other documents it was customary to state whether grantor or grantee were a yoeman, or to mention his occupation. This was a means of defining the social standing of a person.

Negro slaves were very few until after the Indian war of 1754. Bound white servants, however, were numerous. Some of these were orphans or of illegitimate parentage. Others were young persons brought from Europe under indenture. To pay the cost of passage across the Atlantic they were sold into servitude, the average term of which was five years. Until his time expired, the servant was virtually a slave. If he ran away and was retaken, he was made to serve his master until after his term had regularly expired, so as to make good the cost of recovery. Some of the servants, after becoming free, made as good citizens as any other people. Some others had a record as petty criminals, or were of loose moral character. If, as frequently occurred, the woman servant had bastard children by another man than her master, her term was lengthened. But immoral behavior was not confined to the servant class.

The first dwelling houses were small round-log cabins. The roof was of long riven shingles held down by weight-poles. The floor was of puncheons, or even the natural earth. But among the more well-to-do settlers larger and better houses of hewn logs soon made their appearance. That of Captain William Jameson of the Calfpasture, built in 1752, was eighteen feet by twenty-four in the clear, one and one-half stories high, and the contract price was $22.50.

In many an instance the settler was master of some trade, which he could now make a side-line support. One man was a weaver, another a mill-wright, another a cooper, and still another a carpenter or cabinet-maker. A very important man was the blacksmith. He did not limit himself to repair work, but was really an iron-worker. He manufactured nails, horseshoes, edged tools, and copper-glazed bells. He also made farm implements, except such as were wholly of wood.

The tilled acreage was small, because the pioneer grew little more than the supplies consumed on his place. The farming tools were few and simple. The plow with wooden mouldboard and the brush harrow were almost the only ones to which a horse was attached. Wagons were scarce for a while, but were fairly common at the time of the Revolution. Indian corn, unknown in the British Isles, was the only staple the pioneer had to learn how to grow. The Ulster people were proficient in the weaving of linen, and the flax patch was on every farm. Only the people of means could afford to wear clothes made of imported cloth. Others wore homespun made of flax fiber or wool, or a mixture of the two, and skin garments were also used. Hemp was peculiarly a money crop, and was encouraged by the colonial government. It was suited to the deep black soil of the river bottoms. The price was $5 a hundredweight, and there was also a bounty of one dollar for the same amount. Few planters produced so much as 1,000 pounds. And yet we do not identify any Alleghany pioneer as presenting any claim to the bounty. The remoteness of this locality is the probable reason.

The pioneer farm was well stocked with horses, cattle, sheep, and hogs, but the grown animals were not so large as those of the present day. The smaller ones needed protection from the bears, panthers, and wolves.

Profanity was very prevalent, and conversation was coarser than it is now. Gambling was also common. And yet very many of the pioneers were either genuinely or nominally communicants of the Presbyterian Church, this being the religious profession of nearly all the Ulstermen. The opportunity to attend religious services did not keep pace with the march of settlement, and there was much falling away in matters of conduct. For some years there was no house of worship any nearer the settlers in Alleghany than Windy Cove near Millboro, built about 1752. We have no information as to the first appearance of a church building within the limits of this county.

The ability to read and write was very general among the Scotch-Irish immigrants. Owing to frontier conditions this was not so much the case with the generation following. But although schools were fairly common in the settlements, they were not public schools. The ruling element in colonial Virginia held that education is a private and not a public interest, and schooling had to be purchased in the same manner as clothing or groceries. This is why a school-house is never mentioned in the public records, except in an incidental way. The nearest school we hear of in this manner was one on the Calfpasture in 1760. Charles Knight was to have $60 for teaching one year, every half-Saturday or every other Saturday to be free time. In case of a foray by the Indians, Knight was to be sheltered in the neighborhood stockade without charge.

It was customary to begin a will with a long preamble of a pious tone. And yet the settlers of Augusta were very much given to litigation. Some persons seemed to be almost constantly in court. Most of the suits were for debt. Not a few were for assault and battery. Many others were for slander. It was a common thing for a person to claim damages for being called a thief. It was even more common for both men and women to complain of being accused of immoral behavior. Some of these charges are gross in the extreme, and are set forth in the bills of complaint with an explicitness that is astonishing. A number of lawsuits, of all the kinds mentioned, were brought by the early settlers of the Alleghany area.

The Scotch-Irish believed themselves entitled to a high degree of personal liberty. They were not meek in submitting to either legal or military authority. The justices of Augusta were sometimes "damned" or otherwise insulted while sitting on the bench. They were repeatedly disturbed by rioting in the courtyard or by ball playing. Sheriffs or constables were sometimes interferred with. One constable says he was "kept off by force of arms." Another says "the fellow gave me 'heel play.'" A third says his writ was "not executed case of by a hay fork."

And because the frontiersman was little amenable to restraint, only the militia officer who possessed a high degree of tact and an inborn sense of leadership could exercise much control over his men. The private was inclined to obey his officer only when it suited him to do so. He was individually brave and likely to be a good shot, but sadly deficient in the discipline that makes a reliable soldier. The white male adults were enrolled in militia companies, and these mustered four times a year. The day of general muster was the fourth Tuesday in September.

Previous to the French and Indian war small printed forms were used for writs. From then until the Revolution, legal papers were made out in pen and ink, usually in a neat, legible manner. Because of the high cost of paper, very small pieces were used, and the lines of writing are near together. The ink used by officers and professional men was of a very durable sort. Quill pens were the only ones known. Fine sand took the place of blotting paper.

By 1770 the mines of Wythe county had become an important source of bullets and shot. The manufacture of powder was begun at an early day, and small powder mills were in existence as late as 1850. The first powder mill we hear of in the Alleghany area was at Mann's fort. Saltpeter could be made on the very spot. Sulphur, called brimstone, was the only ingredient that had to be imported. In 1819 there was a powder mill on Blue Ridge Run in Rich Patch mountain.

The thinness of population, the few and very small towns, the slowness of travel, and the comparative absence of newspapers caused the life of the community to move at a slow pace. So late as 1775, there were but two newspapers and fifteen postoffices in all Virginia. Postage was so high that many letters were sent by private persons, although this was contrary to an English law. There were no envelopes, and postmasters read the letters that passed through their hands. Letters left on the bar of a tavern until the right claimant should appear were likewise read by anyone who cared to look at them. Until 1755, there was no regular postal service with the British Isles, and if a letter did not weigh less than one ounce it cost one dollar to have it delivered there.

Money was computed, as in England, in pounds, shillings, and pence. But on this side of the Atlantic, these words applied to values and not to coins. In Virginia currency, the pound was $3.33, the shilling 16 2/3 cents, and the penny 1 7/18 cents. It was because of the lower value that English money did not circulate in the colony. The hard money in actual use was Spanish, French, or Portuguese, and came from the West Indies. Thus we find frequent mention of the pistole, the doubloon, and the louis d'or, or "loodore." These were gold coins, worth, respectively, $3.92, $7.84, and $3.96. The largest silver coin was the Mexican dollar. It was also called the "piece of eight," because divided into eight reals, the real being equivalent to the Virginia ninepence. The earliest mention of the dollar in the Augusta records is in 1752, when Adam Dickenson of the Cowpasture thus acknowledges a payment on a note: "Rec'd of the within 28 dollars." It is because the dollar was so well known in the colonies that it was adopted as the basis of the Federal coinage of 1784. And as six shillings made one dollar, the dollar divided very readily into terms of Virginia currency.

But with respect to the gold coins, computation was by weight, and this is why money scales are often named in inventories of personal property. Paper money of colonial issue began to appear in 1755. The ten-pound bill was only 2½ by 3 inches in size. Warehouse certificates for tobacco were also used as money and did not need indorsement.

When a nominal money consideration is written into a legal document of the colonial time, the sum mentioned is usually five shillings. The legal rate of interest was five per cent. There were no banks, and to safeguard money it was hidden. Peter Wright hid some money on Peter's Mountain in so secure a manner that it was not found until a comparatively recent day.

Since the early settlers arrived by way of Philadelphia, and also because their merchants often purchased goods in that city, there is frequent mention of Pennsylvania money, in which the pound was $2.50.

Under the names of "levy" and "fip." the real and half-real of Mexico continued to be legal tender in the United States until about 1850.

The purchasing power of the dollar was very much greater in the colonial period than it is now. This accounts for the seemingly low prices of land and livestock. On the other hand, some articles were relatively more expensive than they are now. Whether, on the whole the pioneer had any advantage over ourselves in the problem of living may be fairly well determined by a study of the remaining paragraphs of this chapter. Nearly all the prices named are taken from the law documents of Augusta for the period before the Revolution.

A farm of 517 acres on Back Creek rented three years for $6.46. For 149 acres on the Calfpasture, a man was to pay $13.33 yearly for three years. Wheat varied little from fifty cents a bushel. The average price for rye, oats, or corn was about thirty-three cents. Potatoes are quoted at twenty cents. Flour by the barrel ran all the way from $3.25 to $8.33. Butter was worth five to eight cents, while beef and mutton averaged hardly more than two cents. Half of a bear carcass is mentioned at eighty-three cents and a whole deer at thirty-six cents. In 1749 a "haf buflar" was sold for $1.25.

Condiments nearly always came from the seaports and were very expensive. As late as 1763 salt was $2 a bushel at Richmond, and it cost eighty-three cents to bring it as far as Staunton. In 1745 it is mentioned at sixty-seven cents a quart. Coffee was $1 a pound and tea $1.56. Pepper was seventy-five cents a pound and allspice fifty-four cents. Nutmeg was seventeen cents an ounce and cinnamon fifty-eight cents. White loaf sugar from the West Indies was usually twenty-five cents. Brown cane sugar was much cheaper. Bottled honey is named at thirty-one cents a quart.

A mare could be had for $15, although an extra good horse might come as high as $40. The average price of a cow was about $5, although a young woman, perhaps through sheer necessity, sold two cows and a yearling for $10. A hog or a sheep could ordinarily be had for $1. The one mention of a goose is at forty-two cents, and nothing is said as to other poultry. A board bill for one month could be satisfied for $3.00. Common labor ran from thirty-three to fifty cents a day, although twenty-five cents would pay for one day's corn husking, and thirty-three cents command the services of a person who could tend store and post books. The price for a man with his wagon and two horses ran from fifty cents to $1 a day. Rails could be split for 37½ cents a thousand. A blacksmith would make a mattock for sixty-seven cents. A carpenter charged William Dean eighty-three cents for making his churn, $2.50 for laying his barn floor, and $6.67 for covering his house. A bedstead could be made for $1.25, a loom for $5.00, and a coffin for $2.17. Two pounds—$6.67—would build one of the big stone chimneys of that day, and four pounds built a log dwelling, although David Kinkaid paid in 1752 $30 for his new house. A year's schooling cost $10. Aminta Usher, servant to Loftus Pullin of the Bullpasture, worked for $20 a year.

A weaver would come to a person's house and weave cloth at six cents a yard, but Irish linen cost $1.08 a yard, velvet $3.33, sheeting $1.25, flannel forty-one cents, and ribbon seventeen cents. A handkerchief of cotton cost twenty-five to thirty-three cents, while one of linen cost seventy-five cents. Men's stockings, which came above the knee and were there secured under the ends of the trowsers with a buckle, cost eighty to ninety cents. Headgear was high, or low, according to the means of the wearer. A woman's hat is mentioned at $5, but a cheap felt hat could be purchased for thirty-three cents. Leggings were $1.04, pumps $2, and men's fine shoes $1.40. Gloves are listed at fifty-eight cents, a necklace at thirty-three cents, and a woman's fan at twenty-five cents. James Carlile's blue broadcloth coat cost him $5.42. A pair of steel buckles for shoes or knees cost twenty-five cents, but the man of fashion insisted on silver for both buttons and buckles, and had his name engraved on the buttons. Common buttons were forty-two cents a dozen, silk-garters were forty-two cents a pair, and thread was half a shilling to a shilling an ounce. Leather breeches, very generally worn by laboring men, are priced at $3.17 a pair.

In 1762 the Carpenter brothers were credited four shillings (sixty-seven cents) a pound for their beaver skins . To make and nail 100 clapboards cost $1.46 in our money in 1767.

The doctor was charged thirty-three cents a pound for his casteel soap, sixty-seven cents an ounce for his calomel, and thirty-three cents for a roll of court plaster. Nails were sometimes sold by count, ten-penny nails coming as high as $1.50 a thousand. Ginseng brought sixty-seven cents to $1 a pound. The hunter had to be a good marksman, when he paid twenty-one cents a pound for lead and fifty-six for powder. His gunflints and fishhooks cost about one cent each.

The pioneers had little of our modern hurry, but were alert as to what was taking place in their own neighborhoods. On matters relating to the colony in general, they were slow to move unless aroused by their better informed leaders. As to anything like a national feeling between the populations of the several colonies, there was nothing worthy of the name.

A journal kept in 1749 by two Moravian missionaries gives us a glimpse into the lower valley of Jackson's River after three years of settlement. Coming up the South Fork in what is now Pendleton county, they reached the head of that stream on the night of November 13th. Here they found what they call an "English cabin," because occupied by an English-speaking family. They slept on bearskins spread on the floor in front of the fire-place. Like all the settlers the family had bear meat, and like some of them it had no bread. But on the morning of that day, a German woman had given the missionaries some bread and cheese. These eatables they shared with their entertainers.

Next day they went down the Cowpasture to where Williams-ville now stands. This time their host was suspicious and not very cordial, but in the morning he put them across the swollen Bullpasture. They soon fell in with George Lewis, who was traveling on horseback in the same direction they were going. This man set them across the river at twelve fords. They seem to have parted with him when they left the vicinity of the river to begin the ascent of Warm Springs Mountain. A rain began falling and it was dark when they reached an empty hut in the valley beyond. They had nothing to eat, but made a fire and dried their clothes. In the morning they hurried to the nearest cabin, and had a breakfast of hominy and buttermilk. They speak of their host as a good Presbyterian, but do not give his name. He was probably James Ward, who took out the first tavern license at Warm Springs. The missionaries do not say a word about the thermal waters. They were in a hurry to get on. They did not speak English fluently, and along this part of the way there were no German settlers. Jackson's River was crossed by swim-ming and with some difficulty. At the close of this day, after crossing Dunlap Creek, they reached a house, perhaps that of Peter Wright. Here they slept on bearskins, the same as the members of the family. While crossing a mountain on their way to Craig's Creek, they heard an "awful howling of wolves."

These Moravians relate that the people along their route were living like savages, wearing deerskin clothes, and making hunt-ing their leading pursuit. The style of living is spoken of as poor in the extreme. Pounded corn was separated into meal and hominy. Bear oil was a substitute for butter. However, these men came in the very infancy of the settlement of this region, and during the "wild and woolly" stage of its evolution.

We have devoted some space to an account of pioneer life in this region, because until within the recollection of our elderly people the impress of pioneer conditions was still very visible. When the war of 1861 began, labor-saving machinery was little in use, and the railway locomotive had but just entered our confines. Men were still wearing homespun and firing flintlock guns. In no small degree the customs of the pioneer day had not been superseded.

V

TWENTY YEARS OF INDIAN TROUBLE

THERE IS ample proof that at some time, possibly remote, a settled aboriginal population occupied the valleys of Alleghany county. But when the white man appeared on the scene, the only Indians were the bands that came to hunt or were passing north or south to fight the warriors of some other tribe. The dusky visitors did not fail to call at the frontier cabins, where they expected to be given something to eat. This unwelcome hospitality was quite a burden on the settlers, although, if the case had been reversed, the Indians would have fed them and done it willingly. It was through such contact that the native learned to express himself in the English tongue. And the fact that he thus became familiar with words of insult and profanity is very significant as to the everyday language of many of the borderers.

There was no love lost between the two races. The white despised the red as a heathen, and had no use for him. Because the native did not actually live in these valleys, and did not cultivate the ground, the newcomer could not see that the claim of the Indian to the soil was worthy of any serious consideration. In his dealings with the redskin he showed little tact or patience, was prone to make trouble, and was inclined to be shamefully treacherous. But the Indian was proud as well as free. When he gave title to land he thought he was conveying no more than a right to a joint occupancy. He held that while the white man was tilling the soil he himself should continue to enjoy the privilege of hunting and fishing. In his eyes it was an indignity to be driven away from the hunting grounds of his fathers. He did not give up his claim without a prolonged struggle, but the struggle was hopeless. The natives were a handful, the newcomers were a host. Nevertheless, it was the Indian who inflicted the greater loss of life and property. He was cruel in war, after the manner of all barbarians, but the frontiersman was equally cruel.

Open war broke out in 1754. It arose from the rivalry between the English and the French for the control of the Mississippi basin. The French were the more tactful with the tribesmen and were much the more successful in winning them to their side.

The shameful defeat of General Braddock exposed the whole frontier of Virginia to the vengeance of the native. To Colonel George Washington, then only twenty-three years of age, was assigned the defense of the border. His position was trying in the extreme. He was not loyally upheld by the fuming, stingy governor, who never ventured anywhere near the frontier. The legislature was as meddlesome and ineffective as the royal governor himself. With a few hundred militia, untrained, insubordinate, and poorly equipped, Washington was expected to hold a line 300 miles long. In spite of his exertions, there were times when it seemed as though all the country west of the Blue Ridge would have to be abandoned by the settlers.

Since the colonial government did not take efficient measures to protect the frontier people, hundreds of them flocked into North Carolina. Those who remained at their homes were in almost constant danger except in the winter season. The trails and the mountain passes were watched by men who were called "Indian spies." They were forbidden to make fires to warm themselves, lest the smoke might give notice to some lurking enemy. One of these scouts, speeding over the bridlepaths and shouting "Indian sign" to every white person he met caused the families thus warned to make a hurried flight to the nearest stockade or blockhouse. There they "forted" during the times of special danger. Fierce dogs, trained to recognize the body odor of the Indian, were an additional means of protection.

And yet the pioneers were very careless. They were restive at being cooped up in the stockades. They were negligent in sentinel duty and took imprudent risks. When Washington visited the valleys of the Cowpasture and Jacksons' River on a tour of inspection, he wrote that not one of the forts he came to was in a proper condition for repelling an enemy. There was not one which could not have been surprised with ease. The members of his escort conducted themselves in a most foolhardy manner.

For the defense of each frontier neighborhood there was a blockhouse, with or without an encompassing stockade. The windows of the fortified house were too narrow for a foeman to crawl through. The door was bullet-proof and strongly secured. There were loopholes in the wall for the defenders to shoot through. It was necessary that the water supply be near, and the approach to it was sometimes by a covered way that was virtually a tunnel. The Indian was very reluctant to storm a blockhouse. If he could not set the roof on fire with a flaming arrow, he resorted to blockade or sttrategem.

The leading stronghold in the Alleghany area was Fort Young, built in 1756 according to specifications furnished by Washington. It stood on the site of the iron furnace at Covington, and was quite close to an important ford in Jacksons River. And yet one wonders why it was placed so near a bluff. The fort had entirely disappeared by 1840.

Mann's fort was the same as Fort Breckenridge, and must also have been a stockade. Its position was in the river bottom at the mouth of Falling Spring Run, and on the south side of that stream between the river and the railroad track. By a council of war held at Staunton, July 27, 1756, no reënforcement was ordered, because the fort was deemed properly protected by the garrison already here.

Carpenter's fort was probably no more than a fortified house. It stood on a low bluff near the mouth of Potts Creek. The abundance of arrowheads and the fine specimens of stone implements found in the vicinity indicate a flint quarry, or more probably an aboriginal village.

But according to Hugh Paul Taylor, who should be excellent authority, another Carpenter's fort stood on the bottom at Low Moor that was afterward the Karnes place.

At the McKinney farm on the Cowpasture is a remnant of a fortified stone house. On the bluff above the mill of McAlllister and Bell at Covington was a blockhouse, which is distinctly remembered by John W. Bell.

From the defeat of Braddock in July, 1754, to the close of the Dunmore campaign in the fall of 1774, there was never a time, unless in winter, when the Alleghany area was not in danger of Indian attack. There were at least three separate raids. But with respect to the accounts which have been handed down to us, there is some confusion as to place and time. The incidents of a given story may not all belong to the same year, and it is all but impossible to relate the events as they actually occurred. Thus, according to the *Preston Register,* the first of the attacks we shall presently mention, took place in 1756. According to Hugh Paul Taylor, it occurred in 1764. The latter date is clearly impossible. The Pontiac war had already closed, and the Indians had been forced to sue for peace. And yet Taylor wrote his narrative as long ago as 1826, and he was a relative of the Captain Paul he speaks of. On the other hand, one wonders why men should be trapping beaver on New River in such a dangerous time as 1756. If the date were 1759, this would be easier to understand. By this time the French had been driven from the Ohio valley, and the Indians were discouraged. The probability is that the invasion of October, 1759, included the region around Covington, and that some of the events related by Taylor belong to that date.

In its session of August 21, 1755, the Augusta court summoned Joseph Carpenter to answer the charge of selling ammunition to the Indians. He replied that he did not know the natives he thus supplied were hostile. Yet within one month, Captain John Dickinson had a "scrimmage" with nine Indians, killing one of them and losing one of his own force. This collision probably took place on the Greenbrier.

If we follow the document known as the *Preston Register*— and its authority is very high—the most destructive raid upon Jackson's River occurred near the middle of September, 1756. On the 11th or 12th of that month, Ensign Madison was killed, probably near Fort Dinwiddie, which stood northwest of Warm Springs. Two days later, nine persons were killed. These were Nicholas Carpenter, Stephen Sewell, James Mayse, James Montgomery, Nicholas Nutt, John Byrd, George Kincaid, Mr. Boyle, and a man named Fry. Joseph Swope and a man named Wilson were wounded. The captives were Mrs. Byrd and six children, Mrs. Kincaid and three children, Mrs. Persinger and two children, and five children of Charles Boyle; also a young son of Swope, and two boys named Brown. Joseph Carpenter, David Calloway, and Mr. McConnell, and a Carpenter boy were captured, but escaped.

Not all these people belonged near Covington. One or more of the men may have been soldiers whose homes were elsewhere. The Byrds lived a little below Fort Dinwiddie, and the disaster to them happened while the family was trying to reach the stockade.

Sewell, Persinger, and Swope, and probably two or three other families had fled here from the Greenbrier. Nor, with the exception of the Byrds, do we satisfactorily know the circumstances of the tragedy. It would seem that not all the other killings and captures took place at one spot or on the same day.

According to the narrative by Taylor, three men, named Pitman, Swope, and Pack, were trapping beaver on New River. Here they detected a war party of fifty Delawares. The band divided, about twenty proceeding in the direction of Jackson's River, the others toward Catawba Creek. To give warning to the settlements, Swope and Pack ran in the latter direction and Pitman in the former. The first band came down Dunlap Creek, crossed Jackson's River above Fort Young, and went on by night to Solomon Carpenters' place on the Low Moor bottom, the blockhouse being in charge of a man named Brown. The attack was made in the daytime. All the white people were in the fields except two of Brown's sons, young Jeremiah Carpenter, and a woman. The three boys were captured. Brown carried the news to Fort Young, but as only a few men were there, a messenger hurried to Fort Dinwiddie, where Captain Audley Paul was stationed. That officer gave pursuit with twenty men, and on Indian Creek in Monroe he met Pitman, who had been running all night, and now joined the pursuers. The band that committed the havoc on Jackson's River was not overtaken. The other band, however, was found encamped at the mouth of Indian Creek. Paul and his men waited until daybreak and then fired a volley, not knowing the Indians had three prisoners. The attack would have had better success but for the impetuosity of a soldier named John McCollum, afterward killed in the battle of Point Pleasant. He yelled out, "Take steady aim and send them to hell." The Indians were thus given notice, and though several were killed most of them got away. A captive taken on the Roanoke was rescued, as was also Catharine Gum, a servant to Captain Paul.

After this disaster, a council of war was advised that forty men be stationed at Fort Breckenridge.

Some of the persons then carried away never returned. Mrs. Persinger was never again heard from. A tradition in the family says that a part of her dress was found on a rock. This is entirely credible, since it was a practice of the Indians to shorten the skirts of a woman prisoner, in order that she might travel faster. According to the same statement the piece of cloth was found high up on Blue Spring Run near what was afterward the farm of Henry Persinger, Sr. If there is no error as to the locality, it would show that the Indians did not think it best to return by way of Dunlap Creek. Another tradition in the same family is that may years later sonme Indians claiming kinship with the Persingers visited Alleghany and told of some lands in Minnesota to which the Persingers here had by equity a share in the title, but that the tract became delinquent.

In May, 1757, the Indians came again to Jackson's River, where they killed Andrew Arnold and Henry Lawless. In July of the same year James Allen and a Swope were wounded. Perhaps all these men were serving in the militia. It is highly probable that most of the settlers who escaped death or capture the preceeding year refugeed to some place of greater safety. We do know that the husband of Mrs. Persinger went back to Rockingham, and did not return for at least fourteen years.

In 1759 the French power in America was completely broken and there was now a pause in the Indian raids. Yet the tribes remained angry and restive under the short-sighted contempt with which they were treated by the arrogant British officers on the frontier. Under Pontiac, an Ottawa chieftain of unusual ability, the red men made a final attempt to drive the whites from the country west of the Blue Ridge. The league among the tribes west of the Ohio was made with great secrecy. When, in the summer of 1763, it did reveal itself, it came like a thunderbolt from a clear sky.

To Cornstalk, a Shawnee leader, was assigned the task of dealing with that section of the frontier which included Alleghany. With a strong band he fell upon the unsuspecting settlements on the Greenbrier, and within two days they were blotted out of existence. In their progress to Jackson's River the Indians were outstripped by Conrad Yoakham, who gave warning to the people around Fort Mann. He found it hard to make them believe his story, yet they gathered into the blockhouse and sent a courier to Fort Young. Captains Moffett and Phillips set out with sixty men to their relief. The scouts kept cautiously along the riverbank the entire distance. But when the main body of the little army reached the horseshoe bend immediately below their destination, they thought to gain time by marching across the neck. As a result of this imprudence they fell into an ambuscade and lost fifteen of their number, the survivors retreating.

This battle of Fort Mann was the most severe engagement that is known to have taken place within the limits of Alleghany. The stockade was not taken, but the Shawnees followed up their victory in the field by going eastward down Jackson's River. They were seen from Fort Young and an express rode at full speed to William Dougherty's on the Cowpasture a few miles above the Alleghany line. Thanks to this warning, no scalps were taken in that valley.

The war with the Pontiac league came to an end in the fall of 1764. The Indians were decisively beaten and were required to give up the whites they had carried away.

For ten years there was nominal peace. In the spring of 1774 the relations between paleface and redskin were again strained to the breaking point. In June the Virginia militia were called out. In the first week of July a settler on Jackson's River a little south of the present line between Highland and Bath was fired upon and slightly wounded. The Indians pushed on to the Cowpasture and made demonstrations around Fort Lewis. It seems scarcely possible that the Alleghany area could have escaped a similar visitation, yet we have no account of its being ravaged. Early in September an army of more than a thousand men assembled on the Levels of Greenbrier, and then began a march through the forest to the mouth of the Great Kanawha.

The memorable battle of Point Pleasant was fought October 10, 1774. It led to the speedy closing of the Dunmore war. There is no evidence that hostile Indians ever again crossed that section of the Alleghany Front that borders this county. Yet the frontiersmen could not feel at all certain that the Indian peril had come to an end so far as Alleghany was concerned. Even so late as 1788, John Stuart of Greenbrier feared that red men and foreigners might drive out all the people west of the mountains. Six years later yet, he was authorized to station a force of not more than six scouts at the mouth of the Greenbrier. Until the treaty of Greenville in 1795 the Indian war-cloud continued to lower over the Alleghany area.

A legend of this county states that Katharine Vanstavern taught the children of the four families living on the site of Clifton Forge. An admirer was Harry Gorman, a graduate of William and Mary College. Two Indians came one day to the door of the schoolroom. Gorman fired on them from the woods, killing one and causing the other to run away. This very naturally led to an engagement between the lovers. But before they could be married Katharine was seized by five red men, bound, and taken in a canoe to their camp lower down Jackson's River. Gorman was then out on a hunt and witnessed the proceeding. He collected a party, came upon the Indians while they were asleep, and after several of the latter were killed, the maiden was rescued. She became in due season the wife of Gorman. This legend may rest on fact, but if it does it cannot be taken at face value. Cornelius, the first of the Vanstaverns in this section, was born in Dalaware in 1756. His daughter Katharine married Joseph Carson in 1822, a date much too recent to fit into any Indian foray into the valley of Jackson's River. Even then no hostiles would have made a camp lower down on that river. It would have been too easy a mark for attack, and the course of the stream was not in the direction of the Indian country.

Another story relates that some quiet, peaceable Indians lived on White Rock near Low Moor and traded at the distillery of Michael Karnes. The farmers of the vicinity met at the still by appointment, hunted up the natives, and exterminated them. But Michael Karnes was a resident of Bedford in 1771, though he seems to have moved here within the next six years. No Indians had permanent homes in Alleghany when the first settlers arrived, and none would have ventured to live here so long as the average borderer regarded any red man, friendly or hostile, as a target for a rifle ball. For years after the Revolution it was not safe for an Indian even to visit the home of his fathers. It may be that the tradition is confused with the massacre of an unoffending party of Indians on Middle River about 1753.

VI

BEFORE 1822

THE FORM OF GOVERNMENT in colonial Virginia remained in force, with but little change, until the third state constitution went into effect in 1852. This was thirty years after the establishing of Alleghany.

There was a property qualification for voters, and the suffrage was very much restricted. Even then the citizen could vote only for the man who represented him in the General Assembly. He had no voice even in choosing the officers of his county.

Until 1776 the governor was chosen by the British crown, and he was its personal representative for Virginia. He lived in much pomp and wielded a great influence. He signed all patents for public land. He appointed all the commissioned officers of the militia. After 1776, the governor was elected by the General Assembly. Less style was now attached to his office, but its powers remained much the same.

The county court was a close corporation. When a new county was created, its justices were nominated by the court of the parent county. When vacancies were to be filled, the court made its own nominations. In either case the men thus nominated were appointed by the governor. The county clerk, the constables, and the overseers of the roads were appointed by the court.

The sheriff was nominated by the county court from among the senior justices, but was commissioned by the governor. He was treasurer as well as sheriff, and his term of office was only one year. His official duties were performed by deputies, and as the justices served without pay, the custom of passing the office around so frequently put some money into their pockets.

The county surveyor and the coroner were also appointed by the governor. In colonial times, the coroner was a more important person than he is now. He was a conservator of the peace and held office during good behavior.

The county court had extensive powers. It was a court of law, and it passed judgment on all offenses except felonies and high treason. When the criminal was a negro slave, it could decree the death penalty and order the sheriff to hang the culprit.

Another close corporation was the vestry, and there was one in each parish. Sometimes there was but one parish in a county. The vestry had charge of the local interests of the Church of England, and it kept an eye on the behavior of the people. It had the care of the poor, and it bound out the children of illegitimate birth. When a new county was formed, the members of its first vestry were chosen by the qualified voters. But with a curious inconsistency, the vestry thenceforward filled its own vacancies. Its executive officers were the two church wardens chosen from its own membership. One of their duties was to levy taxes for the support of the established church. The vestry system broke down during the war for American independence, and as the Church of England was disestablished in 1785, there was no occasion to revive this institution. To some extent, the overseer of the poor took the place of the church warden.

Until the close of the Revolution, therefore, every citizen of Virginia had to pay taxes to the support of the established church, no matter whether he were a member of it or not.

In 1852 there was a radical change in state and county government. The governor was now elected by the people. County officers also became elective. Each magisterial district now elected four justices to the county court, these men drawing a per diem allowance while on duty.

So far as the war for American independence is concerned, the annals that relate strictly to the Alleghany area are very meager.

With respect to Virginia there were three stages in that contest. There was first the campaign against Dunmore. This was confined to the counties on the Chesapeake, and it came to an end early in 1776, with the expulsion of the town-burning tory governor. Next came the invasion by Arnold and Cornwallis, limited to the country east of the Blue Ridge, and to the ten months closing with the surrender of Cornwallis at Yorktown in October, 1781. The last stage was the warfare with the Indians. For nearly three years after their experience at Point Pleasant, the tribes beyond the Ohio remained quiet. But being worked upon by British emissaries, whose home government did not scruple to turn loose the redskins on women and children as well as men, they once more began to raid the settlements beyond the Alleghanies. The war on the frontier lasted intermittently until after the treaty with England in 1783, and it involved the Cherokees of the South as well as the Ohio Indians. The most practical danger to the Alleghany settlements was from the Indians, but in this region they do not seem to have come across the Alleghany Front. In the spring of 1778 they assailed Donally's fort near where Lewisburg now stands but were beaten off with loss.

It would seem that most of the men from the Alleghany area who fought in the Revolution saw service only on the frontier. Among the militia officers in the campaign of 1781 we do not certainly identify any Alleghany man excepting Thomas Wright, an ensign under Captain Thomas Hicklin of Colonel Sampson Mathews's regiment.

During the war the machinery of local government moved about as usual. Yet, there was much hardship. There was no good money except specie, and this went largely into hiding. The paper bills issued by the Continental Congress soon began to depreciate, and in the spring of 1781 it took $140 in paper to go as far as one dollar in coin. The price of a dinner in a tavern advanced to $30. The taxes were very oppressive, and although they could be paid in produce, some persons refused to pay them at all, and some officers refused to make collections.

To draw the line between patriot and tory, a law of 1777 required that an oath of allegiance be administered to the citizens. Richard Mayse was assigned to this duty in the territory covered by the militia companies of Captains Dean and Robinson of Jackson's River.

This region seems to have been nearly free from tory disturbances, such as took place on the South Branch to the northward or in Montgomery county to the southward. In fact, the only exception of which we have documentary knowledge is related by Colonel George Skillern, whose plantation was about two miles above Buchanan. In a letter to the governor of Virginia, dated June 26, 1781, he states that about four years earlier, Captain Lapsley had taken Solomon Carpenter and Samuel Lyons as recruits, telling them they were to have three and one-half shillings a day as members of General Washington's bodyguard. On their arrival at army headquarters in New Jersey, the men found this representation untrue. They then deserted, came home, and hid in the mountains. At the date of the letter it was supposed there were forty to fifty of the refugees. Attempts to disperse them and capture their leader had failed. Carpenter and Lyons came to Skillern's house under a flag, offering to serve two years in the militia, subject to call, or to join George Rogers Clark for two years. Skillern recommends that the terms be accepted. Carpenter, a bold, daring, active man, had lived among the Indians, and intimated that if his proposition was not accepted he would go back to them. His comrades were active woodsmen, well armed with rifles, and might be a source of danger. The writer adds that there were parties of tories and deserters in the counties of Montgomery and Washington, and that they were probably in correspondence with one another.

We do not know what action was taken on this letter, but Skillern's advice was probably followed. The lead mines in Montgomery were very important to the Americans. In the spring of the same year the tories of that county were threatening to seize them, and then to join Cornwallis, when, as was expected, he would pursue Greene's army into Virginia.

Our knowledge as to the men of this county who served in the Revolution is very deficient. One of them was William Keyser, who came from Gloucester county. John Wright, seventy-eight years old in 1832, enlisted in 1778 for a term of three years in the Continental line. Jacob Persinger enlisted as a second lieutenant in 1775, serving under Captain Matthew Arbuckle and Lieutenant Andrew Wallace. He left the service in November, 1776. His tour included Pittsburg and Point Pleasant, and Muddy Creek in Greenbrier.

Items from the order-books of Botetourt, in 1770-1780, are these:

John Galloway, constable on Jackson's River, 1770.

Constables for the "bent" of Jackson's River: first precinct, Thomas Wright; second precinct, Andrew Hamilton.—1770.

John Potts, road surveyor from top of Montgomery Gap to McMunsey's mill.—1770.

William Christian to list the tithables on James River and the

Pastures from the mouth of Craig upward and including "green Brier" settlement, 1770.

William Hughart, Robert Glaspey, and John Robinson report it impossible to put in a road from Jacob Persinger's to the fork of Dunlap, 1770.

James McCollister, constable vice John Young, 1771.

John Robinson, living on Dunlap near county line recommended as justice.—1771.

Jacob Persinger, road surveyor from county line by Cowpasture to Red Hill vice William Dougherty, 1771.

John Bowyer makes certificate of entry on four tracts of 400 acres each; two in the fork survey on Jackson's River and the Cowpasture, one on Dunlap, two miles above the mouth, one adjoining Dickenson's meadows in Falling Spring valley, 1772.

Matthew Arbuckle, who lives on the James near the mouth of the Cowpasture, to list the tithables up Jackson's River and Cowpasture to the county line between North Mountain and Jackson's River and up that stream to William Hughart's, 1773.

John Robinson to take the tithables from William Hughart's up Jackson's River to county line and the Western waters, 1773.

James Montgomery of Rich Patch to show why he does not maintain his children in a Christian manner, 1775.

Road from forks of Dunlap to Camp Union (Lewisburg) established, November 15, 1775.

Thomas Carpenter recommended as ensign, 1779.

Robert Armstrong granted tavern license, 1780.

VII

FROM 1822 TO 1861

THE ACT OF ASSEMBLY creating the county of Alleghany was passed January 5, 1822. The same act created also the county of Pocahontas. It is affirmed, and probably on good authority, that the eastern county was to be named Pocahontas, and the western, Alleghany. The titles were transposed through the carelessness of the engrossing clerk.

In 1843 a portion of Monroe, lying between the Alleghany Front and Peter's Mountain, and extending some eight miles northward from the present line, was annexed to Alleghany. In 1847 the boundary was so modified, where it crosses the Cowpasture, as to transfer Shepherd Gilliland and Orlando Griffith from Bath to Alleghany. In 1856, a very small part of Alleghany, designated as the "Mountain House," was annexed to Craig. With these exceptions, the boundaries remain as defined in the Act of 1822.

The line is therein defined as starting on the top of Potts Mountain, where the road from Fincastle to Sweet Springs follows it, and continuing with the said road to the top of Peter's Mountain. There was thence a straight line to the Greenbrier border on the top of the Alleghany. The Greenbrier line is followed to a point where a straight line may include in the new county Captain Henry Massie on Falling Spring Run and Archibald Morris on Jackson's River. From Massie's there was a straight course to the line of Rockbridge, crossing the Cowpasture just below William Griffith's. The Rockbridge line is then followed to a point in the Rockbridge-Botetourt line, so that a course beginning there will pass at or near the confluence of Jackson's River and the Cowpasture and strike the nearest part of Rich Patch Mountain, leaving the house and yard of Captain John Jordan in Botetourt. The boundary then follows the highest parts of the Rich Patch next to Craig's Creek, including the inhabitants of the Rich Patch in the new country, to a point where it unites with Potts Mountain, the latter being then followed to the point of beginning.

As late as 1886 there was an Act of Assembly to settle a dispute relating to the Alleghany-Monroe boundary.

The first meeting of the county court was held at Covington, March 18, 1822. Thomas Massie and Joseph D. Keyser were empowered by the legislature to administer the oath of office to Michael Arritt, John Callaghan, Jesse Davis, and John Holloway, who were the other attending members of the board of justices.

William Herbert was the first sheriff and surveyor, Oliver Callaghan the first county clerk, John Crow the first coroner, and William S. Holloway the first commissioner of the revenue.

The recommendations by this court for the officers of the 128th regiment of militia were these: Colonel, John Crow; Lieutenant Colonel, John Persinger; Major, William H. Haynes; Captains, Moses H. Mann, Anthony Brennemer, George Arritt; Lieutenants, Jacob Fudge, Moses Smith. For the First Battalion, John Callaghan was recommended as captain, Cornelius Vanstavern as lieutenant, and David Johnson, William Mann, and Joseph Pitzer as ensigns. For the Second Battalion, Robert Griffith was recommended as captain, William G. Holloway and Barton Shawver as lieutenants, and George Pitzer and Alexander Johnston as ensigns.

The number of men liable to poll tax was 534. The first levy was $1,361.70, out of which there was an appropriation of $1,068 for the first county buildings. In 1834 the levy was $488.24. In that year there were in all Alleghany county seven coaches, five carryalls, and two gigs.

In 1827 bounty was paid on five grown wolves and six cubs. In 1846 the wolf bounty was advanced to $12 for grown animals and $8 for cubs. In 1860 there was a dog tax, varying from $1 to $3, and this was applied to county purposes.

The first tavern license was granted to Fleming Keyser. Tavern rates in 1840 were 50 cents for dinner, 25 cents for supper or breakfast, 12½ cents for one gallon of oats, or for stable room and hay for one horse. The prices which a landlord might charge were in these days minutely regulated by the county court.

In 1832, Hans Jenkins, a free negro, was adjudged guilty of killing John Gillispie. At this time the payment per day for a jail guard was 75 cents.

The first legal execution in Alleghany took place August 12, 1842, on or near the site of Fort Young. The person hanged was the slave Daniel Wright, alias Blue. On the 28th of the preceding June, while at work in the harvest field, he had mortally wounded his master, Colonel John Persinger. By the will of Jacob Persinger, the father of John, Blue would have become free November 4, 1851. In accordance with the legal procedure in slavery times an estimate was made of the value of the slave, and it was fixed at $320. This was paid by the county to Persinger's heirs. William H. Terrill was attorney for the slave, and the court ruled that he be paid $15 out of the Persinger estate. The trial was very prompt, being held July 9, only a few days after the capture of the negro.

In 1835 the only postoffices were Covington, Callaghan, Jackson's River, and Morris's Hill. In 1858 the voting places were Covington, Clifton Forge, George Stull's, John V. Taylor's, Jabez Johnston's, Fork Run, Griffith's Mill, and Robert Skeen's hotel. But in 1840 there was a poll at John Martin's on Dunlap Creek.

Between 1820 and 1861, a number of foreign-born persons were naturalized. Almost all were from the British Isles. During the building of the Virginia Central Railroad in 1856-1857, several hundred Irishmen were employed on it, and some of them became residents of Alleghany.

The population figures, for the census years, 1830, 1840, 1850, and 1860, were, respectively, 2,816, 2,749, 3,515, and 4,765.

The census of 1840 found in this county 2,144 free whites, sixty-four free colored persons, and 547 slaves. The males were, respectively, 1,123, twenty-seven, and 318; the females, 1,021, thirty-seven, and 229. The number of persons above the age of seventy was thirty-five. Two were above ninety, and there was one centenarian. The number of men employed in farming was 656. There were seventeen professional men, three pensioners of the Revolution, 111 persons in trade and manufactures, seven in commerce, and five in mining. There were 849 horses and mules, 2,686 cattle, 3,647 sheep, and 4,578 hogs. The value of the poultry was $1,901. The farm crops included 25,449 bushels of wheat, 58,860 of oats, 70,828 of corn, 9,142 of rye, 1,392 of buckwheat, and 9,372 of potatoes. The wool clip was 5,782 pounds. The sugar product was 4,335 pounds, and the tobacco, 42,500.

The crop of hay was 792 tons. Dairy products were worth $3,762, and orchard products, $2,660. The value of homemade goods was $5,832. There were five stores with a capital of $24,000. The output of flax manufacture was $1,179. The four tanneries had a capital of $800, and produced 210 sides of upper leather. The four flouring mills had an output of $28,950. The five distilleries had a capital of $2,360, and a production of 3,400 gallons. There were twenty-one sawmills and twenty grist-mills. Three persons made hats and caps, employing a capital of $500 and producing goods to the value of $1,500. The one furniture-maker had a capital of $40 and an output of $200. The one gunmaker made twenty-four guns. The one pottery had a capital of $400 and a production of $300. 20,745 pounds of soap and 5,955 of candles were made.

In 1850 there were 2,763 white persons, fifty-eight freedmen, and 694 slaves. The men and women above the age of seventy were sixty-four. In the census year there were thirty marriages —all white—eighty-two births, and thirty-four deaths. The farms were valued at $519,592, and the farm machinery at $15,797. The acreage of improved land was 20,144. There were 741 horses and mules, thirty oxen, and 801 milch cows.

By 1860 the real and personal valuation of Alleghany county had risen to $3,156,238. There were now fifteen church buildings, of which nine were Presbyterian and four were Methodist.

The above paragraphs will enable the reader to picture for himself a contrast between the Alleghany of today and the Alleghany of seventy-five years ago.

To give some idea of values at the beginning and also at the end of the period covered by this chapter, we quote the following appraisements. That of the estate of Joseph D. Keyser was made out in the spring of 1859, and consequently before the value of slave property could have been affected by the John Brown raid at Harper's Ferry.

AN INVENTORY OF 1823: ESTATE OF JOHN LEWIS
OF SWEET SPRINGS

Blanket	$ 2.25	Broadaxe	1.00
White coverlet	5.00	Box of carpenter's tools	25.00
Double coverlet	10.00	Sickle	.50
Five table cloths	10.00	Old wagon	18.00
Linen damask tablecloth	4.50	Whipsaw and crosscut saw	8.00
Six cushioned chairs	10.12	Set of harness	3.00
Three window curtains	15.00	Four horse plows	20.00
Two feather beds and furniture	77.50	Harrow	5.00
		Horse wagon	55.00
One feather bed with two blankets, two pillows, and bolster	22.75	Three old wagon tires	16.50
		Hogs, 100, all sizes	200.00
Trundle bed and furniture	15.00	Young bay mare	52.50
Old falling leaf table, cherry	6.00	Steers, 35	550.00
		Cows, 18, with 19 calves	190.00
New cherry table	8.00	Sheep, 48	48.00
New map of North America	25.00	Two small oxen	12.00
		Bull	20.00
Two brass-headed andirons	4.00	Hay, 7 stacks	175.00
Hand towel	.50	Boy, 3 years old	125.00
Cupboard	9.00	Girl, 12 years old	312.00
Lady's secretary	20.00	Woman, 37 years old	345.00
Books, 95 volumes	66.25	Blacksmith, 45 years old	675.00
Washstand	4.00	Wheat fan	4.00
Set of crockery and table furniture	80.00	Rye, per bushel	.50
		Wheat, 3 stacks	100.00
Grindstone	2.00	Hay, per stack	$20.00 to 25.00
Crowbar	2.50	Corn, 25 acres (August 25)	312.50
Loom and tacklings	10.00	Cherry plank, 234 feet	7.02
Home-made carpet	35.00	Three hides	2.00
Wolf trap	6.00	Cow and young calf	10.00
Walnut, 300 feet	6.00	Saw for sawmill	8.00
Heifer, two years old	7.00	Total of inventory	$7,971.49

AN INVENTORY OF 1859: ESTATE OF JOSEPH D. KEYSER

Billy, 60 years old	$ 100.00	Sow	10.00
Henry, 26 years old	1,200.00	Corn crusher	25.00
Milly, 50 years old	400.00	Harness for 4 horses	25.00
Girl, 5 years old	500.00	Bedstead, feather bed, and bedding	25.00
Boy, 8 years old	700.00		
Young calf	3.33	Tobacco, per pound	.07
Young bull	25.00	Stack of hay	15.00
Stock hogs, 24	96.00	Clock	5.00

Item	Price	Item	Price
Set of blacksmith's tools..	40.00	Boar	12.00
Chairs, one dozen	6.00	Four-horse wagon and body	45.00
Center table	6.00	Cart	15.00
Bed, straw tick, and clothing	10.00	Harrow	2.50
Bay mare	100.00	Furniture in 3 cabins $4.00 to	10.00
Old mare	20.00	Sofa	15.00
Colt	80.00	Corn, per bushel	1.00
Six milch cows	92.00	Parlor chair	1.00
Yearling calf	10.00	Grindstone	4.00
Hayrake	7.00	Wheelbarrow	5.00
Sheep, 35	43.75	Large mirror	8.00
		Crosscut saw	3.00

VIII

ALLEGHANY IN THE WAR OF 1861

Between 1850 and 1860 the population of Alleghany nearly doubled, chiefly as a result of the coming of a railroad as far as Jackson's River, and the consequent enlarged development of the mining industry. When the war of 1861 began there were nearly or quite 7,000 people in the county. This, however, was an average of but three families to the square mile. Alleghany was still predominantly agricultural and was rated as one of the poorer counties of the Old Dominion. The only village—a small one at that—was the county seat.

During the first two years of the war Alleghany was not a scene of active military operations. But in August, 1863, a column of Federal cavalry under General Averill penetrated the county as far as Callaghan's. After making a demonstration toward Sweet Springs, Averill moved at daybreak on the morning of the 26th, his purpose being to push across the Alleghany Front to Lewisburg. After moving twelve miles in this direction he was worsted in a severe action at Dry Creek.

Next year Averill entered the county three times, always by way of Jackson's River. On the second occasion, General McCausland put his force in line of battle between Covington and Island Ford, but instead of attacking Averill crossed the Alleghany Front to the northward.

The last of these raids was in December. Averill then pushed to Salem and New River, doing great damage to the railway now known as the Norfolk and Western. In his return he was in great danger. Confederate forces were hurrying from both east and west to cut off his retreat, but by great nimbleness of movement the Federal commander escaped through the jaws of the trap. His return to Covington was December 19th. The Home Guards were to burn Island Ford bridge, but their picket was captured, and it was Averill's men who burned the bridge to hold back their pursuers. The thermometer registered three degrees below zero, and Jackson's River was out of its banks. No adult townsmen were at home, but the Federals are said to have behaved well, although they were not at all backward about going into the houses to escape the freezing weather. In continuing his retreat next day, Averill burned the river bridge at Covington. This was the third important bridge to be destroyed during the war, the railroad bridge over the Cowpasture having been burned May 17, 1862.

The next visit by a Federal force was June 3, 1864, when General Hunter passed this way in his retreat from Lynchburg. A light Confederate force deployed in the piney fields that then lay in the direction of Mallow, and made so bold a front that the Federal advance guard did not press matters to a conclusion. Hunter then took his troops up Dunlap Creek to Sweet Springs and thence to Union.

In all these movements, there was no actual engagement except the trivial skirmish just spoken of.

The people of Alleghany adhered to the Confederate cause to such an extent that in the first year of the war there were more soldiers than voters. In the south of the county, however, this feeling was not quite unanimous, and several men refugeed within the Federal lines.

The shortage of farm labor was most acute, there being times when there was scarcely a boy at home above the age of twelve. The forces campaigning within the county, whether Federal or Confederate, made heavy inroads on the slender supplies of foodstuffs and forage. It was a custom to take the provisions to the woods when a hostile visit was known to be impending, but on Averill's return from Salem, the people of the county seat had no notice, and his hungry troopers made eatables very scarce. No serious stringency was felt in 1861 or 1862, for in those years the county was invaded only one time. A pinch was felt in 1863, and still more in 1864, partly because of the horses carried away by Averill in December, and also from a drouth lasting from the day of Hunter's visit until into August. Even more acute was the pinch in 1865, despite the return of peace in April. Work animals were scarce, and there was so little to eat that the county was threatened with starvation. The railroad to Jackson's River was hardly serviceable, and the public roads were in bad condition. But the weather this year was very seasonable, and by the time summer arrived supplies could be had through the United States commissary.

While the war continued, the makeshifts were many. There was no foreign sugar, and in Alleghany very little maple sugar. Sorghum became known in 1862, and from 100 to 200 gallons could be made at a time. Cloth of any kind became scarce. Cotton was apportioned to the families. Uniforms for the soldiers were sewed together by hand, the home-made woolen being colored with vegetable dyes. Little salt could be obtained. Houses were sometimes almost undermined to get at the nitrous earth, from which saltpeter was made and sent to the powder mills.

In general the soldiers from Alleghany served in the famous Stonewall Brigade.

The most noted of the local commands was Carpenter's Battery. It was organized at Covington, April 20, 1861, when it numbered eighty-two or eighty-three men. Next day its services were tendered to the state. A few days later still the men were taken by wagon to Jackson's River Station, and thence conveyed by rail to Staunton. Here they were ordered back to Covington to be uniformed and drilled. The command was mustered in at Harper's Ferry as Company A, 27th Virginia Infantry, 1st Virginia Brigade. At the outset the company officers were Captain Thompson McAllister, First Lieutenant Joseph Carpenter, Second Lieutenant George McKendree, and Third Lieutenant H. H. Dunnott. Dunnott was from Delaware.

The affair at Falling Waters, in which no loss was sustained, was the first of the many encounters in which the company took part. At First Manassas it was heavily engaged, losing six men killed and sixteen wounded, but taking a leading share in the capture of some of the guns of Rickett's Battery. These were turned on the fleeing Federals by Lieutenant Carpenter, who had studied artillery under Stonewall Jackson, graduating from the Virginia Military Institute in 1858. Lieutenant Dunnott was the first Confederate officer to be captured in the war. He soon escaped, only to die of fever near Kernstown.

About a month after the battle of Manassas, Captain McAllister resigned. He was fifty years of age, and the hardships of campaigning bore heavily on him. His taking leave of the company was much regretted, since he had handled it most skillfully in the late battle.

Joseph Carpenter, John C. Carpenter, George McKendree, and

William T. Lambie were now, respectively, captain, and first, second, and third lieutenants. Captain Carpenter was killed at Cedar Mountain and was succeeded by John C. Carpenter, McKendree becoming first lieutenant, and S. S. Carpenter and Charles O. Jordan second and third lieutenants.

In August, 1861, the company was transferred to the artillery service, and was equipped with four six-pounder field pieces, made at the Tredegar Works at Richmond. After Second Manassas it exchanged these small guns for four captured pieces, two twelve-pounder Napoleons and two ten-pounder Parrotts. It was further supplied with new limbers and caissons and new harness. After the fight at Kearneysville, the Cutshaw Battery was merged with the Carpenter.

After First Manassas, the engagements in which Carpenter's Battery took part were these: Romney, Kernstown, McDowell, Winchester, Port Republic, Malvern Hill, Cedar Mountain, Kelly's Ford, Second Manassas, Ox Hill, Sharpsburg, Kearneysville, Fredericksburg, Chancellorsville, Gettysburg, Payne's Farm, Mine Run, Spottsylvania, Monocacy, Wade's Depot, Opequon, Fisher's Hill, Cedar Creek, Five Forks, and Spottsylvania.

At First Winchester the Battery lost seven men and at Malvern, nine. At Gettysburg its loss was five killed and eighteen wounded. At the Bloody Angle in the battle of Spottsylvania it lost ten men. At Wade's Depot, the loss in men was nearly as great as at Gettysburg. Seventeen horses were also killed, and three guns were captured or made unserviceable. In the later battles the losses were ruinous. At the Opequon, Carpenter's Battery lost nearly forty men besides twenty horses. In the rout at Fisher's Hill the loss was thirty-three men, and in that of Cedar Creek two of its guns were taken. At Five Forks all the guns were lost, and what little remained of the organization, now commanded by Corporal John Willey, surrendered with General Lee at Appomattox.

Out of a total enrollment from first to last of about 150 men, forty-six were killed and 124 were wounded. Since in a number of instances a soldier sustained casualties in different engagements, it follows that very few members came out of the war unscathed. But the Battery was a very efficient fighting machine and inflicted great damage in return.

Other units in the Confederate Army were companies C and D of the 27th Virginia Infantry, the former under Captain Lewis P. Holloway, the latter under Captain Harry Robinson. Company D, eighty-five strong when organized, was known as the "Virginia Hibernians," because composed of Irishmen who had come here as workers on the railroad. Another command was Company D, 60th Virginia Infantry. Still another was the 1st Virginia Battalian, otherwise the Irish Battalion of the Stonewall Brigade. It is said to have contained 400 Irish, and was organized by Major Gardner Paxton of Rockbridge, who drilled his men in Alleghany once a month.

A few men from this county served in still other commands, particularly Bryan's and Chapman's Batteries and Company G, 22d Virginia Infantry.

We now pass to the leading documentary features of the War of 1861, as given in the county order-book.

1861

Grand jury, March term: Peter Boyer, Samuel Boyer, Dennis Callaghan, George Carson, Peter Dressler, Jordan Helminstoller, Elias Hook, Michael Karnes, Joel Kindell, Asbury Matheny, William F. Morton (foreman), William Scott, John H. Stone.

The entire court was present at the first session of the war period, held April 27th. The members were Andrew Fudge, John I. Haynes, Madison Hook, Beale V. Keyser, G. McDonald, Lee Persinger, Charlton Shirkey, Thomas T. Shumaker, George Stull, and Davis Williamson. At this session it was announced that two volunteer companies were organized and on duty in a tented field, and that other companies would soon be organized.

There was an appropriation of $6,000, raised by a loan, for the equipment and support of these volunteer companies. The board to adjust and settle all claims arising out of this fund were C. Bias, James Burk, William R. Clark, Thomas J. Daggs, Charles Dressler, William G. Holloway, Madison Hook, Edwin Jordan, John Mallow, James M. Montague, Lee Persinger, John L. Pitzer, and William M. Scott.

The war sheriff was John J. Stuck.

The poll tax per tithable was $3.50. A levy of two per cent. on the salaries of officers was laid.

1862

Andrew Damron was authorized in March to remove, if necessary, the public records to a place of greater safety.

Levy, $6,375.53.

William C. Clark was directed in August to buy 2,500 bushels of salt in Washington county.

A great scarcity of wagons is reported.

William P. Rucker was arraigned in November under a charge of treason for acting as provost marshal under the Wheeling government, for compelling citizens to take an oath to uphold the Federal government, for burning the railroad bridge over the Cowpasture, for appropriating horses and wagons, for carrying off slaves, and for mortally stabbing Michael Soice in April, 1861.

1863

William C. Clark was employed in January to buy 800 bales of cotton yarn, 1,000 yards of oshaburgs, and 3,000 yards of brown domestic. The actual purchases were 225 bales of cotton and 800 yards of cotton cloth.

Out of 595 slaves the county was required to furnish twenty-seven between the ages of eighteen and forty-five to work in the service of the Confederacy.

Committee of safety appointed in August: Peter Byers, William F. Clark, William Damron, Joseph Irvin, Thompson McAllister, and Charlton Shirkey.

Ordered that C. F. Johnson be paid $25 for removing the county records.

Stated by the court that early in the war ten per cent. of the population had volunteered for the Confederate service; that the families of 200 of the soldiers were now in need of support; that there had been two invasions by the cavalry under Averill; that many slaves had absconded; that if the quota of forty slaves asked by the War Department were insisted upon, desertions from the army would follow.

1864

William F. Clark is authorized to borrow $10,000 to buy 2,000 bushels of corn for destitute soldier families.

Announced that the Federals under Averill, Duffie, and Crook in their advance, and Hunter in his retreat, had taken everything they could lay their hands on; that the drouth this year had been unprecedented; that it was impossible to supply the people and the soldiers unless the Confederate government should release the payment of tax in kind, and permit payment to be made in money.

Wheat is selling at $8.11 in September.

The tax on real and personal property is 1½ per cent.

1865

William F. Clark is impressing agent.

A good deal of felony is reported.

Each person hauling salt from Buchanan is to be paid by the salt agent twenty-one cents per 100 pounds—April 17th.

At a special term a resolution is passed, stating that the surrender of General Lee has greatly demoralized the citizens, and that both soldiers and citizens are taking government property by force. Captain John C. Carpenter is ordered to take possession of all government property now in private hands and turn it over to the state.—April 24th.

"The Court having exhausted all means for the impressment of grain for the soldiers' families, and it being demonstrated that there is not enough grain in Alleghany to support their families till harvest, it is ordered that Thompson McAllister purchase abroad 200 barrels of flour, or its equivalent in corn, he being authorized to borrow gold or silver coin to pay for the said flour, and to execute a negotiable note, if borrowed from a bank." The county is responsible, since its outstanding bonds are under $2,000.—May 3d.

Grain distributors to refuse Confederate money in payment of grain and to accept only specie or its equivalent.—May 15th.

No further meeting of county court till August 21st.

Elections to be held for Congressmen, State Senators, and Delegates, second Thursday in October, at courthouse, Clifton

Forge, George Wright's, Skeen's, Fork Run, William Damron's, George Stull's, Griffith's Mill.

Thirty road precincts.

1866

Election of officers of 128th regiment of militia—May 21st.

1868

Of 100 negro convicts on turnpike and railroad, over one-third have escaped, making insecure the lives and property of the citizens. They obtain citizen clothes by force or threats. The military is looked to for protection.—September 21st.

$50,000 voted in aid of Chesapeake and Ohio.—November 23d.

IX

HIGHWAYS AND RAILWAYS

WHEN the Alleghany area became known to the whites, Indian
paths followed the valleys and crossed the ridges. The native
road was sometimes broad enough to admit a wagon, and often-
time it was deep because of long-continued use. A stream was
ordinarily crossed at the mouth of a branch, because a bar will
occur at such a place. The settler was quick to use the native
path whenever it would serve his purpose. Some portions of
these aboriginal highways undoubtedly still exist as county roads.

But the buffalo was also a maker of paths. This animal lives
in herds, and when the grazing gives out in one place the whole
herd moves on to another, taking a very straight course. At
first sight it would look as though the buffalo and not the Indian
was the first road-builder. So far as the Alleghanies are concerned, this is not the case. The entire Alleghany country is by
nature an unbroken forest. The buffalo keeps to the open,
grassy country, and has no use for a densely timbered region.
The large expanses of open ground found here by the early ex-
plorers were caused by fires set by the Indians, so as to ensure
an ample supply of large game. Hence the buffalo district was
extended far eastward from the plains of the Great West, and
the mound-building ancestors of the historic Indian tribes fell
away from their agricultural habits. There is no doubt, however, that the Indian appropriated some of the buffalo paths for
his own use.

When the pioneer went to laying out a road, he acted on the
principle that a straight line is the shortest distance between two
points. He preferred to go directly over a ridge instead of wind-
ing through a hollow, where he would have to contend with side-
cutting, laurel thickets, and ledges of rock. He had no time for
grading, and a road through a narrow pass offered too good an
opportunity for Indians to lay in ambush. The woods had less
underbrush than now, and it was comparatively easy to open a
serviceable route. As for bridges, they were rare for some time.

Crude, stumpy, rocky, and innocent of grading as the first

roads must have been, the public opinion of the day required that they conform to a certain accepted standard. Many an overseer was presented by the grand jury for failing to keep his section of road in order. Whenever a road forked, the colonial law required that an "index" be set up for the information of the traveler.

The earliest roads were used almost wholly as bridle-paths, the usual mode of travel being on horseback, and the packsaddle being the usual means of conveying goods. Yet there was now and then a pioneer, even among the earliest, who had a wagon, and the more important roads had to be broad enough to permit a vehicle to pass.

Two classes of highways received very early attention. A road was needed along each river, for it was directly along the watercourses that the early settlers located. In the valleys were the forts for their protection, and the indispensable gristmills. Other roads ran over the mountains, or, if possible, around them, so as to reach the neighboring valleys. The most important of such roads were those leading toward the courthouse, which was the chief commercial point for a wide region.

With respect to the Alleghany area, it was in 1748 that we find the first order for a road. A view was then ordered from Peter Wright's to Adam Dickenson's. Wright lived on the site of Covington and Dickenson on the Cowpasture near Nimrod Hall. Three years later an order calls for a road from Wright's mill to the Cowpasture near Hughart or Knox, these men living above Dickenson. This would indicate that no road had yet been built. Also, in 1751, a road was ordered from the Cowpasture to Borden's Tract in Rockbridge. The builders designated were James Frame, William Gillespie, Hugh McDonald, Robert and James Montgomery, William McMurray, James and John Scott, and James Simpson. Some of these men appear to have been living on the Cowpasture within the Alleghany line. In 1766, William Gillespie and James Beard were overseers for a road down the river from Dickenson's to a point eight miles from "Pedlar foard." In 1769 a road was ordered from "Little Warm (Hot) Springs" to the forks of the road on Dunlap Creek. The viewers were Robert Armstrong and John Bollar.

In 1766 Joseph Carpenter and William Whooley were directed to survey a road from Fort Defiance to Handley's mill. The

Fort Defiance named in this order could not be the place of that name in the present Augusta county. The following men were ordered to turn out to work the road, and we give the names in the original orthography: Solomon, Thomas, Nathaniel, Zopher, Joseph, Jr., and a second Thomas Carpenter; Peter and Thomas Wright; John Umphries; Ezekiel John; Edward and John Mc-Mullin; James Williams; Joseph Leaper; John Tieler; William McMurry; William Whooley; Peter Christian; Robert Galesby; Patrick Coridge.

In 1770, the first court of Botetourt named and described thirty-nine road precincts. One of these lay partly in the Alleghany area, and the first overseer was James Montgomery. In 1772 Peter Wright and Robert Armstrong were ordered to survey a road from Wright's to Sweet Springs.

We have now given all we know as to the steps taken to build public roads within the present limits of Alleghany previous to the Revolution.

About 1790 Jefferson wrote on what he believed the practicability of reducing the land haul to twenty-five miles between Dunlap and Howard's creeks. About 1811 improved highways were chartered between Lexington and Lewisburg by way of the mouth of Dunlap, and by 1830 the sum of nearly $172,000 had been expended on roads and bridges between Covington and the Kanawha. In 1825 there was a tollgate at Callaghan's. Ten years later there was a stage three times a week each way between Staunton and Lewisburg by way of Callaghan.

During some forty years there was great interest in the building of good highways and many turnpike companies were chartered. In 1817 a company with a maximum capital of $1,000,000 was legalized to make an improved road from Lexington to Kanawha Falls by way of the mouth of Dunlap. The Covington and Lexington Pike was incorporated 1826. In 1824 John Callaghan was given permission to build a road from the bend of Jackson's River across the Rich Patch to McClung's mill in Botetourt. The Lexington and Covington and the White Sulphur and Sweet Springs turnpike companies were incorporated in 1831. The former was allowed to charge one cent a mile to a man with his horse, and four cents to a man afoot for crossing a river bridge. In 1832 the Covington and Red Sulphur company was given a chance to raise $40,000 by means of a lottery. In 1837 the Staunton and Covington pike was incorporated. In 1840 and 1846 the Dunlap Creek Turnpike Company was incorporated to build from or near the mouth of Ugly to John Crow's tavern. The authorized capital of $6,000 would today scarcely make a respectable beginning. The grade was not to exceed four degrees, and the breadth of the highway might vary from eighteen to thirty feet, according to the nature of the ground. In 1851 came the Fincastle and Covington and in 1855 the Covington and Falling Springs companies.

At an early day there were attempts to make the crooked Cowpasture a navigable waterway. This was the subjects of Acts of Assembly in 1819 and 1835.

The James River and Canawha Canal, incorporated 1784, was projected to extend to Covington. A convention was held at Covington, October 19, 1846, to discuss the improvement of the James and the Great Kanawha. There were delegates from Alleghany, Bath, Botetourt, Greenbrier, Kanawha, Mercer, Pocahontas, Roanoke, and Rockbridge. The meeting was in favor of bringing the canal to Covington and then securing a railroad. If these things could not be accomplished, it was claimed that the region would be almost depopulated by emigration to the West. It was shown that most of the counties represented were virtually without a market, owing to the prohibitive cost of transportation. Coal, wheat, and fruit could not be sent away, and the efforts of the farmers had to be centered on stock growing. With the canal brought to Covington, it was asserted that there would be a probable increase yearly of 15,000 tons of traffic in farm produce and 8,000 tons of merchandise. The cost per ton in moving freight could thus be reduced from $5 to $1.50.

In 1850 the canal company was authorized to borrow $360,000 to extend its route to Covington. In 1853 this sum was increased to $640,000, yet navigation was never carried above Buchanan.

It was ten years before relief came in the form of a railroad. The influence of the new mode of transportation on the growth of Alleghany county is significantly shown by comparing the increase between 1830 and 1850 with that between 1850 and 1860. In the first period of twenty years the rise in population was not quite twenty-five per cent., even with the annexation of quite a slice of Monroe and a corner of Bath. In the second period of ten years the rise was over ninety-three per cent., in spite of a loss of a part of the county to Craig.

Construction work on the Virginia Central began at the Richmond terminus about 1840. Railroad building progressed slowly in that early day, and the line did not reach Jackson's River until 1857. But the panic of that year caused an indefinite suspension of work, and a far greater hindrance was the war of 1861.

Construction was not resumed for about ten years. The Covington and Ohio Railroad was chartered February 26, 1866. This was really a rechartering, for in 1853 the Board of Public Works was enabled to incorporate as the Covington and Ohio and to build to the Ohio not above the mouth of the Great Kanawha nor below the mouth of the Big Sandy. In 1860 a loan of $600,000 was authorized so as to extend the rails to Covington. Soon after the war the Virginia Central was renamed the Chesapeake and Ohio and came under the control of Collis P. Huntington, who had developed his executive ability in the stimulating atmosphere of the flush times of California. By 1867 the railroad had reached Covington, where it rested till July 4, 1869, when the first train left that town for White Sulphur. In 1872 it had come to the bank of the Ohio river. Later on it was extended to Cincinatti, Louisville, and Chicago. Eastwardly, it was extended to the mouth of the James. By connecting the seaboard with large centers of population in the Mississippi Valley, and also by traversing an extensive coal field, the Chesapeake and Ohio soon developed into a line of much consequence.

For seventeen miles beyond Covington the Chesapeake and Ohio runs obliquely through a very rugged district, and it traverses two long tunnels before it fairly begins the descent of the western slope of the Alleghany Front. An early survey ran up Dunlap Creek to its head, crossed an easy saddle between two mountain ridges, then descended for a while the valley of Second Creek, and by another saddle came upon Indian Creek, following that stream to New River. Had this route been chosen, there would have been no tunnels and no prohibitive grades. There would also have been a good tributary region all the way to the mouth of the Greenbrier. But the interests of Greenbrier county, and of White Sulphur Springs in particular, were powerful enough to deflect the undertaking into the difficult route actually followed.

In 1881 the Richmond and Alleghany Company acquired possession of the James River and Kanawha Canal, and by utilizing the towpath for a roadbed, so far as it was serviceable, it built a railway from Richmond to Clifton Forge. The new road came in 1890 into the hands of the Chesapeake and Ohio corporation. Because there is a steadily downward grade toward Richmond of less than five feet to the mile, the James River Division has become a very important freight-carrying line. Within ten more years, the Chesapeake and Ohio built a branch line to Hot Springs, twenty-six miles northward, and another to Bess, twenty miles up the valley of Potts Creek. Starting from Covington, Low Moor, and Longdale are four other spurs, used wholly for freight.

A little study of the topography of Virginia will make clear the strategic position of the county seat of Alleghany. Nowhere else between the Potomac and the New is there a pass by which a railroad can reach the foot of the Alleghany Front without crossing a mountain. And, as we have just observed, a railroad may overcome even the Alleghany Front by going up Dunlap Creek. Northward is the long valley of Jackson's River, and at its source nothing more than a saddle-ridge like that at the head of Dunlap separates it from the long valley of the South Branch of the Potomac. Physical geography indicates that this route should be used by a north and south line connecting the main valley of the Potomac with New River. In fact, the end of the Potts Creek branch is separated by only a few miles from the end of a spur of the Norfolk and Western. Only the selfish interests of two corporations have stood in the way of spanning this interval. So far back as 1872 the South Branch Railroad was projected to run northward from Covington. The incorporators were A. A. McAllister, H. W. Massie, R. L. Parrish, William Skeen, J. H. Oliver, J. J. Hobbs, and B. Rarus.

Returning for a moment to the subject of public roads, the most important of the Alleghany thoroughfares is the one called by courtesy a turnpike, which crosses the county on its way from Hot Springs to White Sulphur Springs.

A good road, partly macadamized, now connects the cities of Covington and Clifton Forge. A few years since, a fine road was built up Dunlap Creek to a point about seven miles below the Monroe line.

Until 1902, the highways of this county were kept up by dividing them into sections, and the upkeep let out by contract to the lowest bidder. Since then, a very different system has been in vogue. In each magisterial district is now a road superintendent with a complete road-working outfit.

The highways of Alleghany county aggregate about 330 miles, and compare favorably with those of any other county in Virginia. Previous to the recent war the cost of keeping them in order was about $40 a mile.

X

CHURCHES, SCHOOLS, AND JOURNALISM

THE ALLEGHANY AREA was settled very largely by Scotch-Irish, and the first church in this field was the Presbyterian. In 1775, and probably earlier, the Rev. Edward Crawford was coming here twice a year to administer the sacrament. He was thus followed by John McCue, Benjamin Grigsby, Christopher Clark, and Jeremiah Burns.

A formal organization took place in 1819, the year in which Covington was officially designated as a town. The ministers present were John McElhenny and Andrew B. Davidson. Peter Wright, Conrad Fudge, and John Brennemer were installed as elders. There being no resident minister for some time, the duties of the elder were very real and sometimes arduous. He visited the sick, having sometimes long distances to travel, and conducted such religious services as were held.

By the end of 1834, the congregation in Covington occupied its new building on Main street. Later on, it was succeeded by a brick church on Water street. This, in turn, will soon be superseded by the larger building now in course of construction. The Covington church has had nine pastorates, James Rice, the third of its ministers, being here twenty years.

Oakland church was built as a mission to the Covington church about 1847, and became independent in 1871. In 1882 most of its members transferred themselves to Clifton Forge, where a church was then built. It was followed by a new church in 1907. From 1880 until 1902, the pastor at Clifton Forge was Emmett W. McCorkle, who preached also at Low Moor, Iron Gate, Oakland, Rich Patch, and other places, the growth of the denomination in his territory being marked.

The other Presbyterian churches in Alleghany are those of Iron Gate and Low Moor, and the rural churches of Palestine on Dunlap Creek, and Falling Springs and Sinking Springs on upper Johnson's River. But as in the case of other denominations, services are sometimes held in union chapels.

Methodism must have apppeared in Alleghany by 1784, and it

has a strong following. Both the Methodist Episcopal Church and the Methodist Episcopal Church, South, are represented, the latter having by far the larger membership. Granbury Memorial at Covington is the mother church of what was once a large circuit of the Southern Methodists. The building cost $30,000, and there are 500 members. There is also Epworth Chapel in East Covington. There are churches at Iron Gate and Low Moor, rural churches in the west of the county at Alleghany Station, Damron's, Callaghan's, and Emory. The Methodist Episcopals have a strong congregation in Covington, dating from about 1907, and the small rural ones of Pennell's Chapel, Dark Hollow, and Shoaf Chapel on Potts Creek.

The Baptists organized at Covington in 1841 with only fourteen members, and for a long while they were few. Their present building was enlarged to its present commodious size in 1902, The first was built in 1875. The church affiliates with the Augusta Association. In Clifton Forge the Baptists built their first church in 1882, and their second in 1896. There is also Lone Star Chapel on Potts Creek.

The Church of Christ has a house of worship at Covington, the Disciples at Clifton Forge, Iron Hill on Snake Run, and Antioch near Alleghany Station. The first church in Clifton Forge dates from 1886. The Covington church was organized in 1912.

The Episcopalians organized at Covington in 1887, at which time their representation in this county was exceedingly small. They built Emmanuel Chapel in 1890. At Sweet Chalybeate Springs are Forest Chapel and a rectory, but not in use since the closing of the resort.

The church buildings of the Roman Catholics are Our Lady of Mount Carmel at Low Moor, built 1882; St. Joseph's at Clifton Forge, built 1891; and Sacred Heart at Covington, where the chapel built in 1892, gave place in 1907 to a house of worship purchased from the Methodists and altered to meet Catholic requirements. Sacred Heart at Hot Springs is the fourth of the four churches served by Father Gaston, whose rectory is at Clifton Forge.

The Church of the Brethren have a congregation at Arritt's on Potts Creek.

There are a few union chapels, one of which is Mount Olivet, on Potts Creek near the Craig line. The Odd Fellows hall at Beaver Dam Falls is also used as a church.

In 1840 Virginia had the bad preëminence of showing the highest percentage of illiteracy among the states of the Union. In this county the number of free whites of school age was 776. The number of pupils in the five common schools was eighty-eight, and these included the twenty-nine whose tuition was paid out of the income from the Literary Fund. Of the whites above the age of twenty, the illiterates were 104. But in 1843 the schoolhouses were thirteen. In that year was appointed the first board of school commissioners for Alleghany. Its members were Joseph Damron, Andrew Damron, Charles King, John McD. Mann, Alexander Rayhill, Sampson Sawyers, Henry Smith, Isaac Stull, and James Warren.

In 1843 there were thirteen schoolhouses, and the sum spent on public education was $243.22.

In 1850 eight public schools were reported with eight teachers and 153 pupils. The one academy had three teachers and thirty pupils. The total number of persons at school was 414. The illiterates were 249.

In 1912 the taxable valuation of Alleghany was $7,791,706.01, not including $2,063,656 for Clifton Forge. The school report for 1911 gives $60,521.32 as received for school purposes in the county, and $13,496 additional in Clifton Forge. Including Clifton Forge, the white population of school age was 4,427 and the colored 1,033, the enrollment being 2,141 and 977, respectively. There were fifty-four separate school buildings, costing $120,800. These figures have since been considerably increased. But the exhibit shows a regrettable indifference to schooling on the part of some of the people of the mountain neighborhoods. Until a recent date the public schools of the county were neglected and the teachers poorly paid. There is now an Alleghany Teachers Association, which includes all the teachers of the county and seeks to raise the standard of instruction.

The following statistical items were given us by Division Superintendent James G. Jeter, who has been thirty-two years an educational worker at Covington.

Outside of the county seat, there are now forty-six schools in Alleghany county, taught by sixty-nine white and four colored teachers. All but six of these teachers are women. Of the entire number, thirty-three belong in this county, so that the number coming from without is forty. The schools of more than one room are eighteen, one of these being for colored pupils. The school population is 3,969 white and 802 colored, while the attendance is 2,231 white and 370 colored. The illiterates above the age of ten are 194 whites and sixty-three colored. Of the white illiterates only seventy-one are girls. There are twenty-five school libraries. The cost of the schools for the year 1921-22 was $124,500.95. The rural schools are doing well, and the compulsory law, lately enacted, has materially increased the enrollment. These schools are given the same opportunity as the town schools, and their teachers are paid the same salaries. In Covington are thirty-three white and six colored teachers, the number in the high school being seven. All teachers in the grammar school hold state normal professional certificates.

The Industrial School and Farm for Homeless Boys lies two and one-half miles west of Covington on Dunlap Creek and within sight of the railroad. It is an enterprise of the Episcopal denomination. There is no other institution of this kind in Virginia. It is not a reformatory, but a home run without locks and bars, and is under the care of Christian men and women. The farm covers 1,197 acres, partly creek bottom, and the value of the land and the eighteen buildings is about $200,000. The endowment is about $50,000. There are thirteen persons in the official force. Printing, carpentering, and other trades are taught. The home provides a shelter, Christian training, academic and industrial scholarship, and a bread-winning trade. More than 200 boys have been admitted, and more than that number were turned away in a single year. At the present purchasing power of money, $200 maintains a boy one year. One of the latest campaigns carried on in connection with the recent war activities is an effort to raise $10,000 to admit to this school ten of the homeless boys of Alleghany county.

Journalism in Alleghany is a short story. The first newspaper in Covington was the *Sentinel,* an independent weekly. Since the close of the World War it has suspended publication, and the office confines itself to job work. *The Virginian,* owned by Richard F. Beirne, is a daily, and the office is well equipped for job work in general. The weekly edition is called *The Dispatch*. *The Clifton Forge Review* is unusually strong in reading matter, and has a large circulation in the east of the county.

Alleghany is not the home and does not apppear to be the birthplace of a literary celebrity. But we cannot refrain from quoting the following lines by a writer of Covington. They were suggested by the last words of Theodore Roosevelt: "Turn out the light."

"Turn out the light." The dawn has come
The glory of another land surrounds me.
And earth-made radiance has no place
In my awakening.

America, my cherished land
Heed this, my final bidding,
"Turn out the light," on creed,
And institution, and subtle powers,
That thrive not in the wholesome sunshine of the truth,
But spread beneath the artificial rays
Of faction's greed and envy.

Stand guard, my country
For the hour has come,
To stamp the vital impress,
Upon thy brother and thyself,
Of well-conditioned liberty.

Shame not thy sons with lesser manhood
Than some gave to France;
But work and live and love America,
To such great ends,
That deeds of state and fireside,
Land and sea are purified each day,
In God's white light.
And every destiny,
The warp and woof in Glory's fields.

XI

THE INDUSTRIES OF ALLEGHANY

THERE ARE five persons in the average family of this county. If the land were equally divided there would be 235 acres to each family. If this average farm were truly typical of the surface of Alleghany, very much of it would be a mountain slope covered with timber. Another part would run into a dry, slaty ridge of slight agricultural or forestral value. Still another considerable part would be so taken up by deep ravines and steep creek bluffs as to be untillable. Yet there would remain, after all these heavy deductions, some upland that is tillable, though more or less stony; some limestone upland affording good pasturage; and finally some bottom land. And furthermore, if this parcel were in the hands of a practical farmer, who divided his attention between tillage crops, livestock, and poultry, and had also an orchard and some bees, he would make a quite comfortable living, and with a normal growth of timber on the mountain-side he would be independent with respect to the fuel question.

All this is equivalent to asserting that Alleghany is capable of supporting an agricultural population as large as the total population of the county. There would indeed be no corn and wheat for export. The most progressive methods of our time would dictate that the farmer of this region must in the future stress those lines of production for which this rugged mountain land is best adapted. The possibilities of the American farm, whether on the Appalachian hillsides or in the level West, have not yet been reached, and they will be reached in the latter section sooner than in the former.

Sixty years ago, Alleghany was a farming community and was supporting itself, although it had but one-third as many inhabitants as now. But the railroad had come only just within its border. The West was still new, and its appeal was very strong. Alleghany now lies on what is, in effect, a transcontinental line of railway. Its agriculture is overshadowed by its commercial and manufacturing interests. Here, as elsewhere, the rural neighborhoods tend to lose in population, notwithstanding the numerical growth of the county when considered as a whole. With the wages paid in the local industries the farmer cannot now compete, and all he can do is to mark time. But since there is everywhere a limit below which the agricultural population and the agricultural production cannot be permitted to fall, there will yet be a turn in the tide, and with the assured advantage of a local market, the farming output of Alleghany is destined to be of more value than is the case now or hitherto. The local agriculture of tomorrow will be more intensive than now, and will specialize on dairying, fruit culture, and market farming. The day when the frontiersman pulled up the old cornstalks and dropped kernels for new hills into the holes thus made has long since vanished.

There is already an active and enterprising fair association. The fairground is at the county seat. The exhibits are varied and highly creditable. In particular, fine specimens of vegetables and fruits are displayed.

Two miles north of Covington is the Evergreen dairy of 1,200 acres. The same distance southeast is the Mallow stock farm of 500 acres. These holdings are of the best river-bottom in Alleghany.

Although this county was for a long time mainly agricultural, it was never wholly so, except in the early years of settlement. So long as America was a land of small industries, not always carried on in the towns, this county had its fair share of these. Mention has been made of the two powder mills at Barber and on Blue Spring Run, which were in operation even before Alleghany was organized.

There were once several potteries near Arritt's on Potts Creek, but they were abandoned many years ago. The pig iron and forged iron, which began to be produced probably somewhat earlier than 1800, was sent down the James on flat boats, and in this way some lumber and farm produce was marketed. The early furnaces and forges produced only one to three tons of metal a day. The triphammers and wooden blowing-tubes were driven by waterpower, and until 1873 charcoal was used as fuel. At the high tide of the iron industry, after the coming of the railroad, perhaps 2,000 men were employed.

At Clifton Forge there was a cable across Jackson's River,

the ore being brought from a mine under a cliff in bucket-loads of one-third barrel each. The bucket slid down the cable by gravity, and was drawn back by a windlass worked by hand-power. Pig iron then sold at twenty-five cents a pound. Much of the labor was by slaves hired from more eastern counties.

When Colonel John Jordan was the iron magnate of this region, he operated several furnaces, and these made heavy drafts on the forests for the charcoal that was then needed. His first was the Lucy Selina, built in 1827. Another gave its name to Clifton Forge. A third was the Dolly Ann. Still another was the Mud Tunnel. Colonel Jordan built a furnace toward the head of Blue Spring Run, but it was never put into blast, although it was connected with the public road by a graded way.

Since the war of 1861, there have been fewer and larger furnaces. The Longdale Company was organized in 1869, and though a second furnace was opened in 1880, bringing the daily capacity to 120 tons of pig iron, operations closed in 1910. A spur railway was built up the valley of Simpson's Creek to give access to the ores on the west side of North Mountain. Furnaces were built at Covington in 1891 and at Iron Gate in 1893. The latter has been owned since 1902 by the Alleghany Ore and Iron Company.

Low Moor is now the principal seat of the iron industry. The original furnace was built in 1873 and the present one came into blast in 1893. The Low Moor Company controls 45,000 acres of mineral lands in Virginia, one of them being the Orispany mine east of the Rich Patch in Craig county, and a railroad was built to it. The daily capacity of the Low Moor furnace is seventy-five tons of foundry iron.

The Clinton red ore, fourteen to twenty-four inches thick, yields thirty to fifty per cent. of metal, while the Oriskany brown hematite yields forty to fifty per cent. However, the ores within Alleghany have not proved to be sufficient for the capacity of its furnaces, and a portion of the supply has come from without. The abandonment of the Jordan mine on Potts Creek was stated to be on account of the unsatisfactory nature of its ores. Yet with the exhaustion of the high grade ores in other states, the deposits in this county may at length be worked more extensively than now.

Covington is the manufacturing center of Alleghany, and its industries have been described in another chapter.

The Ohio C. Barber Fertilizer Company opened its works at Barber in 1913. To furnish hydro-electric power for its plant, and to gain access to the marl-cliff at Falling Springs, the waters of the stream were diverted into a pipe. When in active operation, the works run day and night and employ twenty men. The daily output is 120 tons of pure lime, and most of this is sent South. The workmen are mainly native Alleghanians.

If Covington is the manufacturing center of this county, Clifton Forge is the transportation center. It succeeded Covington as a division point in 1880, and has been the largest place in Alleghany. Its position is highly important, being at the western terminus of the freight-carrying James River Division. West of this city the Chesapeake and Ohio is double-tracked. As this book goes to press, it is announced that at a heavy outlay the yard-space at Clifton Forge will be greatly enlarged, and that the grade at the Mallow curve will be much reduced.

XII

THE COUNTY SEAT

COVINGTON, the seat of government of Alleghany, and one of the leading industrial towns of Virginia, lies at the confluence of Jackson's River and Dunlap Creek. The elevation is 1,222 feet. The loftiest of the bold ridges on the horizon is Carpenter's Mountain. From a copious freestone spring on the western slope comes the water supply for the town. By rail it is 280 miles to tidal waters at Newport News. The distance to New York is 444 miles, and to Chicago 664 miles.

The level land comprising the business quarter became in the spring of 1746 the homestead of Peter Wright, a settler from New England. His house stood near the river on the ground occupied by the Deford Tannery. For seventy years there is no indication that the bottom was anything else than the plantation of a leading pioneer family.

In 1756 Fort Young was built in the bend of the river on the south border of Wright's farm. Since it followed the specifications laid down by a council of war sitting in Staunton, we may consider that the stockade was sixty feet square, and that the palisades composing the wall were fourteen feet in length. The two bastions were about twelve feet square. This fortification commanded a ford in Jackson's River. A primitive road led to Staunton by way of Warm Springs. Another passed over Carpenter's Mountain and led to the settlements in Botetourt county. A bridle-path led to the settlements on the Greenbrier. An Indian trail near by ran up Dunlap Creek and continued to New River.

Fort Young was consequently an important post, and seems to have been garrisoned quite continuously until after the close of the Revolution. An incident of 1759 relates that an ownerless horse appeared on the opposite bank. The river was past fording, but a bottle of rum was offered to the soldier who would swim the swollen torrent and halter the animal. Two brothers, William and Thomas Mann, won the bottle.

Peter Wright soon built a gristmill, a very important institution in pioneer days. In 1819 there was a little cluster of houses, and Covington was then designated as a town by Act of Assembly. Just prior to this the locality was known as Merry's Store. In 1818 two inspectors—for flour and tobacco—were appointed for Merry's warehouse. Each man drew a salary of $100 a year. Dr. John Merry, who had succeeded the Wrights in the ownership of the farm, was philanthropic and public spirited. His house is yet standing as the front part of the residence of George A. Stephenson. Some of the large hewed logs that compose the wall are walnut.

Alleghany became a county in 1822, and west of the Blue Ridge a county seat in Virginia has always meant a town. In 1823 Bernard Pitzer was authorized to dam the river above the mouth of Dunlap. A bridge was put across the river in 1836, or shortly afterward, and in 1845 was rebuilt at a cost of $15,000. The toll was one cent for a cow, three cents for a man, a horse, or an ox, six and one-quarter cents for a man and horse, and twelve and one-half cents for twenty hogs or sheep. For vehicles, the maximum rate was fifty cents, the minimum six and one-quarter cents. In 1837 Elisha P. Williams was given leave to set up a wool-carding machine at a waterfall in the vicinity.

Covington was incorporated by an Act of Assembly in 1833. Six years later the Act was repealed, but it again became valid in 1840.

The town of 1819 was laid off into lots supposed to be seventy-five by 150 feet, but as the surveying was by compass and chain it was not very accurately done. The name is said to have been in honor of Peter Covington. He was the oldest citizen, and was a descendant of Peter Wright. For the first half century and more, the town was aristocratic and conservative. The Intermont Hotel was the center of a great deal of social life. But after the coming of large manufacturing interests, the society of Covington has been democratized to a striking degree.

Until after the war of 1861, Covington was no more than a village. In 1855 there were only about forty-three houses grouped on two streets. Some were of brick, but the larger number were log dwellings. Of the 43, nine are still in existence. Perhaps the largest house was the one which seems to have been previously owned by Hugh Paul Taylor. It stood on the postoffice lot and like all the houses of that day it was built close to the street.

This dwelling was of brick and contained eight rooms. Another landmark, torn down only a few years ago, was the log building known as Rogers' shop. The county court held its first sessions here, and for a long while it was occasionally used for religious worship. On the site of the Citizens' Bank stood in 1855 a large brick hotel. Where is now the Peoples' Bank stood Skeen's Hotel, partly brick and partly log. Tilled fields came close up to the lots in the diminutive village.

In 1870 the railroad had arrived, and yet the Covington of that date is discribed as a little, old, poor-looking town. At the lower end was a colored suburb. Around the station were several saloons, these being permitted nowhere else. Reincorporation took place February 18, 1873. The first mayor was Lewis Payne. The members of the first council were Andrew Damron, J. J. Hobbs, R. L. Parrish, A. B. Persinger, J. L. Pitzer, and William Skeen. In 1892 the town was authorized to bond itself in the sum of $10,000 for side walks and sewerage. So late as 1890, however, the population was only 704.

About 1889, a boom epidemic was sweeping the entire length of the Valley of Virginia, and Covington caught the contagion. Several small industries made a beginning and although the net results of this hot-house process were small and not altogether permanent, it was at this time that the county seat of Alleghany began its career as an industrial center.

During the third of a century that has elapsed since 1890, Covington has grown by leaps and bounds. The population in 1900 had risen to 2,950. In 1910 there were 4,234 inhabitants, and in 1920 there were 5623. Clifton Forge is still in the lead, yet if the rate of increase in the two cities were to remain the same during the present decade, Covington will have 7,613 people in 1930 against 6,612 in Clifton Forge.

Since Covington grew eight-fold in 30 years, it has very much the appearance of a new town, and it has the spirit of one. The streets are broad. Six miles of them are hard-surfaced, and this mileage is soon to be increased. There are many handsome residences and house yards, and the business buildings are in general a credit to the place. The cut through which the main line of the Chesapeake and Ohio approaches the town from the west is spanned by two bridges. Near the lower end of town a subway passes under the railroad tracks. A covered wooden bridge over Jackson's River connects the main town with the suburb of Rosemont.

The original courthouse, put up in 1823, was succeeded in 1877 by a brick building, and this, in 1911, by the present handsome and commodious structure of stone. The cost was $50,000. In one corner of the well-grassed inclosure is a beautiful monument to the memory of the Alleghany soldiers who served in the Confederate army. It was erected by the United Daughters of the Confederacy, at an expense of $3,000, and was unveiled at the dedication of the courthouse, September 15, 1911.

The Federal postoffice is a tasteful structure of brick on a lot of ample size.

The high school is housed in a building of 12 rooms, and the cost was $30,000. The graduates may enter without examination the University of Virginia, Washington and Lee University, Hampden-Sidney College, and the Randolph-Macon College of Lynchburg. Each teacher is required to hold the degree of Bachelor of Arts. The grades have a separate building near by, that cost $47,000 and in another part of the city is a school for the colored children, costing $15,000. Each of the three institutions has its own principal and a trained nurse. In all, there are about 36 teachers, and they are well paid. The pupils number about 1,500.

The Methodist Episcopal Church, South has Granbury Memorial church in the heart of the city, and Epworth Chapel east of the railroad. Near the latter is the house of worship of the Methodist Episcopal Church. The Presbyterians are building a new brick church, which will be the costliest of any in the city. The Baptist Church is new and commodious. The other churches for the white people are the Protestant Episcopal, the Roman Catholic, and the Church of Christ, all three being of medium size. The colored inhabitants have a fine brick Baptist Church west of the railroad, and a Methodist Church east of it.

A formal business directory is not appropriate in a book like this, which may not be superseded by another of its kind in a long while. A directory begins to fall out of date almost at once, and as a dependable guide is soon valueless. Suffice it to say, in general, that nearly every kind of business establishment is well represented in Covington.

The three banks—the Citizens National, the Covington National, and the Peoples, all have modern and handsome buildings, and their assets are nearly $4,000,000. These succeed the Farmers and Miners Savings Bank, chartered in 1866.

The one newspaper is the *Virginian*, a daily.

The hotels—both near the station—are the Alleghany and the O'Gara.

Among the larger business houses are two department stores and a wholesale grocery company.

More than all else, it is the manufacturing industries that have made Covington what it is. The industrial plants are 17, have a capitalization of more than $5,000,000, and give employment to a large majority of the wage-earners of the town.

It is these enterprises that have given the place its phenominal growth, and have been the means of transforming Alleghany from a predominantly agricultural county of low valuation into a wealthy and predominantly industrial county.

The local industries are the West Virginia Pulp and Paper Company, the West Virginia Pulp Products Company, the Robeson Process Company, the Southern Textile Company, the Low Moor Iron Company, the Covington Machine Company, the Covington Brick Company, the Deford Tanning Company, the Snead Foundry, Nettleton and Company, the Alleghany Ice Company, the Alleghany Beverage Company, the Alleghany Milling Company, McAllister and Bell, Incorporated, the Covington Broom Company, and the Clifton Forge Bottling Works.

Among the industries of Covington the West Virginia Pulp and Paper Company easily leads. Its grounds are in the north of the town and on both sides of Jackson's River. The buildings, yards, and offices cover thirty acres of space. Since active operations were begun, in the spring of 1900, the plant has been considerably enlarged, and is now one of the most complete of its kind in the world. The pulp is produced solely from spruce timber from the company's woodlands on the headwaters of the Cheat in West Virginia. The works require each day about 200 cords of wood, 300 tons of coal, eighty tons of pyrites, 15,000 barrels of lime, and ten tons of bleaching powder. The daily output is more than 100 tons of paper, and this is used by many of the leading weekly and monthly periodicals of the great American cities. Fine book, parchment, lithograph, and map poster papers are also made. But not all the pulp is converted into paper. A considerable amount is made into fiber and card boards, traveling cases, etc., by an allied corporation, the West Virginia Pulp Products Company. Another associated industry is the extract plant operated by the Robeson Process Company. The waste liquor from the pulp mill is piped across the river to the Robeson works, where it is turned into glutrin. This by-product is used as a disinfectant, as a briquetting agent, and as a binder in making sand cores for foundries. Without intending the least discrimination against the other industries of the county seat, it must in fairness be added that during the twenty years past the West Virginia Pulp and Paper Company has shown a most commendable civic spirit. It has placed on one and the same level its own interests and the interests of its employees. Good wages are paid. If a workman wishes to rent a house belonging to the company, the rate charged is simply what will cover interest, taxes, and other legitimate charges. If he wishes to build a cottage, money is advanced for the lot and for building purposes. Matters are often submitted to a vote of the workmen particularly interested. But no labor union is represented here, and the quantity and quality of the output are better for the absence of any. It may be said without exaggeration that it will be hard to find a large manufacturing establishment that works more smoothly than the paper mill at Covington. From 1,200 to 1,500 people are regularly employed, and the yearly payroll is in the neighborhood of $2,000,000. The freight charges paid to the railroad were in 1921, $1,150,000, mainly on the raw material received. From thirty to forty carloads of pulp wood are consumed daily, and twelve carloads of coal consumed. The same year the company paid $95,000 in taxes.

The silk industry was brought here from New Jersey by the Southern Textile Company. It is a branch of one of the largest silk corporations in the world, and has 200 female employees.

The Deford tannery dates from 1892 and is the largest steam tannery in Virginia. Its grounds cover seventeen acres, and it furnishes a good market for bark and hides. The capacity of the sheds is about 15,000 cords of bark, much of which is obtained from this county. The finest grades of leather are made and the tannery can turn out about 300 hides daily. The employees number 150 and are chiefly colored people.

The furnace at Covington makes foundry iron, and its output is over 100 tons daily, almost exclusively from ores mined in this county. The plant includes several coke ovens.

The machine shops date from 1892, and have grown into the largest plant of the kind between Newport News and Huntington. Much of the metal used is supplied by the local furnace.

The growth of the towns and villages of Alleghany creates a large demand for all kinds of dressed lumber. The planing mill industry was begun in 1887 by E. M. Nettleton, who came here from Ohio.

The Covington Roller Mill gets its power from a dam in Jackson's River, the legislative permission for which was granted in 1797. The present mill is modern in equipment and makes four grades of flour. The capacity is 125 barrels of flour and 500 bushels of ground feed.

The Alleghany Milling Company began work in 1904. Its mill has a daily capacity of 150 barrels of flour, 600 of meal, and twenty tons of feed. Three grades of flour are made. The company also handles fuel, fertilizers, salt, and farm implements. Electricity supplies the motive power.

The Covington Brick Company has been doing business twenty-five years, and its daily capacity is 25,000 brick. The supply of clay is found close to the kilns.

The Alleghany Ice Company began work in June, 1908, uses distilled mountain water, employs about eighteen men in the busy season, and has a present capacity of twenty-five tons a day. The plant is capable of meeting the demands of a city of twice the size of Covington. Delivery is by auto truck and this is found an improvement over delivery by wagon. There are branches at Hot Springs, White Sulphur Springs, and Alderson.

The Snead Foundry employs eleven men and has an output of one ton of metal a day.

The Covington Broom Factory began operations in April, 1918. It has a building thirty by fifty feet in size, equipped with up-to-date machinery. At present it employs four hands and turns out eight dozen brooms a day. It expects soon to increase its force to ten men and its capacity to twenty-five dozen.

Not quite all the enterprises that have been launched in Covington have persevered, yet the rapid growth of the town and the present congested condition of the dwelling houses show the great success that has generally attended the existing industries. The working people very frequently own their own homes. The unsightly spectacle of long rows of ill-used tenement houses, looking as much alike as peas from the same pod is hardly to be seen here. The wages paid are exceptionally high as compared with other places in Virginia. The relations between employer and employed have as a rule been very harmonious. With the exception of a single industry, the workmen are not identified with any labor union, and the prevailing opinion of the town is not in favor of such organizations. In number, the foreigner is a negligible element in Alleghany county. The people of both Covington and Clifton Forge show by their names that they are chiefly of native American stock. Of those not born within this county, some have come from states of the North and West, but a far larger share from other counties of Virginia. The colored population of Covington is about twenty-five per cent. and is industrious and law-abiding.

The incoming and outgoing railway freight is very large, and the station buildings are of a character befitting the volume of traffic. The spacious passenger house is surrounded by a broad cement platform. From each direction on the main line, five passenger trains are scheduled to stop at Covington. Three other trains run in each direction on the Hot Springs branch, and on two days of each week passenger trains run up and down the Potts Creek line.

If Covington considers itself the "Pittsburgh of Virginia," it has a valid claim to the title. Its paper mill pays more taxes than any other industrial establishment in the state. This town is the fourth largest freight-paying station on the Chesapeake and Ohio system, being exceeded only by Chicago, Cincinnati, and Richmond. The business men of Covington are alert, progressive, and hospitable, and there is present the push which is ordinarily regarded as a characteristic of the West.

XIII

CLIFTON FORGE

ON THE north side of Jackson's River, at the mouth of Smith Creek, is a small rectangular expanse of bottom land, hemmed in by a hilly plateau. On the opposite side is a quite narrow belt of low ground, behind which the surface rapidly rises to a mountainous height. A few miles westward is Fore, or Little Middle Mountain, shutting out a view of the loftier Warm Springs Mountain beyond. The scenic setting of Clifton Forge is therefore very rugged.

In 1770 and 1772 the tillable portion of the town site was patented by Robert Gillespie. He sold in 1829 to Henry Smith of Scotland, who was soon joined by Andrew Williamson. The latter with his family crossed the Atlantic in a small boat. When the railroad came in 1857 the place became known as Williamson's Station. On the upper side of Smith Creek the first land owners were Benjamin and Joseph Haynes, who were here in 1797. In 1839 Clifton Forge became a voting place, but in 1868 the river was still unbridged.

As early as about 1800, there were several furnaces and forges on the upper James. Coke was not then to be had and all smelting was done with charcoal. The daily capacity of these primitive concerns was one to three tons of metal. The triphammers were driven by waterpower. But the iron industry assumed larger dimensions after Colonel John Jordan of Lexington appeared on the scene. His Lucy Selina (now Longdale) furnace was in operation about 1825. To reach it conveniently, a good wagon road across North Mountain was a necessity. When the county court of Rockbridge balked at what seemed too formidable an undertaking, he told that body that if they would give him the men he would build the road. The offer was accepted, and the main highway between Lexington and Covington is the result. In 1828, John Jordan and John Irvine petitioned the court of Alleghany for permission to bridge Jackson's River two miles above the mouth of the Cowpasture. In the same year the county records speak of Clifton forge, and it would seem that it was one of the plants operated by the Jordans. We are informed that it stood on a hill on the south side of the river. Others place it at the gap opening toward Iron Gate. It was perhaps here that in 1813 Colonel Jordan sold to Abijah Warren a lot in "Newprospect."

By 1850 stoves, stovepipe, pots, and skillets were being made on the upper James. But from an agricultural viewpoint, there was little development on the lower course of Jacksons River.

In 1857 the Virginia Central Railroad had come to the bank of Jacksons' River, a mile above the present station at Clifton Forge. For a whole decade the iron rails did not extend any farther. Then came a resumption of railway construction, and by 1881 the Richmond and Alleghany had built up the James to a connection with the Chesapeake and Ohio. Clifton Forge became not only a railroad junction but a division point. Its growth was necessarily rapid, and in 1884 it was incorporated as a city, thus becoming politically independent of Alleghany county. A new charter was granted in 1900 and it was amended in 1904. In the former year West Clifton Forge was incorporated. The census of 1900 gave the city 3,212 inhabitants. In 1910 there were 5,740 people, and in 1920, there were 6,164. In the suburb of Selma, south of the river and outside of the corporation, there are 400 people.

During the boom epidemic of 1888-90, Clifton Forge experienced an attack of the prevailing malady. A few industrial enterprises were launched, but none proved permanent, and the railroad interest is decidedly the mainstay of the town. Because of the very broken character of the country around and the indifferent quality of much of the soil, the agricultural output within a six-mile radius is not enough to support more than a village. Some of the farm products consumed in the city are brought from beyond the eastern foot of North Mountain, a distance of about thirty miles. However, five dairies are represented in Clifton Forge.

The business quarter of the city stands on the area of bottom land already mentioned, yet a very considerable part of this level space is necessarily occupied by the shops and the extensive sidings, to say nothing of the railway offices and the commodious station grounds.

The city of Clifton Forge has a mayor and twelve councilmen and such other officials as are required by a city of its size. A circuit court for the trial of all civil and criminal cases meets in February, May, July, and November. The home of the municipal government is the city hall on Main Street, its tower clock being a very noticeable object from the station yard. Engleside Park is a recreation ground. The cemeteries are Oak Hill for the whites and Crown Hill for the colored people.

The churches are Baptist, Christian, Episcopal, Methodist Episcopal South, Presbyterian, and Catholic, besides two Baptist Churches for the colored people. A high school and the Moody School minister to the educational needs of the white children. For the colored children there are two schools. Other religious socities are a Young Men's Christian Association, a Young Women's Christian Association, and the Clifton Forge Federation of Bible Classes. The fraternal lodges are those of the Freemasons, Odd Fellows, Knights of Phythias, the Eagles, and the J. O. A. M. and the B. P. O. E. There are also lodges of the United Confederate Veterans, the United Daughters of the Confederacy, and the Sons of Confederate Veterans. There are a Masonic Temple and an Elks Home. The clubs are the Fairfax, the Clifton Forge Gun Club, the Clifton Forge Women's Club, and the Eagle's Club. Places of amusement are a theatre and four pool rooms.

The business houses of Clifton Forge include two banks, the First National and the Clifton Forge National, a wholesale grocery company, two department stores, a lumber company, a machinery and foundry company, a telephone company, ten garages, two ice plants, a bottling works, and a daily newspaper, the *Clifton Forge Review*.

Other stores and places of business are fifteen groceries, six general merchandise stores, five stores for dry goods and notions, five cleaning and pressing shops, four coal yards, four jewelry stores, four tinshops, four variety stores, four real estate offices, three hardware stores, three furniture stores, three plumbing shops, three feed stables, three drugstores, three dealers in cut flowers, two feed stores, two junk stores, two bakeries, two laundries, two photograph galleries, two printing offices, two shoe stores, two undertaker's rooms, two florists, two confectionery stores and one bicycle shop.

The professional men are thirteen physicians, eight lawyers, and four dentists.

There are two electric contractors, twelve draymen, five shoemakers, five tailors, six contractors and builders, five barbers, one auctioneer, one gunsmith, and two men who are blacksmiths and wheelwrights.

The one hotel is the Gladys Inn at the railroad station. There are also several rooming houses. The railroad company supports a hospital. The employees of the Chesapeake and Ohio corporation are grouped into nine unions.

XIV

ALLEGHANY AS SEEN IN A TOUR

A GOOD way to describe any territory is to take the reader through it on an imaginary tour. We shall do so in this instance, and as the tour is not a literal performance, we choose an ideal day and pass from one point of observation to the next with even more than the speed of the airplane.

We enter by way of Warm Springs valley, which extends into this county four miles. The fine limestone lands of this long oval basin were taken up by non-residents before 1750. At the head of Falling Springs Run, which waters the south end of the valley, are what were once known as the Dickenson meadows, from their first owner, Colonel John Dickenson, who lived on the Cowpasture below Millboro Springs. Close by is the tract of 3,329 acres patented by Thomas Massie.

The floor of this valley is 1,000 feet higher than Covington, being 2,200 feet above sea level. The climate is exceptionally good, because of the encircling mountain wall, and the perfect air-drainage afforded by several watergaps. The mean temperature is thirty-one degrees in the winter, sixty-nine in summer, and fifty-one for the year. The extremes of heat and cold are less pronounced than is usually the case in the eastern half of the United States, and there is not the close atmosphere and the winter keenness of the Atlantic coast.

Falling Springs Valley, as the section lying in Alleghany is known, produces cabbages and potatoes of large size and superior quality. The pippins are said to be quite equal to those of Albemarle county. A little above the exit of Falling Springs Run are the eight acres of cress pools belonging to the Virginia Cress Company. A season's crop is about 1,500 barrels, and it is shipped to the Eastern markets.

The pass in Valley Mountain by which the run leaves the high basin ends in a marl-cliff over which the water used to plunge in a beautiful cascade, thus described by Thomas Jefferson: "It falls over a rock 200 feet into the valley below. The sheet of water is broken in its breadth by the rocks in one or two places, but not at all in its height. Between the sheet and the rock at the bottom you may walk across dry. This cataract will bear no comparison with that of Niagara as to the quantity composing it, the sheet being only twelve or fifteen feet wide above and somewhat more spread below."

The height of the cliff is somewhat overstated by Jefferson. Yet the altitude is imposing, when viewed from the summit, and Moses Mann used the precipice as a shot tower. From considerations of the picturesque, it is a matter of regret that the waterfall is now a thing of the past. About ten years ago the current was turned into a flume in order to give free access to the soft rock which the stream had built up from the leaching of the limestone strata of the upper valley.

Looking westward from the top of the cliff, the broad lower valley of Falling Springs Run is seen to extend two miles in airline distance to the village of Barber, where are located the works which are slowly eating into the marl-cliff. Barber is at the mouth of the run. Beyond Jackson's River is a tangle of hills and ridges, with glimpses of the Alleghany Front seven miles away. South and southeast from Falling Springs valley is a mountain district, rugged and sparsely peopled. It extends all the way to the great bend in Jackson's River below the mouth of Potts Creek, and extending to Clifton Forge.

We proceed to the mouth of the creek, where we find a cluster of dwelling houses around the lime plant. There are also a church, a two-room school, and two stores. Just below the village the river bends sharply to the east. Southward the bottom lands are narrow and are not continuous. Northward, to beyond the line of Bath county, five miles above, the bottoms are more extensive, and passed into private ownership as early as 1746.

One of these early settlers, living just below the Bath line, was Robert Armstrong. In 1750 he was visited by Dr. Thomas Walker, who was on his way to Staunton from a land-prospecting tour. The doctor and his companions had gone as far to the southwest as Cumberland Gap, and had just now come over the Alleghany Front from Greenbrier River. An entry in Walker's journal reads thus:

"July 8th, having shaved, shifted, and made new shoes, we left our useless Raggs at Ye camp and got to Walker Johnson's about noon. We moved over to Robert Armstrong's in the afternoon and stayed there all night. The people here are very hospitable and would be better able to support travelers was it not for the great number of Indian warriors that frequently take what they want from them, much to their prejudice."

When the railway spur was built from Covington to Hot Springs, the workmen demolished an Indian burial ground that lay in its path. This mound was a little south of the railroad bridge over Falling Spring Run, and was examined by an expert from the Ethnological Bureau at Washington. It is a common surmise that a mound containing Indian skeletons marks the site of a battle. On the contrary it means that there was once a village nearby, the mound being the result of successive interments. Indian battles were very small affairs. The victorious party usually lost few men or none, and it did not bury the killed on the other side.

The fine half-moon bottom at Barber was the nucleus of an important pioneer settlement. The price paid by William Mann in 1762 was nearly $10.00 an acre if measured by the purchasing power of the dollar in our time. And yet those were troublous days, for there is a tradition in the Mann family that after the water had been turned off from the mill wheel and the miller had gone home, the Indians would sneak in after dark, turn on the water, and grind a grist for themselves. The sound could be heard at the blockhouse, but the inmates esteemed it the part of prudence not to interfere. The Indians would not turn off the water when they went away. On this farm, Moses, the son of William Mann, operated a mill for making gunpowder and bullets.

A mile above Barber may be seen, a little way off at the right, the long foot-hill elevation known as Mad Ann's Ridge, because associated with the exploits of Ann Bailey. Toward the river are limestone caverns. It is averred that William Mann lived in one of these a while, and that it is where one of his children was born. But the oldest of the Manns living in that vicinity know nothing of any such tradition.

Still higher up the river is the Natural Well. In the river bottom is a roundish opening, very suggestive of the mouth of a well. Below, the cave-wall widens very greatly, and at a depth of almost twenty feet is a copious supply of good water, reached by a well sweep. The water is also piped to a neighboring house.

A mile before we reach the county seat is Dry Run, a suburb of about thirty houses. A little more than the same distance beyond is Mallow, another suburb of about the same size, but less compact. Close by is a large dairy farm.

The Potts Creek road leads through the Carpenter bottom and crosses Jackson's River by a covered wooden bridge. Where the low ground ends a mountain begins. It looks strange to have to climb a mountain just to go up a valley, but in the road which follows Potts Creek from its mouth are several fords. At the foot of the ridge on the farther side, we come to Potts Creek for the first time, and here we cross a railroad over which trains run only two days in the week. Looking down Potts Creek in the direction of the Alleghany poor farm we notice a very high and almost perpendicular cliff of bare rock. Other cliffs of like character occur elsewhere on Potts Creek and also on Jackson's River above Covington. In all these instances the face of the precipice is anything but smooth.

Soon we pass, on the farm of R. B. Rose, a weather-beaten log house probably built much more than a century ago. It was once the home of the pioneer Kimberlin. Yet even he was not the first settler, for he was preceded by a Potts, who was living here at least as early as 1767. Local tradition says his clearing was the first one in the valley. Although Potts did not long remain, the creek has gone by his name ever since. It was first known as Carpenter's Creek.

Within two miles we cross Blue Spring Run, a swift, sizable stream which comes from the direction of Nuckoll's Knob, an eminence on the eastern horizon that is quite blunt on its northern side. It is so lofty that the view from the summit on a clear day is well worth the climb. A mile or so up the run there used to be a grist mill run by a crabbed person named Sinkhorn. Still higher up the run, on the land of Jacob Bush, was once another powder mill. It was abandoned just about one century ago, yet the field in which it stood is still known as the "powder mill field."

Returning to the creek road and going up a rise is a burial ground. The first interments are those of Jacob Persinger and his wife. A quarter of a mile to our right, and near the bank of Potts Creek, is a house, the oldest portion of which was built by the Persinger who spent eight or ten years of his early life among the Shawnee Indians. The hewed logs which were put into this section of the now weather-boarded house are very large, and the boards in the wainscoating of the sitting room are of a width rarely seen nowadays. But in the enlarging and remodeling of this ancient house, the original features are much obscured. Quite near the house was once a long kitchen, and the slaves slept in the loft above. The old hunter had a still in which he made firewater. But because of a tragedy which occurred on this farm, the new owner removed the still and put the stillhouse to a better use. It was harvest time and Colonel Persinger was telling a slave named Blue to grip the grain in a different manner. Blue replied with blasphemous profanity that he would not do so. When next the slave was asked to give his master the cradle, he told the colonel to come and get it if he wanted it. Persinger then stepped into the grain four or five paces in front of the negro, and when the latter had come up with him he made a high cut, which the colonel attempted to parry, but the blade struck him back of his right knee and cut to the bone. The assault was witnessed by several persons, these declaring in the trial that Blue was insolent generally, did much as he pleased, and had previously made threats against Persinger. Blue escaped to the mountain, but was soon captured, and forty-five days after the assault he was hanged. Colonel Persinger died from loss of blood a few days after the hurt. Both master and slave had been drinking that morning.

About three miles higher up the valley we come to the house of Elias Bowyer, and this aged citizen points to a cave entrance in a rocky cliff near the creek. A settler named Evans had preceeded Mr. Bowyer's grandfather in the ownership of the farm, his clearing being only half a year later than that of Potts. In the Indian days, Evans and his wife used the cavern as a sleeping room, climbing to it by means of a pine from which the numerous limbs were not cut close to the trunk. This device of pioneer days was called a "Jacob's ladder." The cavern lies high and dry, and is fairly roomy, when one is once inside.

Near Mr. Bowyer's house a little stream comes down from

Potts Mountain. It is called Solomon's Run from this circumstance: A slacker of the Revolution by the name of Solomon came to this side-valley to avoid military service. He lived in a shack and subsisted mainly on venison. He had to be very sparing of his ammunition, and he dried his venison, so that each carcass might last a long while. One day a settler happened to meet Solomon, who now learned that the war with England had been a thing of the past for five years. He had been a hermit seven years. The slacker went back to his old home, but he could not at once resume eating bread, as it made him sick.

Potts Creek is very crooked, although the valley is not a limestone belt. Soon we come to one of the several bridges. A white house a little lower down the stream is the Arritt homestead. The gristmill still further down is the leading one in this valley. We cross a rise, and then we come to the Jordan mines in a section of the creek bottom. They are no longer worked and nearly all the seventy-five to 100 houses that stood here have been taken away. It was a busy place while the works were active, and many of the miners were of foreign birth. A few vacant buildings still remain. Still further on is the hamlet of Bess, twenty miles from Covington. Here is the terminus of the Potts Creek railway. This part of the valley is more populous than it is below. The water all along Potts Creek is freestone, and the soil is good enough to make this valley one of the most interesting in Alleghany from an agricultural viewpoint.

When we are still a mile or so below the county line, we come to the old pike that ran from Sweet Springs to Fincastle. In its palmy days it was a busy thoroughfare, but travel has almost deserted it in favor of a newer road. On each side of the ford where the road crosses Potts Creek, still a quite respectable stream, stands one of the old-time hostelries. The one on the east side is log, the other is brick. On the top of Potts Mountain, a few miles to the east, was once the "Mountain House," and some vestiges of the tavern still remain. Nearly seventy years ago, the Mountain House was mentioned in the Act of Assembly, by which a small corner of Alleghany was annexed to Craig.

We turn westward, and before we have gained the summit of Peter's Mountain, a bend in the almost abandoned road brings us against the county line. On the mountain top the road forks.

The left branch leads to Sweet Springs, and were we to follow it we would within half a mile pass very near the spot where was once the house of William and Ann Royall. Of them the reader will find an account in a later chapter. The other branch, leading to Sweet Chalybeate Springs, is the Stringer Road, because built with an eye to business by John Stringer. The grade is most abominably steep, and in scarcely more than a mile we are in the limestone lowlands and at the house where Stringer kept tavern, but which is now the farmhouse of Daniel J. Callaghan. Stringer built the road to shorten the distance from White Sulphur to Fincastle, and bring more business to his tavern; and in this he was successful.

In a short mile from the old Stringer house, and by a grade still downward, we come to the Sweet Chalybeate, formerly called Red Sweet Springs. It was a noted resort in the antebellum days, but one of the effects of the World War was to put an end to its long history as a watering place. As long ago as 1773, people visited here for the sake of the waters. The guest capacity of the resort is 350 persons, and the mineral waters, which pour out of the earth at the rate of 250 gallons a minute, are serviceable in neuralgia, rheumatism, and debility. The Red Springs Company was incorporated in 1836 by Philip Rogers and others with power to own not more than 5,000 acres of land and employ a capital of not more than $100,000. Though not only old, but old-fashioned as well, the cluster of large buildings will still answer for years of service of some sort. The expansive lawn is well shaded and the entire vicinage is pleasing to the eye. It seems a grevious economic waste that all this house room should not be in use.

A mile below Sweet Chalybeate, Snake Run comes in from the northeast. The stream is small, but the valley is long. A century ago it was settled by the Carsons, Carters, and Stones, and their descendants are numerous. It is related that the tributary derives its name from the following incident: Some families living farther west fled in this direction to get away from the Indians, and while camping in this side-valley one of their children was bitten by a rattlesnake. Let us hope the bite was not fatal.

We are following Sweet Spring Run. Toward Peter's Mountain the lands are limestone and largely open, and are well peopled. Along our road, houses are much more numerous than we shall find them presently, and among them are a few summer bungalows, one of which carries a name.

We pass Beaver Dam Falls, an actual beaver dam once being here. In this vicinity a field on the creek bottom has a record of producing 105 bushels of shelled corn to the acre.

In three miles from Sweet Chalybeate we come to a large, old-fashioned, weather-beaten building. It is the "old Damron place." Very near by, Sweet Springs Run flows into Dunlap Creek, both streams having their sources in Monroe. The red Americans styled this little river the Eskataba, which means "clear running water." But unlike the English settlers along the Atlantic, the Scotch-Irish pioneers of the mountains would retain almost none of the expressive Indian names. So they called this stream Meadow Creek, from the natural meadows they found about Callaghan Station. It took its present name from the Dunlap who temporarily owned a patent of 875 acres that included these meadows.

In three more miles we come to a huge landmark of "ye olden time." It was once the famous turnpike hostelry known as Crow's tavern, and was frequented by some of the renowned statesmen of the era before the civil war. It is related that in 1839 President Van Buren rode here from Washington on horseback to attend a picnic. He came unguarded and unattended.

At this point our road forks, the left hand branch leading up a small creek to Alleghany Station, three miles away, and thence to White Sulphur Springs. In his *Virginia Collections*, written near ninety years ago, Howe says that, "near the home of Mr. John Lewis, there is on the roadside a large shelving rock called Peter's rock, where says tradition, he (Peter Wright) sought shelter in a snowstorm. Here he lay for several days, until the snow was four feet deep." According to the late John A. Carson, the rock is by the side of this road, a mile below Alleghany Station. Wright nearly starved and had begun to chew his moccasins to extract some sustenance from them. But fortunately a deer came struggling through the snow, was promptly shot, and the hunter then went to chewing raw venison.

We take the thinly peopled road leading to Covington. Before reaching Callaghan Station it used to cross Dunlap by five fords. These were abolished in 1915-17, when a state road was built a part of the way. Near Callaghan the low ground broadens and houses are more numerous. A mile further, but not on the railroad, is what remains of the tavern opened by Dennis Callaghan. In the stagecoach days it was a famous lodging place. The locality was first known as the Forks of Dunlap, because the main stream is joined by a large tributary from the northwest. It has been Ugly in name ever since the eighteenth century, but the title appears to come from a settler named Ogley. William Knox was living in this valley as early as 1781. From here to the vicinity of Covington the waters of the Dunlap basin are as yet unpolluted.

Below Old Callaghan, Dunlap Creek presses through the gorge between Peter's Mountain and a continuation called Lick Mountain. The old pike did not use this gorge, but kept along the west foot of Lick Mountain, coming to Jackson's River above Barber on its way to Warm Springs. The railroad turns away from Dunlap two miles above Callaghan Station, and begins a sidling approach to the Alleghany Front. The ten-mile distance to Alleghany Station is through a very rugged and sparsely peopled region. Between two long tunnels and very near the Greenbrier line is the little village of Alleghany, the railway station for Sweet Springs.

From Old Callaghan it is five miles through the gorge to the county seat. Let us digress a moment to tell of the Midland Trail, the newly arranged thoroughfare connecting the east of Virginia with the states of the Ohio Valley.

This trail enters Virginia at the top of the Alleghany Divide, at the very point chosen by Washington in his waterway scheme to join Chesapeake Bay to the Ohio, using James River, Dunlap Creek, and a portage over the Alleghany to reach the Greenbrier, and thence the Kanawha and the Ohio. It follows very closely the old emigrant trail, by which hundreds of wagons, a century ago, poured into the basin of the Mississippi. From this entrance on the Alleghany to the crest of the Blue Ridge the trail crosses the great valleys up which the Scotch-Irish pioneers came from Pennsylvania in the middle third of the eighteenth century. Until the Revolution the Alleghany was the western limit of settlement, escept for the few daring souls who pressed beyond and paid dear for taking the risk.

Many of the leaders of the West were nurtured in this area, and the names of the early pioneers who settled along Dunlap, Jackson's River, the Cowpasture, and the Calfpasture River, are to be found as household names in the West. That the descendants of these pioneers will welcome an open road to the cradle of their ancestors is a foregone conclusion.

A short distance west of the old Callaghan tavern is Oak Hall, built by Lord Hilton of England, who lived here a while in an effort to regain his health. Here was born his son, the wealthy Earl Fitz William. A mile beyond Oak Hall are vestiges of the ironworks built before 1800 by Edward Ramsey, said to have been a near relative to the Ramsey who invented the steamboat.

Passing again through Covington and Mallow, we come to Island Ford, two miles below the latter point. Here our road crosses Jackson's River by a covered bridge, the stream being closely hemmed in by mountain walls. A little lower down are the chimneys marking the site of the Island Ford Tavern. From here to the Iron Gate, bottom land occurs only in pockets, the most extensive being the one formerly owned owned by the Karnes family, and now the site of the town of Low Moor. The one industry of this place is the large iron furnace operated by the Low Moor Company.

Here we turn squarely to the right to visit the Rich Patch, our road following not only a small stream but a spur railway, built to reach some deposits of iron ore, but not now in use. In two miles we come to Rich Patch Mines, where wooden ironworks falling into decay, are surrounded by many small red houses. Several of them are still occupied, and there is a school in the village. But the furnace has been silent for years. To financial embarrassment, rather than a failure of ore, is attributed the collapse of the mining industry at this point.

We go nearly five miles farther, the steady ascent putting us 800 feet above the level of Low Moor. Just back of the store we come to is a small level field which is said to have given a name to the locality. When the white settlers came, it was an Indian old-field, and the rankness of the vegetation, caused by the wash from the neighboring heights, gave it the name of the "rich patch." The old Fincastle and Covington pike passed this way, and undoubtedly it followed in the main an Indian path. This must have been the trail taken by two Moravian missionaries in 1749, when they journeyed from the site of Covington to Catawba Creek. They speak of "mountains all around," and they heard "an awful howling of wolves." But the section of the old pike leading over Carpenter's Mountain has been abandoned, and though it reached Covington in seven miles, by the Holloway ford, the people now have to travel fifteen miles.

The name Rich Patch is often given to the mountain ridges along the Botetourt line, which is only a mile away. But properly it applies only to the narrow, elevated district just east of Carpenter's Mountain. The limestone soil makes it a good grazing district. Here have long been settled the Bennett, Fridley, Hook, Humphries, King, Stull, and other families.

We retrace our steps to Low Moor and proceed to Clifton Forge. From the high ground at the north of the city, it is seven miles as the crow flies to Griffith Knob on the border of Bath. In the intervening distance is an uneven plain, low ridges breaking the surface. The soil is thin and the tilled land limited in amount. And yet there is evidence of very early settlement.

Between Clifton Forge and the wilderness of Padd's Creek in Bath the only place is the town of Longdale, chiefly a creation of the iron industry. From this point a long railway spur runs up the valley of Simpson's Creek to some ore deposits. This branch is a freight carrier and the valley it ascends contains but few farms. A glance at the map shows that the Simpson's Creek valley is like a wedge driven into Rockbridge, of which it is geographically a part. This eastern end of Alleghany is unattractive to the agriculturist, yet the hills are stored with iron ore and the deposits have been in use more than a century.

Just east of Clifton Forge is the watergap in Waite Mountain known as the Iron Gate, and through it flows Jackson's River. Although the pass is both short and narrow, and the mountain not lofty, the view is striking. On the right side of the river is a railroad track and a public road. When a person is half through the gorge, he sees on the other side of the river a thick, massive, symmetrical arch of white rock, rising from the river-level. Far above is a series of four thinner arches. The face of the outcrops are perpendicular, and elsewhere the face of the gorge is so abrupt, that it looks as though it might tax the agility even of a goat to make the ascent. South of the river the formations are less clearly defined.

Immediately below the pass is the town of Iron Gate on the edge of Botetourt. It is another center of the iron industry.

Iron Gate, where the census enumerator in 1920 found just one individual less than 700 people, lies on the river bottom next to the Rockbridge line. It was incorporated in 1890 and 1896, and placed wholly within the border of Alleghany. A new charter was granted in 1906. Being comparatively new, the town is regularly laid out. Low Moor occupies a similar position on another tract of river bottom, but Longdale, a much smaller place than either, lies in the hill district northeast of Clifton Forge.

XV

ANN ROYALL AND ANN BAILEY

ANN NEWPORT was born near Baltimore in 1769. In 1772 her parents moved to the mouth of the Loyal Hanna in the west of Pennsylvania. There the family lived in a log cabin only eight feet broad and ten feet long. It contained a bed, a puncheon table, and four stools, but there was neither a trunk nor a box, nor was there a tablecloth in the hut. Ann never saw a metallic pin until she was a grown woman. On the frontier thorns were used as pins and mussel-shells as spoons. But in possessing knives, forks, and spoons, the Newports were better off than most of their neighbors. From the door could be seen a tree in which was the nest of an eagle.

It has been conjectured that Newport was a tory and fled to the frontier to get closer to British influence. Be this as it may, the Americanism of the daughter was sound to the core. The father was a man of some education and taught his girl to read, but they were living in a wilderness, and Ann grew up almost as a child of nature.

Mr. Newport died before Ann was grown, and the widow married a man named Butler. An Indian raid in 1782 made her a widow a second time, and three years later she was at Staunton, Virginia, near which town she seems to have had relatives. With her were two living children. The second was James Butler, who moved to Indiana after he was grown.

It is now necessary, for a moment, to leave the widow and her family, in order to take up another thread in the narrative.

Major William Royall was a zealous patriot in the American Revolution, and he raised the first company for the defense of Virginia. Out of his own pocket he sent a schooner laden with flour for the relief of the people of Boston, after that city had been closed to commerce by order of the British government. During his seven years of military service he paid his own way, receiving no remuneration from his state or from Congress. In the summer of 1781, Major Royall was a member of the House of Delegates, then sitting at Staunton, on account of the invasion by Cornwallis. A report came that the British cavalry was moving on that town by way of Rockfish Gap. The legislators rushed out of Staunton with breakneck speed. But the Scotch-Irish of the vicinity turned out in force, old men as well as boys, and they proposed to give Tarleton a practical knowledge of their skill with the rifle, in case that brutal trooper should attempt to force his way through the Blue Ridge.

Royall was so ashamed of his fellow legislators that he told the people of the Valley he would settle among them after the war was over. He had been a wealthy planter of Amelia county, but he was as good as his word. His patents in the vicinity of Sweet Springs covered more than 2,000 acres. He built a house on the western slope of Peter's Mountain, a little below the old turnpike leading from Sweet Springs to Fincastle, and almost on the present line between Alleghany and Monroe. The commodious log dwelling stood until about 1850. The spot has been reclaimed by the forest, but the house-yard may still be traced, and a rock-heap marks the position of the chimney.

To find relief from a skin ailment, Mrs. Butler went with her children to Sweet Springs. Major Royall invited her to become his housekeeper, and she accepted. Ann seems to have interested the old planter at once. She had a bright, retentive mind.

In 1797 the hermit-philosopher and the forest-bred girl were married. Their sixteen years of wedded life were childless but happy. The wife idolized her husband and his views were her views. Whenever the district court sat at Sweet Springs the house was full of guests. Toward the end of his life Royall was an invalid and was tenderly nursed. He died in 1813, making his wife and a nephew his executors. With the exception of one tract of land, he left his wife during her widowhood the use of all his estate. The will was at once disputed by another nephew and ten years of litigation followed. The relatives of Royall would not accept the widow as a social equal. They even denied that there had been any marriage, but this contention was overthrown by the courts.

Mrs. Royall was now quite alone. She missed the influence her husband had exerted over her. For a time books lost their charm and she had a great desire to see the world. It was doubtless the persecution by the relatives of Royall that made her say she could not love the mountains any longer. Yet it was an article in her creed that "one learns more in a day by mixing with mankind than he can in a year shut up in a closet."

She sold a house and two lots and began her travels. From 1817 to 1825 she was much of the time in the South, especially in Alabama, for which state she had a liking. It was while she was there that the lawsuit was decided against her. She was dispossessed of her inheritance and even jailed as an imposter. The shock made her ill and to relieve her mind she began writing her first book. Yet she did not let this work interfere with going to Washington to secure the pension, to which as a widow, she was entitled. The cost of the journey was in large degree met by her traveling companions. A family at Alexandria, the head of which was a freemason, took her into their home for six months, regardless of remuneration. But later on she repaid these kind friends.

Mrs. Royall's first visit to the national capital was in July, 1824. The first statesman she met was John Quincy Adams, who paid her five dollars for an advance subscription, asked her to call on Mrs. Adams, and promised his aid in securing a pension. This promise he faithfully observed. She spent six weeks in Washington, and then journeyed to New England to collect further material for her book and to secure more advance orders. Under the title of *Life, Manners, and Customs in the United States,* her first book was published at Hartford, Connecticut.

During the next five years Mrs. Royall visited nearly every town of consequence in the twenty-four states which then existed. Meanwhile she wrote a novel, *The Tennessean,* and nine more volumes of descriptive sketches. This prosperous period was brought to a close by the enemies her writings had created. Through a forced interpretation of a moss-covered law, Mrs. Royall was convicted of being a common scold, fined ten dollars, and bound over for one year. She was the first woman in America to be subjected to such an indignity. She would have retired to a farm, but had no means to purchase one. A trip South in 1830 yielded meager returns in a financial way, and on her return she was nearly worn out.

In 1831, Mrs. Royall took up her residence in the city of Washington, then a straggling town of cheap houses, muddy streets, unhealthful marshes, and perhaps 15,000 inhabitants. The national capital was her home for the remainder of her life. For the greater portion of this time she lived in a rented house standing in the northeast corner of the present grounds of the Library of Congress. There were shade trees in the yard and a good well. Then as now, the city covered a large surface and the widow could keep poultry. One day Richard M. Johnson, while vice-president, helped her catch a hen as he was passing the house.

Mrs. Royal was now sixty-two years of age. To keep the wolf from the door she set up a printing press in her own house, taking out a sink to make room for it. As sole editor and proprietor, she began the publication of a weekly newspaper. Her choice of title was not a good one. The name, *Paul Pry,* is calculated to make one think it was a yellow sheet, devoted to sensation and scandal. On the contrary, it was clean. The first issue appeared December 3, 1831. The price was $2.50 a year, and local subscriptions were secured mainly through her own efforts. But within a year she had agents in nearly every city and large town. The typesetting and presswork were done by a foreman assisted by two boys from an orphanage. The first page was given to literary articles, the second and third to editorials, news, jokes, and miscellaneous matter, and the fourth to advertisements. In 1837 the title was changed to *The Huntress.* In the new form the paper was a distinct improvement, though less a financial success, owing to the antagonism of Calvinistic Protestants. Nevertheless, Mrs. Royall continued its publication until July 2, 1854, her death taking place three months later at the age of eighty-five.

In personal appearance Mrs. Royall was short and very plump. She had pink cheeks, fair hair, very bright blue eyes, and in her dress she was scrupulously neat. She was a good talker, was quick to laugh, and had a keen sense of the ridiculous. She was loyal to her friends, and young men admired her for her courage and her aptness in repartee.

Mrs. Royall did not possess the great advantage of a systematic education. Her mental qualities were keen but undisciplined. She was also deficient in spiritual insight, calm judgment, and coherency. Yet her forest training gave her quickness and accuracy of observation, and a contempt for the sham and insincerity of fashionable life. She was fearless, and her energy, industry, and perseverance were wonderful. She dared to think for herself, and to express her thoughts in sharp-edged words that could not fail to hit the mark. Toward her own sex she was loyal, and because of her kindness to unfortunate women her reputation sometimes fell under unjust suspicion. Her parents had suffered at the hands of the red man, and yet she stood for justice toward him. But the policy of the British crown in turning the Indians loose on the American frontier she denounced as "a foul deed that ought never to be forgiven or forgotten."

Ann Royal was broad and intense in her patriotism, and she fervently desired the preservation of the Federal government. She was proud that the United States extends to the Pacific. She was enthusiastic over the Great West. She admired New England, where her books sold well. The people of New York she found immersed in business and lacking in refinement, and yet less aristocratic than those of Pennsylvania and the South. For the east of Virginia she had little liking, probably because her husband had turned his back upon it. With respect to slavery she was tolerant, and yet she did not think well of the institution. Major Royall was a slaveholder, but emancipated a boy.

Because of her lack of well-balanced intellectual training, her writings do not have the artistic finish to entitle them to rank as true literature. Nevertheless, her books of travel are very readable. Her observations are close and usually very accurate, and her statistical information was gathered with great care. Consequently her books are of much value in telling of conditions that existed nearly a century ago. Her one novel is of less merit.

The pen-portraits scattered numerously through her books and the columns of her newspaper added much to her income. In clear, vivid sentences Mrs. Royall would delineate the personal appearance, the garb, and the inner characteristics of the personages who were more or less in the public eye. Sittings for this purpose were arranged for, just as in the case of sittings in the studio of a photographer. These portraitures made her books sell like "hot cakes."

Her newspaper was a free lance in a political way, and wielded an influence not to be despised. The things it stood for were usually those that make for social betterment. She was quick to detect graft and political schemes. On one occasion she was offered $1,000 if she would keep silent on a certain matter. She replied that she was not for sale.

Her personal knowledge of the public men of her time is most remarkable. She met and talked with every person who filled the presidential chair, beginning with Washington and ending with Lincoln. It was probably on the occasion of his visit to Sweet Springs in 1797 that she saw General Washington. She chatted with John Adams in his own home when he was eighty-nine years of age. Lincoln she must have seen during his one term in Congress. She even met Lafayette on his visit to Boston in 1825. The great Frenchman gave her a letter in support of her pension claim.

During her widowhood Mrs. Royall was very poor, and yet she was always generous. That she managed to travel so much is rather surprising. But when she made up her mind to go anywhere, she set out, and she managed to accomplish her purpose. Her husband was a freemason, and he had told her not to hesitate to call on the brethren of the mystic tie when help was necessary. She never called on them in vain. The Catholics and the Jews also showed her much kindness.

But Mrs. Royall was her own worst enemy. She did not mince her words at any time, and often they stung like a hornet. Her pen was caustic, because she had no patience with side-stepping and subterfuge on questions clear to herself and which she earnestly believed to be for the good of the public. It was the public men she flayed without mercy who were the means of keeping her out of a pension until she was more than eighty years old. Yet she never gave up the fight and was finally granted $40 a month.

Mrs. Royall did not read the Bible and did not have a just attitude toward the Christian religion. She therefore antagonized a large share of the better elements of society, and it is partly because of this fact that her name has fallen into eclipse. But that she was no infidel, the following quotation will show: "The worship of God is paramount to all other duties. I am far from being among the number of those who set at naught the worship of the Deity, however much I may deplore the abominable prostitution of that real religion which is pure and undefiled." The difficulty in her case is that which has been a difficulty with many others. Early in life she began to observe the conduct of persons who were members of the Church, and was appalled at the inconsistencies she noted. And it must be conceded that the churches of her time were involved in various political schemes that were not to their credit. Major Royall was of French descent, an admirer of Lafayette and the French people, and a reader of Voltaire and other skeptics. He was a man of dry wit and was rather cynical. His new neighbors pronounced him eccentric and scholarly. It might therefore be supposed that she imbibed free thought from her husband. But the latter was probably no more than what is commonly styled liberal in his religious views. He owned and used an Episcopal prayer book.

There was also arrayed against Ann Royall the Anti-Masonic party, which for some years was a power in American politics. In its ranks were many of the Protestants. In fighting this political party she gave no quarter and received none. Almost entire editions of her books were bought by her opponents and burned.

All in all, however, America is the gainer that Ann Royall lived in it. Her greatest error lay in her shortsightedness while viewing the tares among the wheat.

*　　*　　*　　*　　*　　*　　*　　*

Ann Bailey, one of the most picturesque characters in American border history, was known as "Mad Ann," because of her waspish temper. Her maiden name was Dennis, and she was a native of Liverpool, England. Like many other persons of her time, she came to Virginia as an indentured servant, and paid the cost of her passage across the Atlantic by being bound into servitude for several years. During this period in her life she was at Staunton. At the age of twenty-three she married James Trotter, who was killed nine years later in the battle of Point Pleasant. William Trotter, her only child, was born near the present village of Barber in 1767.

After Trotter was killed the widow resolved to avenge his death. She left her boy with Mrs. Moses Mann, put on masculine apparel, and became a hunter and scout. She rode a black horse that she called "Pool," an abbreviation of Liverpool. Her other horse she named "Jennie Mann."

It is said of Ann Bailey that she put more than one Indian out of the way. On one occasion her led horse was stolen from her.

She trailed the Indian and found him swimming New River with the animal. The thief was shot in the back. After an outburst of scurrilous profanity directed at the dead foe, Mrs. Bailey called to the horse and "Jennie Mann" swam back to her. At another time tradition relates that she came to Fort Young after dark, hallooed for admission, and entered with a scalp she had taken. Her most famous exploit was the relief of Fort Lee, standing where now is the capital of West Virginia. The stockade was besieged by Indians, the gunpowder gave out, and it was a great risk to attempt to get past the assailants. But Mad Ann volunteered, rode swiftly on "Liverpool" to Fort Union—now Lewisburg—and came back with an extra horse bearing a supply of powder. This feat was performed in 1791, when she was forty-nine years of age.

For a while, Ann Bailey lived in a hut on Mad Ann's Ridge, near Barber. On one occasion Liverpool went on to Mann's without his rider. A party from the stockade proceeded to follow the trail and located the woman by airholes in the snow. She had fallen asleep, either from liquor or drowsiness. According to Ann Royall, who visited her in her old age, she could both drink and swear. In 1785 she married her second husband. Becoming a widow a second time, she went to live with her son, who had settled in Gallia county, Ohio. Eccentric to the last, she refused to live in his comfortable house, and built herself a cabin out of fence rails, living in it with a granddaughter. Here she died in 1825 at the age of eighty-three.

In personal appearance, Mrs. Bailey was short, coarse, and masculine. Yet in manner she was affable and pleasing. She wore a coat instead of a gown, and she was able to read and write. While ranging the forest, she "halways carried a hax and a hauger and could chop as well as any man."

XVI

ALLEGHANY IN THE WORLD WAR

With slight qualification, the people of Alleghany and Clifton Forge were firmly loyal to their country, and were ready to uphold all conservative measures. The war activities at home were thoroughly organized and very effective. The conservation of food and fuel was systematically stressed, and was so well advertised through the mails as to reach all households. There was an enlarged use of wood as fuel. The County Demonstrator was exceedingly efficient. War gardens became very general, and after the return of peace they were not abandoned. Two community plots, comprising ten acres, were planted to potatoes, the proceeds being applied to purposes of public benefit. A fund was raised to pay for the seed and fertilizer, the former being very high in price, but all labor was given without charge.

One of the most practical of the war organizations was the company styled the Alleghany Home Guard. Its membership was drawn from a radius that reached even to Low Moor, and it had a salutary influence for good order. Its organization took place at the courthouse, June 11, 1917, the following officers being elected: president, A. C. Sizer; commanding officer, F. C. Jesser; treasurer, T. B. McCaleb; secretary, Paul B. Lacy. The troop officers, appointed by Captain Jesser, were these: first lieutenant, P. C. Dunbrock; second lieutenant, P. J. Gilmore; first sergeant, A. H. Bowie; second sergeant, P. B. Lacy; third sergeant, George Alexander; fourth sergeant, J. J. Reardon. An entrance fee of fifty cents, and dues of ten cents a month, were assessed on all members. Drills were held weekly in the streets of Covington. Rifle practice was held weekly on a specially constructed range in the basement of the courthouse. During the epidemic of influenza in the fall of 1918, the Guards policed the streets to prevent people from gathering in crowds.

At the end of the war, the fund in the Home Guard treasury, increased by public subscriptions, was used by a committee to erect the bronze memorial tablet in the courthouse yard. This tablet, on which is inscribed the legend, "They died that we might live," perpetuates the names of the eighteen heroes from this county who made the supreme sacrifice. This tablet was due almost entirely to the individual efforts of a committee consisting of P. J. Gilmore, F. C. Jesser, C. B. Cushing, A. C. Sizer, and P. B. Lacy. Even the mechanical work was done in Covington. The tablet was formally unveiled May 30, 1920, in the presence of thousands of spectators, the next of kin to the martyred soldiers being given privileged places. It was buried in masses of flowers carried by the children of the public schools. The names on the tablet are these:

William Bands (colored)—killed in action.

Roy A. Bassaree—Co. K, 128th Inf.—age 25—killed in Argonne Oct. 6, 1918.

Roy H. Bush—Marines—died of wounds in battle of the Marne, Aug. 16, 1918.

Hobson D. Byers—killed in action Oct. 22, 1918.

Joseph A. Byers—killed in action Oct. 8, 1918.

Charles A. Coleman—Co. H.—(Bath)—age 29—killed in action at Grauce Montague, Oct. 16, 1918.

Almer R. Dew—died Sept. —, 1918.

D. D. Goodall (colored)—died.

Mordaunt B. Kelly—killed in action, Oct. 5, 1918.

Bedford C. Lam—(Albemarle)—Co. H.—age 22—died of disease at Camp Hospital No. 10, Aug. 1, 1918.

Marion Landes—died at Camp Lee, —— 16, 1918.

Alvey R. Leffel—Co. H.—age 21—killed in action, Oct. 16, 1918.

Broadus R. Martin—Co. H.—age 23—died of wounds received Oct. 16, 1918.

James M. Nicely—age 23—Co. A, 304th Inf.—died of pneumonia, Oct. 13, 1918.

Herbert W. Nuckolls—died from wounds, Nov. 27, 1918.

William McK. Rose.

Lester Smith—killed in action.

Earl H. Tyree—killed in Argonne, Oct. 1, 1918.

The Home Guard was a volunteer organization, even as to the services asked of the members in safeguarding the community. The enrollment was 150.

The departure of Company H, the first Alleghany unit, was

thus commented on by the editor of *The Virginian:* "One hundred and sixty boys, most of them from our dear old Alleghany, in a magnificent column, swung off to the station. Company H began a journey that will not end until Hohenzollernism is no more. May God bless them! May He bless the cause for which they fight." This command became a part of the 116th Infantry, 29th Division of the National Guard. From July 25 to September 24, 1917, it was at Camp McClellan, and from September 26, 1917 to June 11, 1918 at Anniston, Alabama.

We now pass to a chronological account of the organizations formed in Alleghany for war work.

The first was the Woman's Service League, Mrs. C. P. Jones, Jr., chairman for the county, Mrs. W. A. Rhinehart, treasurer, Mrs. Sallie Staples, secretary. It was perfected May 3, 1917, and had a working membership of 216. The divisions were Covington, Low Moor, and Falling Spring, Mrs. F. U. Humbert being chairman at Low Moor, and Miss Annie Moomaw at Falling Spring. The chairman of the girls' division, which had forty members, was Miss Ida Anderson. The League expended $385 on Company H, outfitting it with comfort kits, the articles for these being contributed by the public, as were also all moneys used by the League in its work. The aid given the Red Cross was $1,259.60, many boxes of surgical supplies and other articles being sent to it as a gift of the League, and finding their way to the Dr. McGuire Hospital Unit. In July, 1917, two French orphans were adopted, $74 being appropriated 'for this purpose. At a cost of $30, the girls' division knitted five sets for the battleship *Virginia,* these consisting of sweaters, helmets, mufflers, and other articles. In August, 1917, the League gave place to the Red Cross chapter then organized. It is impossible to give it too much credit, since it was the foundation on which subsequent work was laid.

The first Food Card Campaign was organized July 11, 1917, with Mrs. C. P. Jones, Jr., as chairman. The registration—805 —was one of the largest in the state, in proportion to the population, and it consisted of housewives who pledged themselves to aid the government by conserving food.

September 5, 1917, Mrs. C. P. Jones, Jr., was appointed chairman of the Woman's Committee, Council of National Defense, and it continued as a permanent organization for all war work headed by Mrs. Jones. It is believed that the record of this committee was not surpassed in all Virginia. The membership was as follows:

Chairman, Mrs. C. P. Jones, Jr.; treasurer, Mrs. W. A. Rinehart; secretary, Mrs. J. S. Earman.

Covington Committee: Mrs. Annie Stokes, Mrs. E. G. Hirons, Mrs. M. M. Collins, Mrs. W. O. Moore, Mrs. Allen Bowie, Mrs. W. A. Luke, Mrs. G. L. Miller, Mrs. J. T. Delaney Mrs. Forrest Payne, Mrs. J. E. Benner, Mrs. Charles Huffman, Mrs. Robert Kincaid, Mrs. G. M. Stull, Mrs. C. R. Karnes, Mrs. Benjamin Cleveland, Mrs. F. E. Payne, Miss Ida Anderson, Miss Nannie Vowels, Miss Mary Bowie, Miss Carrine Noel, Miss Theresa G. Rocke, Miss Geneva Stull.

Low Moor: Mrs. F. U. Humbert (chairman), Mrs. J. M. Lipscomb (secretary-treasurer), Mrs. J. A. Hibbert, Mrs. Frank Smith.

Falling Spring: Miss Catharine Scott (chairman), Miss Margaret Moomaw (co-chairman), Mrs. Hansford Massie, Miss Annie Massie, Mrs. W. O. Tuke.

Bess: Mrs. P. L. Wright, chairman.

Blue Spring Run: Mrs. A. R. Persinger, chairman.

Barber: Mrs. J. B. Griffith, chairman.

Mallow: Mrs. Arthur Bird, chairman.

Sweet Chalybeate: Mrs. Carter Hunter, chairman.

Iron Gate: Mrs. J. R. McPherson, chairman.

Alleghany Station: Mrs. A. B. Mann, chairman.

Jackson's River: Mrs. J. P. Botkins, chairman.

Greenwood: Mrs. J. R. McAllister, chairman.

Jordan Mines: Mrs. E. K. Bowles, chairman.

Rich Patch: Miss Elsie Stull, chairman.

The fourth organization—September, 1917—was the War Library Fund, Mrs. C. P. Jones, Jr., being chairman of the women's committee.

In October of the same year came the Second Liberty Loan, Mr. D. E. Mountcastle, chairman.

Later in the same month was the Second Food Card campaign, with Mr. F. H. Rinehart chairman for the county, and Mrs. C. P. Jones, Jr., chairman for Covington, where the registration was 442, making a total for the county seat of 1,247.

A Y. M. C. A. drive began in November, 1917, with Mr. C. P. Jones, Jr., chairman for the county, and also district chairman for Alleghany, Bath, and Highland. The quota of $4,000 was soon raised.

In February, 1918, the Camp Community Service campaign was conducted by Mr. R. B. Stephenson. The quota for town and county was $800, and the amount raised was $805.

In April, 1918, Mr. C. P. Jones, Jr., headed the Y. W. C. A. drive for $300, and $402.50 was secured.

The Woman's Liberty Loan committee, appointed by the Treasury Department, was formed March 12, 1918, with Mrs. C. P. Jones, Jr., chairman. The committee was the same as on the Council of Defense.

The Third Liberty Loan was in April, 1918, Mr. J. C. Frank, chairman.

In June was the Second Red Cross drive, Mr. E. M. Nettleton, chairman. The quota was $5,000; the amount raised, $8,286.50.

In July, Mr. E. G. Hirons was made chairman of the War Savings Stamps drive, and Mrs. C. P. Jones, Jr., assistant director.

On Labor Day, Mr. A. G. Fauver, a jeweler of Covington, offered a diamond ring to the woman who sold on that day the largest number of stamps. It was won by Mrs. E. G. Hirons.

In October was the Fourth Liberty Loan, Mayor E. G. Hirons, chairman.

November 11, 1918, the United War Work campaign was started, with Mr. and Mrs. C. P. Jones, Jr., as co-chairmen. This was over twice as large as any other drive, the quota for Alleghany being $14,000, and for Clifton Forge, $5,000. For the district, including also Bath, Highland, and Rockbridge, the district quota being $59,000. Mrs. Jones was district chairman. Mrs. E. G. Hirons was chairman of the Victory Girls for Covington, and Mrs. Margaret King of Low Moor was county chairman. The chairman reported $676.50. The Victory Boys, Mr. P. R. Little, chairman, raised $605.53. The West Virginia Pulp and Paper Company and its employees gave $6,508.21. The Machine Shops and their employees gave $332.05. The employees of the Deford Tannery contributed $301.85, this sum being the wages for one day. The Citizens Bank gave $500, and the county, $2,360.50. The colored citizens helped nobly in this, as they did in all other war work, contributing $1,230. Mrs. W. H. Conihay, treasurer, reported $12,119 in cash and $2,029.60 in pledges, a total of $14,148.60. The pledges were due December 2, 1918.

In February, 1919, the Y. W. C. A. investment campaign was conducted by Mrs. C. P. Jones, Jr., chairman. The quota was $100, and the sum raised, $250.

In April was the Salvation Army drive, with Mr. and Mrs. C. P. Jones, Jr., as co-chairmen. The quota was $3,000, the amount raised $3,065.

In June was the Victory Loan, with Mr. J. D. Mustoe, chairman.

The final drive—in July, 1919—though not technically a war activity, may appropriately be mentioned here. It was to provide a place for boys of this county in the Home for Homeless Boys. The need was pressing, and Mr. and Mrs. C. P. Jones, Jr., were appointed by the board of this school to raise a fund. The result was $6,000, which provides a perpetual entrance for twelve boys.

The quota for Belgian Relief—$2,000—was raised. Mr. J. G. Jeter was chairman in 1918, Mr. Ira Dew in 1919. For Near East Relief, 1920, Mrs. C. P. Jones, Jr., was chairman.

The Four Minute Men, of whom C. P. Jones, Jr., was chairman, performed excellent service. The other speakers for Covington were R. B. Stephenson, R. C. Stokes, Dr. Howerton, Rev. C. E. Buxton, G. A. Revercomb, and W. E. Allen. For Low Moor, the speaker was H. N. Sanford.

The members of the Advisory Board on the draft were G. A. Revercomb and C. P. Jones, Jr., for Covington, and F. W. King, of Clifton Forge, chairman.

T. B. McCaleb was Food Commissioner, and R. C. Stokes Fuel Commissioner. The Retail Food Price reports for the United States Food Administration at Washington were made weekly for more than two years by Mrs. C. P. Jones, Jr. This service required much time.

The record of Alleghany for the Virginia War History Commission has been compiled by Mrs. C. P. Jones, Jr., who was appointed by Governor Davis. She has done this unaided, and all departments have been covered in detail. This work has in itself been enormous.

A summary of the financial achievements of the Woman's Committee gives the following exhibit:

War Library Fund; quota $200, raised $216.

Y. M. C. A. drive; raised in Covington $1,200, in county $500.

Y. W. C. A. drives; raised (April, 1918) in Covington $195, in county $207.50; raised (March, 1919) in Covington, $150, in county $100; total, $625.50.

War Savings Stamps; Covington $50,000, county $20,000.

United War Work; Covington $5,000, county $1,500.

Second Liberty Loan; Covington, $15,000.

Third Liberty Loan; Covington $30,000, county, $21,150.

Fourth Liberty Loan; Covington $178,150, county $37,200.

Bonds sold by the women of Alleghany, $281,500.

The same women comprised the committee for all the work above mentioned. They labored in perfect harmony, in the most unselfish manner, and with a spirit and willingness that could not be surpassed. It might therefore seem invidious to single out one of them for special mention, yet even a hasty reading of the foregoing paragraphs will of itself indicate the multiform activities of Mrs. C. P. Jones, Jr., and her great devotion and untiring energy.

The Red Cross was represented by the Covington Chapter, organized August 24, 1917, the officers of which were J. H. Carpenter (chairman), Mrs. O. L. Rogers (vice-chairman), Mrs. T. M. Gathright (secretary), D. E. Mountcastle (treasurer), and Mrs. D. E. Mountcastle (assistant treasurer). The Rev. T. K. Young was chairman the first eight months. The members of the Executive Committee, outside of the above-mentioned officers, were R. C. Stokes, E. M. Nettleton, R. B. Stephenson, J. G. Jeter, G. L. Miller, W. McD. McAllister, J. D. Mustoe, and Mrs. M. M. Collins. The total membership was 3,849. The jurisdiction of the Chapter included all Alleghany, west of and inclusive of Low Moor, and for six months, Hot Springs was within its territory.

There was no canteen, but $500 was contributed to the Clifton Forge Chapter toward the maintenance of the one at that place.

Mrs. O. L. Rogers was director of the workroom, and Mrs. H. B. Justice was chairman of the knitting units. Special badges for working 800 hours or longer were given Mrs. J. M. Noell, Mrs. F. O. Hieronimus, Mrs. T. M. Gathright. There were made 641 sweaters, 1,077 socks, 1,196 hospital garments, two ambulance robes, 500 influenza masks, thirty layettes, six knitted wraps, 200 face towels, 200 handkerchiefs, 180 napkins, seventy-four pairs of wristlets, forty-six scarfs, 1,339 refugee garments, 400 Christmas packets, 450 bath towels, 950 pieces of clothing for the Belgians, 93,250 surgical dressings; also 605 kits were made and filled.

For the furtherance of the Red Cross activities, E. M. Nettleton donated the use of room, W. McD. McAllister contributed furniture, and J. W. Bell and Charles Nettleton gave coal. The Paper Mill made and gave all the necessary boxes and wrapping paper for shipping the above-mentioned products to headquarters.

J. D. Mustoe and R. B. Stephenson were chairmen of the Home Service Committee, which assisted thirty-three families and used $260.13, mostly in loans to soldiers, and the families of soldiers whose pay was held up.

The receipts from all sources amounted to $11,508.59, of which sum $2,509.64 was raised by fairs. The most liberal contributors were the West Virginia Pulp and Paper Company and the Covington Hardware and Furniture Company. The expenditures were $9,928.59, the sum of $4,789.77 going to material and supplies used. There were no unpaid bills.

In each drive there was a house to house canvass, stores and factories being solicited by department heads and foremen. The amounts raised by the drives of November, 1918, and August, 1919, were $8,286.40 and $1,300. The membership dues amounted to $3,413.

The branches of the Covington Chapter were Low Moor, Barber, Blue Spring Run, and Alleghany Station. Hacket was the colored branch at Covington. Hot Springs was a branch for six months. Mountain Brow was the name of the one auxiliary. Low Moor took an unusually active part in work room service. Mrs. F. U. Humbert was chairman at Low Moor, Mrs. G. L. Jamison at Blue Spring Run, J. H. Pence at Barber, and Mary Johnson of the Hacket branch.

The Junior Red Cross was organized in every school-room, the numbers being 102. The chief form of service by these auxiliaries consisted of knitting, sewing, collecting magazines, and making scrap-books. The money raised by them was above $400.

For the First Liberty Loan, no detailed figures are accessible. To the Second, this county furnished 876 subscribers, the apportionment being $551,300, and the subscription $367,900.

For the Third, Fourth, and Fifth Liberty Loans, the apportionments were, respectively, $362,100, $775,800, and $628,800. The subscriptions were $454,200, $822,300, and $621,600; a total of $2,366,000, or nearly forty per cent. of the banking resources of this county. In the Third Loan, the percentage of the population subscribing was 24.37, placing Alleghany the sixth among the 100 counties of Virginia. The five in the lead were Augusta, Henrico, Pittsylvania, Roanoke, and Warwick. In the Fourth Loan, the percentage rose to 26.8, Alleghany being now led only by Norfolk and Warwick. In the Third Loan, the subscription per capita was $28.39, and in the Fourth, it was $51.39. In the former, Alleghany was distanced by eight counties and the city of Richmond; in the latter, by six counties and the city of Richmond. It is significant that in every county which outranked Alleghany was a more populous city, with a heavy concentration of banking capital. The report on the Fifth Loan mentions 2,536 subscribers and subscriptions to Treasury certificates of $700,000 in anticipation of the Victory Loan.

The Woman's Liberty Loan, conducted by Mrs. C. P. Jones, Jr., was for the third drive, $51,150; for the fourth, $215,350, and for the fifth, $155,000, the subscribers to the Fourth and Fifth Loans being 460 and 700.

To tell something of the mind of the Alleghany people during the tense war period, we present first a synopsis of a statement by the rector at Covington; second, a series of extracts from *The Sentinel;* third, a series from *The Virginian,* the quotations beginning just after the Armistice.

*　*　*　*　*　*　*　*　*　*

The general attitude of the Church in Alleghany was a deep realization that a crisis threatened civilization, and that in the name of God, her banners must be set up. Wholeheartedly in response to the country's call, pulpit and pew gave themselves to the work before them, coöperating to the fullest extent. The chairman of every organization and every drive was a devoted church member. Every request made by the Federal authorities was most strictly complied with. Many of the clergy volunteered as chaplains and relief workers. Though none were accepted, they served to a man on the committees at home. The Boy Scouts rendered such service as was possible. Many services of a patriotic nature were held by the churches. In them hung the Stars and Stripes, and in most of them were service flags. The service flag in Granbury Memorial had fifty-nine stars, the one in gold being for Herbert Buckles; the one in the First Presbyterian had fifty stars, with one in gold for Bedford Lam; Emmanuel Episcopal had twenty stars, including a silver star for Major R. F. Beirne; the one in the First Methodist Episcopal had twenty-three stars, the four in gold being for Nelson Byers, Alfred Byers, Mordaunt Kelly, and Roy Leffel; the flag of the First Baptist had five stars.

The farewell to the boys leaving for the camps was all that could be wished. While there was no big welcome home for the reason that they came gradually, there was no lack of happiness or sincerity in their reception when they did return.

It is a matter of regret that without exception the Protestant pastors state that our men came back less religiously inclined than before. A pastor, whose church did a splendid, self-sacrificing work throughout the war period, expresses the wish that the government, by a more careful observance of Sunday, and in many other ways, would endeavor to aid the Church as much as the Church sought to aid the government in its time of need. But the pastor of the Roman Catholic churches in this county writes that the service men from his congregations came back morally and spiritually benefited.

*   *   *   *   *   *   *   *   *   *

1917

The food pirates are a greater menace to the government than all the German spies in the United States. If the government has the right, in protecting the nation's welfare, to confiscate three-fourths of the earning capacity of the men going into the army, why may it not confiscate the foodstuffs in the hands of the sharks? Potatoes are selling at $3.50 a bushel, but there has been a plenty of them all the while. Flour has risen $2.50 a barrel since the President's proclamation.—May 11th.

Dr. H. G. Lind, company physician at Low Moor, is one of six physicians and surgeons in Virginia to go to France at once.—May 11th.

The war with Germany will not be a breakfast affair. This editorial sounds a warning against the apathy that seems to have engulfed so many of our people. Don't take any chances. Do everything in your power to aid the government.—May 18th.

Would it not be well, as our country is at war, to abandon baseball games?—May 25th.

During this war every person should obliterate political lines. Every position of responsibility should be filled by the person best qualified to fill the same, irrespective of his political affiliations.—May 25th.

In this call of patriotism, why is not Virginia found near the head of the list?—June 1st.

Few, if any, in the county failed to register on the 5th. The day passed off quietly, with the exception of the arrest of a negro who is said to have incited the negroes around Rich Patch against the registration.—June 8th.

The official figures show in Alleghany 1,008 white and 270 colored registrees and four aliens; in Clifton Forge 732 whites, 106 colored, and seven aliens. No alien enemies are mentioned.—June 8th.

Buy a Liberty Bond.—June 8th.

Put alien citizens in the army or send 'em home.—June 8th.

The Home Guard organized June 11th. The organization was brought about by J. J. Reardon, formerly first sergeant in Company H, but who was dropped when the boys went to the border. The organization will do all the guard duty and police work possible, and assist in Red Cross work and other patriotic duties.—June 15th.

There must not grow up a spirit of hatred toward those in our midst of foreign blood. Some are unquestionably traitors to the land of their adoption, but time will efface them.—June 22d.

No great cause was ever won without martyrdom.—June 22d.

Practice the strictest kind of economy.—June 22d.

Posterity, glorifying in the results of this war, should pay its share of the expense.—June 29th.

If our great waste and extravagance is eliminated, there will be plenty of food to supply the necessities of every person. Be economical and prudent, but don't be a miser.—July 6th.

William Harding, Alexander Stewart, E. Nelson, and Bernie and Clayborn Davidson of this city are now in France. Stewart and Nelson joined the Canadian troops some time ago.—July 6th.

The Fourth was generally observed in Covington by a suspension of business.—July 6th.

The heroes who die for us on the fields of France will have saved us from national moral decay.—July 13th.

The American people as a mass have regretted the necessity for going to war, but there is also in their hearts a grim, deadly determination that certain objects must be attained. The attitude of the American people today is that of facing a very disagreeable duty, but with no thought of shirking it.—July 13th.

Company H, First Virginia Infantry, assembled at the courthouse the 25th, and entered the Federal service. This is the youngest, and also the only, company in the state up to full war strength. On the roll were 159 privates, besides the commissioned officers, with new recruits coming in.—July 13th.

Monday night is drill night with the Home Guard.—July 13th.

Major Beirne is to address Company H on "How the Heavy Artillery Will End the War."—August 3d.

Lt. A. S. Burnham becomes captain of Company H in place of Capt. R. F. Beirne, who is a major in the artillery service.—August 10th.

Dr. A. C. Jones and Dr. W. M. Revercomb comprise the examining board. Until August 1st, only three out of twenty-eight men were turned down for physical disability.—August 10th.

That man, woman, or minor who is not concerned as to the outcome of the present struggle in Europe is either to be pitied or enlightened. What the future is to be depends upon our action now. It is to the credit of the American people that they have always had a clear vision of the duty of the present generation to posterity.—August 17th.

William Meade, Company E, Second Virginia, accidentally shot himself, August 13th, while on guard duty at Mallow Bridge, rendering amputation of the right arm necessary.—August 17th.

The local draft board has just examined 107 men, few being turned down.—August 31st.

L. P. Pendleton, L. A. Clarkson, and S. L. Clough, all of Clifton Forge, are the first to be taken from this section for the training camp.—September 7th.

Public safety demands implicit obedience to the laws of the land. Absolute free speech is impossible.—September 14th.

To the mind of the American girl, a grave danger lies in the kisses of those French girls.—September 21st.

Company H—three officers, 160 men—left September 24 for training at Anniston, Alabama. 3,000 people were present when the train went out.—September 28.

William Werner, of the New York National Guards, was accidentally killed by Joseph Wiedlitz of the same company, September 22d, while on duty at Eggleston tunnel.—September 28th.

A lady said she was glad her friends were all girls, because "soldiers are so tough." Yes, they are tough enough to leave home and fight the battles which make the world a safe place of residence. God help such girls, for they are more capable of caring for a lapdog than of directing the footsteps of your daughters.—October 26th.

These are very extraordinary times, and in extraordinary times extraordinary proceedings become necessary.—November 9th.

Sergeant Edwin Kincaid of Company H thus writes from Anniston: "The instruction we are receiving here is more like a school than anything I know of. I like it fine here, and have been treated royally by the few people I have met. We are in the best of health with the exception of three cases of measles. I don't believe there is a single one in the company, that if he had to enlist over, wouldn't do the same thing again. Once in a while, one or two of us are blue, but when we hear from home and our best girl, we brace up right away."—November 16th.

1918

Two German suspects jailed at Clifton Forge.—January 25th.

R. B. Stephenson is appointed chairman of the Camp Community Service for Alleghany. Committees are announced for Covington, Barber,

Falling Springs, Low Moor, Iron Gate, Longdale, Selma, Alleghany Station, Sweet Chalybeate, Earlehurst, Callaghan, Potts Creek, Mallow, Rich Patch, and Clifton Forge. D. E. Mountcastle is treasurer.

Midshipmen Earle H. Kincaid of the Naval Academy is chosen to present a book to President Wilson.—February 15th.

Two colored deserters from Fort Monroe are arrested at Low Moor.—March 1st.

Sometimes we wonder whether or not our boys realize the void their departure has left in our community.—April 5th.

Twenty-two men left for Camp Lee, March 29th.—April 5th.

The war is teaching the American people anew the dignity of labor.—April 12th.

Dr. A. S. Freeman spoke April 23d in behalf of the Third Liberty Loan to the most largely attended meeting ever held in this city.—April 26th.

*   *   *   *   *   *   *   *   *   *

Herr Ballin expressed himself after this fashion: "The indicated conditions of the Entente are much more moderate than might have been expected from our situation. We need only think what our terms would have been, had we been the victors. We would have demanded the occupation of Paris and London. We would have dictated peace at Buckingham Palace, and annexed the entire continent from the Ural Mountains to the Bay of Biscay."

We made war for our own protection. If we had delayed another six months, we would by this time be defending our own fireside.

It is the women of America who made victory in the great war a possibility. As soon as the men began to go to the front, women began to take their places in the stores, on the farms, and in the factories. Within a short time, these tasks they had taken on were being done as well, and in many cases a great deal better, than they were ever done before.

The reasons why the Kaiser should be hung are as numerous as the crimes for which under the statute laws of any country there are penalties prescribed.

Were it not for the economic condition of the world, it would be a fine thing to turn the Turk loose on Germany, so that the real refinements of Kultur might be readily felt in the land of its origin.

When our soldiers were called on to go over the top, they did so with a fearlessness never surpassed, and when victorious they carried themselves as men, not as beasts.

Now that the war is over, it will take the combined effort of us all to take care of the wounded soldiers who come home, and to see that they have tasks suited to their equipments; to see that we are patient with $2.20 wheat when we could buy it from Australia much cheaper; to see to it that we take up our tasks where we left them off, and push forward with confidence and faith.

The one thing the Industrial Worker of the World will not do is work. Were it not for this busy trouble-breeder, capital and labor would be able to get together. In our little community we have a wonderful illustration of what can be done by the hearty coöperation of labor and capital.

We contemplate a memorial to our boys, of whom we are as proud as any people can be. If we go about this in the right spirit, we may erect a monument we may always be proud to point to. It will mean much to our city and county.

Among the great majority of our population the true-blue spirit of patriotism runs like a vein of gold.

Everything Mrs. Margaret King has done since she came to Alleghany in home demonstration work has been an unalloyed blessing. She is a future-builder. The next generation will reap tenfold where we reap once.

If you have not forgotten the 60,000 American boys who lay buried in the soil of France, you will be buying Victory Bonds the first time they are offered for sale. It is up to us to see that the job our boys have done is concluded in a workmanlike manner.—March 14, 1919.

An old friend of the editor remarked that he could not get used to seeing a beautiful girl in overalls. A great many discerning men feel this way about the matter.

The courtesy and kindness of our people to strangers is marked and uniform. The visitor is impressed with the fact that the laboring class in Covington is somewhere "near the top of the pot."

If we knock a man down when he says, "To hell with the Flag," we may attract the attention of the whole country to our patriotic action, but we may then go hence and lend our opposition to the Victory Loan, thus doing the very thing the fellow we knocked down only mentioned.

Many of our young men who served their country at home and abroad have developed qualities of leadership, while in the army and navy, which formerly they did not possess, or which were lying dormant waiting for an opportunity of expression. The morals of the soldiers were far better safeguarded in camp than in many places in Virginia, and many men will come home cleaner in mind and practice than when they went into the service. This is also true of other aspects of life. The soldier has come back a changed man, in many cases with higher ideals of community life. We must endeavor to raise the community standard to meet these ideals. If an After War Work Community Program Institute, like the one held in Lynchburg last week, can be held in Alleghany, it will open the eyes of us all to the possibilities of what we can do if we use our war-time spirit in the problems which face us in our everyday life at this time.—April 26, 1919.

If we resume our old careless habit of spending money, wasting food, taking no care of our health, and losing sight of the stupendous benefit which comes from concerted action, we will lose where we ought to gain, and we will not only lose what we have but we will lose what we have not. This is a time to go forward. Let us learn to be thrifty. Let us take care of the money which comes to our hands, for in that way we are good citizens. When you save, your employer has his eye on you and says, "He's looking out for me too when he does that."

Alleghany is asked for $3,000 and Clifton Forge for $2,000 in the Salvation Army drive. Every man who has returned from France is ready and willing to testify for the Salvation Army. The slogan of the campaign is, "Ask the Soldier."

Major R. F. Beirne resumes the editorship of *The Virginian*, remarking that "no town nor county has a finer citizenship than we can boast of here in these mountains. I sincerely believe that the biggest-hearted, bravest, and squarest people in the state are right here in Allghany."—June, 30, 1919.

XVII

THE PRESENT AND THE FUTURE

INCLUSIVE of Clifton Forge the white population of Alleghany was 15,880 in 1910. There were 4,037 negroes and two Chinese. The foreign whites were only 296, and those of foreign parentage, or foreign and American parentage, were 248. Of the foreign element, 124 were from Italy, eighty-eight from the British Isles, twenty-four from Turkey, sixteen from Germany, and ten each from Canada and Russia. The male population was 10,513 and the female 9,404. The males of voting age were 5,673, although only 1,535 cast ballots in the election of 1916. Of the foreign-born 153 were unnaturalized. The percentage of illiteracy was 6.3 among the native whites, 30.9 among the foreigners, and 30.4 among the negroes. The children between the ages of six and fourteen were 4,060. Of these the percentage at school was 72.4 for the county and 79.5 for Clifton Forge. There were 3,760 dwellings and 3,957 families. The farms were 574, nineteen being cultivated by negroes. The tenant farmers were ninety-six, two of whom were negroes. The area in farms covered 35.6 per cent. of the county. The average farm contained 181 acres, fifty-seven acres being improved land. It thus follows that less than one-tenth of the surface of Alleghany is improved. The value of farms and farm property was $2,092,552. Of livestock there were 4,563 cattle, 1,267 horses, sixty-eight mules, 2,487 hogs, 5,520 sheep, and thirty-eight goats. There were 580 hives of bees and 21,690 head of poultry. The acreage in corn was 5,023, and in the cereals 8,323. Of corn, wheat, oats, buckwheat, and rye, the product in bushels was, respectively, 121,048, 28,456, 8,389, 701, and 161. The 4,210 acres in grass yielded 4,376 tons of hay, and the yield of 434 acres in potatoes was 43,159 bushels. The product of sirup was 1,104 gallons, and in the orchards were 50,874 fruit trees.

The arrival of a railroad made the population of this county almost double between 1850 and 1860. The demoralization of the civil war brought the figures for 1870 almost to the level of 1850. From 1870 to 1900 there was a rapid increase in each decade, the gain from 1890 to 1900 being seventy-five per cent. Between 1900 and 1910, the increase, inclusive of Clifton Forge, was twenty-two per cent. Since then, there has been a further slowing down, the census of 1920 reporting a gain over the figures of 1910 of not quite eight per cent.

The latest census gave Alleghany and Clifton Forge a population of 21,496. In 1920, Boiling Spring, Clifton, and Covington districts had, respectively, 2,528, 3,784, and 9,020 inhabitants. The corresponding figures for 1900 were 2,487, 4,505, and 5,759. But the report for Clifton District in 1900 includes the 3,212 people of Clifton Forge and the 367 of West Clifton Forge. In 1920, Clifton Forge had 6,164 people, Covington 5,623, and Iron Gate 699. Covington District outside of the town of Covington had 3,397 people.

An inspection of the census return for 1920 is of interest. The males numbered 10,981, the females 10,515. Of the native whites, 17,484 were of native parentage, 151 of foreign parentage, and 205 of mixed native and foreign parentage. The foreign-born whites were 117, of whom fifty-four were naturalized, twenty-six alien, and thirty-six of unknown status. The Mongolian race was represented by two Chinese. Inclusive of Clifton Forge, the foreign residents were fifty-five from the British Isles, fifteen from Canada, fifteen from Germany, Sweden, and Holland, twenty-eight from the south and southeast of Europe, and eleven from Syria and Armenia. The negroes were 4,037, or precisely the same as in 1910.

The males of military age (eighteen to forty-four inclusive) were 4,409. The persons of twenty-one years old and upward were 10,942. The persons between the ages of seven and fourteen were 3,637, of whom 3,181 were in school. .Those between the ages of fourteen and twenty-one were 3,109, of whom 1,279 were in school. The percentage of illiteracy fell more than one-half between 1910 and 1920, the latter year reporting 776 illiterates of ten years of age and upward. Among the native whites the percentage of illiteracy is now 2.9 per cent. Among the foreign-born it is 8.1 per cent., and among the negroes fourteen. In 1920 the dwellings were 4,064, and the families 4,303, or almost precisely five persons to the family, thus showing that the family of normal size has not become unfashionable in Alleghany.

The wealth of Alleghany county appears in the following table, the figures being those for 1922:

BOILING SPRING DISTRICT

Personal property	$ 326,702.94
Real property	623,848.00
Railroad property	419,089.00
Telegraph and telephone lines and express	13,961.63
Total	$1,383,601.57

CLIFTON DISTRICT (exclusive of Iron Gate)

Personal property	$ 962,795.94
Real property	914,686.00
Railroad property	388,019.00
Telegraph, telephone, and express	13,865.00
Total	$2,279,165.94

COVINGTON DISTRICT

Personal property	$4,504,678.00
Real property	2,665,632.00
Railroad property	630,447.00
Telegraph, telephone, and express	48,121.18
Total	$7,847,878.18

TOWN OF COVINGTON

Personal property	$ 3,147,238.00
Real property	1,996,905.00
Total	$5,144,143.00

TOWN OF IRON GATE

Personal property	$ 320,659.00
Real property	202,408.00
Total	$ 523,367.00

TOTAL FOR COUNTY

Personal property ....$ 9,262,163.88
Real property 6,403,479.00
Railroad property 1,437,555.00
Telegraph and telephone lines and express 75,947.81

Grand Total $17,179,145.69

In the rural neighborhoods the people are largely derived from families that came from seventy-five to more than 150 years ago, but among them are many new families, especially from adjacent counties. In the towns this is much less the case. Many other counties of Virginia are here represented, and there is no inconsiderable number of people from West Virginia, and from various Western and Northern states. Something of a cosmopolitan hue is thus imparted to the town population, and there is present in a marked degree the pull-together spirit, characteristic of new and growing communities. There is no inordinate number of foreign-born residents of un-American feeling to add to the difficulty of maintaining public order, especially in a time of labor disturbances. Much of the illicit distilling of the present moment is not by natives of this county but by lawless individuals from West Virginia. The colored element, which is very largely confined to the towns and does not tend to increase, is of a good type, being orderly and industrious.

The schools are fast improving and Alleghany is becoming more and more entitled to a place among the most progressive counties of Virginia in matters educational. There is less of a desire to keep children out of school, and illiteracy will soon be reduced to a low point. But in some of the remote corners are weak churches in which religious service is not regularly held.

The public roads are likewise improving, although much still remains to be done in the way of grading and hard-surfacing. The amount expended on the highways of this county in 1922 was almost $47,000.

The towns need public parks, well shaded and grassed, for these are to cities what lungs are to the individual. They also need to observe a higher standard of tidiness in streets, sidewalks, and public places generally.

Its position on a great artery of railroad travel, and its near-nees to suppplies of coal, iron ore, and timber have made the county seat a manufacturing city. The abnormal business conditions of the last eight years have worked against the progress which it would otherwise have made. But a continued and indefinite growth is inevitable, and this would be promoted by a railroad outlet to the Potomac in the north and to New River in the south.

In the economic readjustment now taking place in the United States, the farming interest is not yet having its due, and to this circumstance Alleghany is no exception. Yet this county has the great advantage of a home market, the city and town population being twice as large as the rural.

With a good climate, a through line of railway, a population almost wholly native American, and industrial advantages, the future of Alleghany county is very largely in its own keeping.

XVIII

THE FAMILIES OF ALLEGHANY

Outside of the towns of this county, there are more than 300 different surnames among the white population. About five-sixths of these appear to have come into Alleghany since 1850, a very large share being of quite recent appearance. In the towns the proportion of new names is still greater. The names coming into Alleghany prior to the close of the Revolution are either extinct or are meagerly represented in the male line. The same fact seems true of the other families coming prior to the year 1800. Even in the case of families that may not have come previous to the organization of this county, the present representatives are not always able to give a well connected account. The individual who could have told has departed this life, and his descendants are not sure-footed as to the fragments of the story that they relate.

Among the names that have disappeared are Armstrong, Beard, Harnsbarger, Holley, Holloway, Karnes, Knox, Mallow, Morris, Morton, Pennell, and Warren. The actual number of extinct pioneer names is probably greater. For example, the Wrights of this county are a newer family than the Wrights who once lived on the site of Covington.

When the whistle of the railway locomotive was first heard on Jackson's River, almost seventy years ago, there were only 4,000 people in Alleghany. For more than sixty years there had been a heavy and persistent emigration to the West.

For thirty more years the tide was not very strongly arrested. If the population of Alleghany has very greatly increased in the last forty years, it is none the less true that Alleghanians continue to seek new homes in other communities.

The new and near-new surnames in this county are very numerous, and their ancestral descent is to be traced elsewhere. The old family names which have not become locally extinct are relatively few, although they take in a large share of the rural population and a not inconsiderable part of the town population.

In a book of this scope, it is not possible to follow out the local genealogies in an exhaustive manner. Furthermore, the recollections of the aged residents are almost invariably imperfect and sometimes uncertain. Links in the chain have been entirely lost. What they do recall needs to be compared with what can be gleaned from written records. What information the author has thus obtained he has used, and if some family names do not appear in the sketches below, they are not intentionally omitted.

Following the sketches are lists of marriages prior to 1854. Various facts of family history occur in some of the remaining chapters. Some of the families mentioned in the appendix are also mentioned here, but without needless repetition. The findings in the present chapters are the author's.

Michael Aritt, whose wife was Sarah, died on Potts Creek in 1845. His children were George, John, Katharine, and Elizazeth. George was then dead, but left issue. The first daughter married Jacob Armentrout, the second married Henry Myers.

Frederick Armentrout died 1838. His children were Jacob, Joseph, John, George, Abraham, Elizabeth, Mary, and Catharine. Mary had married an Aritt, Catharine, a Cummings.

Robert Armstrong, Sr., was a constable in 1750. Robert, Jr., went to Montgomery county, Kentucky, about 1793, and gave one James Armstrong a power of attorney to sell 270 acres to James Cochran. Archibald, brother to Robert, Sr., died in the same neighborhood in 1800. His son Robert remained here some years and was often foreman of the grand jury of Bath. He gave much attention to raising horses.

The Beards settled on the Cowpasture very near the Bath line, and their name was given to Beard's Mountain. The James Beard who went to Tennessee about 1794 was perhaps the James whose mother made oath in 1755 that her boy's ear had been bitten off by a horse. Slicing off the lobe of an ear was a mode of punishment in colonial times, and a man with a mutilated ear did not wish to be considered an ex-convict.

John W. Bell, still on the active list, has been in the milling business in Covington ever since 1868.

Jacob Bennett, who settled in the Rich Patch a century ago or earlier, is thought to have come from Rockingham. His wife was

Mary. Their children were William, John, Henry, Sampson, Nancy, Jennie, Elizabeth, and Phœbe. John, who married Nancy Persinger for his second wife, and Henry, who married Polly Fridley, both went to Nicholas. Wliliam, who married Kate Stull, remained on the homestead. Sampson moved to Potts Creek and reared a large family. The daughters married, in the order of mention, George King, Charles King, George Wright, and Jacob Stull.

David Bowyer, who died on Potts Creek in 1862 at the age of ninety-five, was a boy of fourteen when he worked the bellows for his father, an army blacksmith in the Yorktown campaign. The anvil was given to the son and remains in the family. He went to Monroe, and then to Potts Creek, where he took up 933 acres. He married Sarah Wolfe, and his children were John, Elias, Polly Harmon, Leah Huddleston, and Betsy Aritt. John married Nancy Craft. What became of Elias is not known.

Dennis Callaghan was famous as the landlord of a turnpike tavern. His son Oliver was the first clerk of Alleghany. Margaret, a widow, died 1847, her will mentioning John and Mary (wife of a Jones) as her children, and William Y. as a grandson.

The father of Daniel J. Callaghan was a native of County Cork, Ireland, and came to Alleghany when the railroad arrived. He soon purchased the Stringer tavern.

Joseph Carpenter came from New York in the spring of 1746, took a survey of 782 acres, and started a corn patch. In the fall he returned with his large family, several of whom were already married. A young buffalo had broken through the brush fence, and was trying to relieve the settler of the trouble of shucking the corn. He was punished for his trespass by being converted into steak. The settler's first cabin was in the bottom on the south side of the bend below Covington. The spot is to the right of the lane leading out from the Potts Creek road, and some distance back. High water induced him to move to the vicinity of the first house beyond the river bridge. A still greater flood sent him to the higher ground at the residence of the late William C. Fudge. About 1753 he, or his son Joseph, married Judith, the widow of John Scott. Financial embarrassment caused him to mortgage 160 acres to Edward McMullen, by whom the tract was sold to William Hughart at a public auction in January, 1771. The pioneer's signature in 1776 is the handwriting of an old man.

Solomon Carpenter, a brother to Joseph, came about the same time, and though his name does not appear as a landowner, he built a blockhouse on the bottom at Low Moor. He was a constable in 1767. He died intestate before 1784, and John Robinson was his administrator.

There were so many Carpenters of the second and third generations that we cannot wholly separate the families of the two brothers, nor distinguish in every case the grandchildren from the children. Children of Joseph were Joseph, Jr., Thomas, Frances, the wife of John Mann, and Hannah, wife of Jeremiah Seeley. It is probable that Zopher, Nathan, Nicholas, and William were other sons. Children of Solomon were Thomas and Jeremiah, and a daughter named Sibby. This Thomas had a son John, mentioned in 1784. Nicholas and William were killed by the Indians, and in the raid of 1756 five Carpenter children were carried away. Zopher, who apppears to have been one of the oldest of Joseph's sons, lived south of Mallow Station.

Nathan, who was killed near Covington, was the original patentee of White Sulphur Springs. His wife, Kate, concealed herself on the mountain which bears her given name. In 1782 she sold to Michael Bowyer her dower interest in the White Sulphur tract of 950 acres, and in 1795, her daughter Frances married Bowyer.

Joseph, Jr., died 1792, dividing his land between his sons, Samuel and William. His daughters were Abigail, Mary, Sarah, Juda, and Martha. The first four were married, respectively, to a Milhollen, a Viers, William Gillespie, and a Shaver. Samuel Carpenter, Sr., son of Joseph, Jr., died in 1842. The children named in his will were Samuel, Joseph, Rebecca, Nancy, and Martha. There was also a William, who went to Missouri as did also Joseph. Samuel, Jr., known as "Colonel Sam," was the last of the Carpenters to live on any part of the original homestead. Martha married John Mallow, Nancy a Dressler. Another married a Tackett and had a son named Gerard M. The commander of Carpenter's Battery in the civil war was a son of Samuel, Jr.

John Carson of Snake Run died 1844. His children were George, James, John, Rachel Landers, and Sarah B. Bush. George was the father of John A., who was county surveyor from 1870 to 1906, and thirty-four years a school trustee and district secretary. His acquaintance with the land titles of this county was remarkably comprehensive.

Lemuel and Thomas Carter, brothers, came from Halifax county to Snake Run in 1828. The children of Lemuel were Jared, Philip, Thomas, James, Bradley, Jesse, John H., Clifton, and Elvira. Those of Thomas were William, Peter, Henry, John, Judah, and Jane, the last named marrying George M. Baker.

The Damrons have been a prominent family of Dunlap Creek. John died in 1828. His wife was Polly, and his children were Elizabeth, Joseph, John, William, Andrew, and Christopher. Elizabeth married Thomas Smith. Joseph was a lawyer.

The Dresslers appear to have been here in 1794.

Mrs. A. M. Evans has been a resident of Covington ever since 1855, at which time she was nearly grown. Her knowledge of the history of the county seat and its vicinity is singularly vivid and exact. Her father built a hotel just north of the station lot, occupying it in 1869. After his death in 1872, his daughters conducted it for twenty years. This gave them an exceptional opportunity to observe local events.

Samuel Ervine, whose wife was Mary, died in 1846. His children were Joseph, Sally Farris, Nancy, Martha, and Matilda Tinsley.

The Fridleys, of German origin, came from Rockingham at a rather early day and settled in the Rich Patch.

Conrad Fudge was born in 1771 and died in 1849. He is said to have been a native of Hanover, Germany, but this is probably true only of an older Conrad. In 1764 the records of Augusta have mention of Conrad and John Fudge. The pioneer in Alleghany settled on a part of the Carpenter survey and married a daughter of Jacob Persinger. He was a blacksmith as well as farmer, and was so thrifty as to leave $1,000 to each of seven sons. His children were Alexander, Jacob (married Elsie Hansbrough), Andrew (married Harriet K. Beale), Jonathan (married Mary A. Spence), Conrad R. (married Nancy Harmon), Jeremiah, Maria L. (married William F. Morton), Nancy (married Archibald M. Kincaid), Catharine, Joseph, Stephen, Mary A. (married Henry B. Harmon), Elizabeth J. (married James H. Perry), and Martha (married James M. Montague).

One or more Gillespies were among the very earliest settlers on the lower Cowpasture. A portion of the ground on which Clifton Forge is built was patented by Robert in 1770. Simon, living in Montgomery county, Kentucky, 1824, was the son of a Simon of this region who was not then living. The younger man gave James H. Gillespie a power of attorney to sell some land on Wilson's Creek.

Gilliland is another very early name. In 1829, James, whose wife was Mary, sold his place on Potts Creek.

The earliest settlement of the Griffiths that we know of was in the bend of the Cowpasture lying next to the knob which bears the family name. William died about 1824. His children were Orlando, Nancy, and Sarah. The last named married James Clendening, who sold in 1832 two tracts on that river to Orlando. This land once belonged to James Griffith.

John Hansbarger died on Wilson's Creek in 1824. His sons were Jacob and Sebastian. Jacob died 1849, and his own children were John H., Elizabeth D., and Rachel, the second daughter being the wife of John A. Black.

In 1797 Benjamin and Joseph Haynes were living where Selma now stands.

Peter Helmintoller of Potts Creek married Polly Johnson. His children were Matthew, Mary, William, "Jerd," Maria, Elizabeth, Susanna, and Wilda. Matthew and Mary went to Ohio. The others married, in the order of mention, Rebecca Plymell, Rebecca Hook, Charles Richardson, "Fad" Kimberlin, James Sollender, and Martha Burk.

The wife of John Hepler, who came from Rockingham, was Rebecca Magart. The children were these: (1) David, who married Basha Miller; (2) John, whose first wife was Sarah, sister to Polly Johnson, wife of Peter Helmintoller; (3) Joseph, who lived in Rockbridge; (4) Elizabeth, who married James Wilson; (5) Sarah, who married William Carson; (6) Mary, who married Lemuel P. Haynes of Caroline county; (7) Harriet, married first to Lewis Fridley, and next to John McPherson.

William Grigg Holloway, county surveyor in 1849, lived at the Holloway ford near Mallow and was the father of Lewis P.

John A. Holley seems to have been living on Ugly in 1824. His wife was probably a daughter of William Knox.

Stephen Hook lived a mile above the Rich Patch store. His

children were Madison, Henry, John, James, Elias, Beale, Sidney, and Caroline. Madison, who married Mary Kimberlin, was wealthy and owned several farms. Sidney married James Whitten, and Caroline married his brother William.

Abraham Huddleston married Leah Bowyer. His children were David (married Agnes Hook), Daniel (went to Greenbrier), Sarah (married Thomas Plymell), Joseph (drowned), John (killed in war of '61), Elizabeth (married David Lockhart), Minerva (married a Bolen), Nancy (married a Smith), William, George (married a Ham), Robert (married a Childs).

Abel Jackson, who married Elizabeth Lockhart, was living on Ugly in 1831.

Barney Johnson married Ann Criss of Botetourt. His children were John (married Sarah Burt of Samuel), Philip (married Catharine Rayhill), Allen (married an Armentrout), Lee, Barney (married Frances Bowyer), Malinda (married Elias Hepler). Allen and Lee were killed in the war of 1861.

Michael Karnes came from Bedford to the site of Low Moor about 1776. He had a mill and a distillery.

The Kimberlin family settled on the farm on Potts Creek now owned by Robert B. Rose, and the log house is yet standing. The wife of James was Nancy, whose will in 1848 mentions William, Eliza A. (wife of Dennison Rose), Nancy Lockhart, and Deanna Byrd. There was also a Lorenzo, not then living, and probably a younger James.

The Kincaids are one of the oldest families in the neighborhood of Covington. Archibald M., a son of Robert, and whose wife was Catharine, died 1837. He was a brother to Robert M., who died in 1840, mentioning in his will Archibald, an infant son of Andrew; also Andrew, Sr., whose children were James C., and Thomas. William D., a brother to John D., died 1838. His children—all minors—were Mary E., Andrew B., Virginia F., Patsy A. L.

The wife of John King of the Rich Patch is thought to have been Barbara. Their sons George and Charles married, respectively, Nancy Bennett and Jennie Bennett. John, another son, went West. There were also sisters.

Solomon Knox died in 1803. His sons were William and Elisha. The latter was a minister. John Knox, whose sons were

William, John, and Wilson, died in 1819. William Knox of Ugly Creek died in 1824. His children were David, John, Reuben, William, Stokeley, James, Leonard, and Alsey. John and William, Jr., were already deceased, the former leaving a son William. David Knox, a neighbor, was not living at this time.

Thomas Landes, whose wife was Nancy, died 1839.

The wife of Isaac Leighton was a Carson. The children were Francis (married Elizabeth Persinger), Daniel, American, Mattie (married Tifford Bratton), Nancy, Elizabeth (married Benjamin Bowyer), Nancy (married William Arthur), James (married the widow of Jared Lockhart).

Conrad Lemon, whose wife was Nancy, died 1843. Their children were George W., Joseph, William H., James Y., Mariah (married a Byers), Caroline (married John Byers), Mary J. (married Jefferson Peters).

David Lockhart died 1845. His wife was Rachel. The children were James L., John, Elizabeth Jackson, Sarah Edgar, and Mary Kimberlin.

Thompson McAllister, born 1811, died 1871, came in 1849 from Adams county, Pennsylvania, and purchased of Rufus Pitzer, Sr., 2,128 acres for about $15,000, adjacent to the Covington of that day. Before coming to Virginia, Mr. McAllister served a term in the legislature of his native state. In his adopted state he was a leader in industrial enterprises. His wife, whom he married in 1839, was Lydie Miller Adams. Their children were Clara Biddle (married Dr. Gabriel McDonald), Abraham Adams, William Miller (married Margaret E. Ervin), Edgar Thompson (married first Alice Cavendish Mann and afterward Clementine Dysard), Annie Elizabeth (married Dr. Joseph Root England).

A. Adams McAllister, born 1841, was denied a college education because of the panic of 1857 and the civil war. He was a sergeant in Bryan's Battery of the Confederate army. In 1865 he was married to Julia Ellen Strattton of West Virginia. Mr. McAllister was a public spirited citizen, energetic, very active in several business lines, and in the church of his choice, the Presbyterian. To bring the paper mill to Covington, he sold to it at a low figure the land on which it is built. He added to the tract purchased by his father, and the real estate holdings became very valuable. His heavy business interests in Covington are now conducted by his sons, William McD., Hugh M., and Julian R.

The name McCallister is the same as McAllister, and is so spelled in the will of James. It is sometimes spelled McCollister. Richard bought 119 acres on Ugly in 1793, and was still living there ten years later. James, of Jackson's River, died in 1801. His children were Hannah—wife of a Barnett—Mary—wife of a Waters—Thomas, John, James, Edward, and Garrett. Several grandsons bore the forename of the grandfather. John died in 1824, leaving Jane, Polly, Nelly, James, and Mary A. The first three married, respectively, a Warren, a Miller, and a Tolbert. Thomas McCallister died in 1829. His own children were Mary A., William, Polly, Reese, Cynthia, and Polly A., the last the wife of a Smith.

Michael Mallow died in 1830, leaving seven children, two of whom were Jacob and John. He lived on a part of the Carpenter survey. Whether he was the same as Michael Mallow, Jr., of Pendleton county, we do not know.

Moses Mann purchased land near Staunton in 1748 and died about 1756. His executor was John, his oldest brother, who seems to be the same John that married a daughter of Joseph Carpenter, and lived on a part of the Carpenter land. He died about 1764, just after winning an ejectment suit against Jeremiah Seeley, his brother-in-law. His son Moses is mentioned in 1796 as a nephew to Andrew Hamilton. William and Thomas were brothers, and were undoubtedly brothers to Moses and John. Their father's name seems to have been the John who died about 1751, leaving a minor son named Thomas. William was a weaver, and also traded with the Indians. For his services in dealing with the red people, Israel Christian in 1762 contracted to pay him fifty pounds ($166.67) a year. He was a sergeant at Fort Young in 1759, and in 1762 purchased for 152½ pounds ($508.33) 320 acres at the mouth of Falling Spring Run. Here he died, March 20, 1778. Thomas lived till 1794.

Jane, the widow of William Mann, died in 1813. Her will mentions her children as John, Alice, Jane, Sarah, Moses, and Archibald. Sarah, the widow of Moses, died 1829. Her own children were Elizabeth L(ewis) (born 1796), Jane T. (born 1797), Hamilton (born 1800), Lewis T. (born 1802), Archibald J. (born 1805), John McD (owell) (born 1805), Sarah W. (born 1808). Jane T. married a Dudley. Benjamina was a granddaughter. Moses H. Mann drowned in Jackson's River about 1864. The Manns of Monroe are an offshoot of the Alleghany family.

Henry Massie, Sr., died 1841. His children were Thomas, Sarah (married a Stanley), Mary (married a Pleasants), Eugenia (married a Gatewood), Hezekiah, Thomas, and Henry.

Patrick Milhollen, who lived on the river east of Mallow, was a commissioner of the revenue in 1825. He seems to have been the husband of Abigail Carpenter.

William Morris, who lived above Covington, died about 1824, and the homestead passed into the hands of Hazael and Elisha Williams. His heirs were Jane, Jackson, Nancy Richardson, Margaret Keyser, Elizabeth Lockhart, and William, Richard, John, Ann, and Benjamin Morris. William Elliott, the husband of Isabella, was living in Jackson county, Ohio.

William F. Morton, a cabinet-maker and a man of local prominence, came from Albemarle and purchased 170 acres of the Mallows. His first wife was a Mallow, the second a Fudge. During the latter part of his life he lived in Covington, where he died during the civil war.

Robert L. Parrish, a native of Fredericksburg, came to Covington in 1866 as principal of the high school, but in 1870 entered upon the profession of law, excelling in land and corporation practice. He accumulated a very valuable library, particularly in Virginia history.

Joseph Pennell, a famous Methodist preacher in his day, lived on Potts Creek near the Craig line. His wife was Harriet. He died in 1849. The children named in his will were Harriet E. and Lynch.

Three Persingers, Christian, Philip, and Jacob, went to Greenbrier from Rockingham about 1751, and a few years later were driven out by the Indians. They seem to have been brothers. In 1760, Jacob was the executor of Philip, and as Christian was not living in 1768, it is a fair inference that the two lost their lives in the Indian war. Barbara was a daughter of Christian, and Catharine was a marriageable daughter of Jacob in 1762. The second wife of Jacob was Catharine, the widow of Jacob Pence, her first husband dying about 1750. Jacob seems to have returned from Rockingham in 1771. In that year he sold to Thomas Kincaid the land in Greenbrier that Christian Persinger had settled on, and made a home on Jackson's River below Island Ford bridge. He died before 1774. Abraham and Philip were sons, and in all probability, Christopher and Henry were other sons. Christopher, who settled on Blue Spring Run, had eleven children. Some of them were Moses, George, Jacob (wife Margaret), John (married Elizabeth Kimberlin, 1778), Elizabeth (married George Karnes, 1793), Mary (married George Fought, 1789), Catharine (married John Wright, 1785), Rebecca (married John Dudding). Of two other daughters, one married a King, and one a McColvin.

Moses, who married Lottie Rayhill and died about 1820, was the only son to remain in Alleghany. He lived on the paternal homestead. His children were Allen, who married a Peters and went to Illinois; Harvey, who married an Alford and went to Texas; Lee, born 1810, married first a Hook and then a Helmintoller, and lived on the Jacob Persinger farm; Maria (married Jabez Johnson); Sophronia (married William Sollender); Charlotte (married George Stull).

Henry, whose wife was Grizzy (Griselda) lived high up on Blue Spring Run and died in 1824. His children were John, Andrew, Jacob, Sampson, Elizabeth, Ruth, Peggy, and Mary. The last three married in the order of their mention, a Humphries, a Patterson, and a Bennett. Jacob appears to be the only son to remain in this county. His wife was Elizabeth, and his children were Henry, Charlotte, William, James, Alexander, John, Andrew, and Jeremiah. The first three married, respectively, Annie Fridley, Henry Myers, and Mary Wolfe. Alexander went to Indiana. The remaining brothers went to Greenbrier and Nicholas. Jacob, in 1798, patented 924 acres on the county line just north of Nuckoll's Knob, and on a portion of this his grandson John—a son of Henry, Jr.—now lives.

Another Jacob Persinger was known as Jacob, Jr., to distinguish him from the father of Christopher and Henry. .He was not related by blood to the other Persingers, and concerning him there is an interesting story. During the raid of 1756 a boy six years of age was carried off from Jackson's River. At one of the Shawnee towns he was adopted by a squaw who had two sons of similar age. Boards were tied to their backs to make them walk erect, and every morning, regardless of the weather, the three boys had to take a plunge bath, after which they ran about nude until their skins were dry. The Indians were kind to this white captive, and punished him only when he presumed—contrary to Indian usage—to assist the squaws in their work. After he grew up, the Shawnees did not ask him to join their war parties against the white people.

After eight years the boy was given up in the general delivery at the close of the war with Pontiac. No one claiming him, he went back to his foster-mother, who was greatly pleased. At a council called to consider the case, the warriors argued that since the youth voluntarily returned, their obligation had ceased. But as the chief ruled that the treaty must be strictly observed, three braves returned him to Jackson's River. He escaped from them and again made his way to the Shawnee village. This time the squaw concealed her adopted son, but at length he was seen by the chief, who said he must go to the white people. The youth now concluded that the Indians had forsaken him, and though he came back to the white settlements reluctantly, he made no further attempt to rejoin the people of the forest, for whom he continued to hold a friendly feeling. It was probably in the battle of Point Pleasant that he was recognized by one of his Indian foster brothers. There was an immediate truce between the two men and a cordial exchange of greetings.

On his third return to Jackson's River, which was probably a year or more after the first, he was claimed by a Persinger woman, who had lost a boy. Mrs. Persinger was but four feet six inches tall, while the youth stood six feet four inches. Her own son had a scar on the foot resulting from the bite of a rattlesnake. Although the returned captive could exhibit no such mark, she took him to her home, where he lived a while, although he was not placed on the same footing as her own children. He now became known as Jacob Persinger, Jr., yet he never believed that he was one of her children. He thought the name of his parents was Godfrey. The Persinger home did not look like the home he recollected, nor were its surroundings the same.

Who was this Persinger woman? It is not easy to see how she could be the second wife of Jacob Persinger, Sr., because she never lived on the frontier until she accompanied him on his return about 1770. The narrative speaks of her as though she were a widow, although Jacob Persinger lived till about 1774. If she were the widow of Christian Persinger and had continued to live on Jackson's River, there are no difficulties in the way.

For a while, the Indianized youth attended a "Dutch" school and had trouble in learning the language. Here is another snag in the story. It suggests that Mrs. Persinger's home was either in Greenbrier or Rockbridge. The early settlers of Alleghany were almost wholly non-German. Be this as it may, the youth was suspicious of the stern discipline then in vogue, and with an eye to possible trouble, he always took his rifle, tomahawk, and hunting knife, whenever he went to the schoolhouse. He afterward attended an English school, but only for three months.

At length the young man purchased a survey on Potts Creek, nine miles above Covington, and here he lived till his death in 1841, when he was above ninety years of age. He always took more kindly to hunting and fishing than to farm work, and thought nothing of sleeping outdoors under a tree. But his hunting was profitable. He became a slaveholder and one of the most substantial residents of the county.

In the Dunmore war Persinger served as a scout, and he campaigned eighteen months in the Revolution. He then married Mary Kimberlin. When the bride found he had only a little, rough cabin, and that the only bed was two bearskins spread on the floor, she insisted that they live in a more civilized manner. The husband readily complied. He put up a better cabin and at length built as good a farmhouse as there was in the valley. Jacob Persinger outlived his wife twenty years. Their children were John, Mary, Andrew, Joseph, Alexander, Elizabeth, Martha, Susannah, Nancy, Sarah, Jane, and Granvill. John, a colonel of militia, was unmarried. Joseph and Alexander went to Missouri, and the latter became a judge. Susannah, who married a Reed, and Jane, who married a Karnes, went to Tazewell. Mary married Samuel Carpenter, Sr., Andrew married Elizabeth Stickleman, Elizabeth (born 1780, died 1846) married Conrad Fudge. Martha married a Rose, Nancy married Charles Callaghan, Sarah married Peter Wright, and Granvill married Henry Clarkson. Soon after the murder of Colonel Persinger in 1842, the homestead was purchased by Lee Persinger, a son of Moses.

Judge Alexander Persinger, born July 11, 1790, served in the war of 1812, became a pioneer settler of Illinois, and in 1818 crossed the Mississippi into what was then Missouri Territory. He was a justice of Montgomery and Boone counties, Missouri, and represented them in the state legislature after 1830.

George A. Revercomb, a well-known lawyer and political leader, is a native of Bath, his grandfather settling at Warm Springs.

William Robinson died in 1794, and his children were Wililam, James, Ann, and Margaret.

Dennison Rose of New England married first a niece of Colonel Jordan and next a daughter of James Kimberlin, succeeding the latter in the ownership of the Kimberlin homestead. He was not related to Joseph Rose, who settled on Blue Spring Run, and was grandfather to Robert P. Rose, the supervisor. The father of Joseph was Alexander, who moved to Botetourt from King George.

James and William Scott were probably brothers. The latter died in 1751, and the widow of Judith married Joseph Carpenter, the guardian of her children. Elizabeth Scott, who died in 1841, was an aged widow, who left $200 to the Presbyterian Church of Covington.

General William Skeen was born in Rockbridge in 1818, and died in Covington in 1893. He excelled as a land lawyer and held many positions of trust.

Children of Daniel Stull of the Rich Patch were Mary, Jacob, and James, who married, respectively, Jacob Bennett, Phœbe Bennett, and Hannah King. Sons of a brother to Daniel were George (married Charlotte Persinger), Jacob (married Sarah Haynes), Samuel, and John.

Hugh Paul Taylor, a native of Rockbridge, died in Covington about 1830. He was a militia officer, and in 1828 was prosecuting attorney. His house stood on the site of the present postoffice. Taylor was the actual author of much of *Withers' Border Warfare*. Mr. Taylor was also an accomplished surveyor, his work in this line being by no means confined to Alleghany county. In 1824 he finished some very important work on the huge Boye map of Virginia, which was on a scale of five miles to the inch.

James Warren was a resident of Covington in 1822.

Jacob and Isaac Wolfe were on Potts Creek in 1825.

Peter Wright the pioneer kept a tavern in 1780. James Wright, who purchased from James Gilliland in 1829 a farm on Potts Creek, was not related to the Wrights of Covington.

The personal property books of 1782 are the oldest that have been preserved in Virginia. The precinct of Captain John Bollar seems to have been wholly within the Alleghany area and the southern border of Bath. The names in his list are given below. T stands for tithable, S for slave, h for horse, and c for cattle. Tithables are not mentioned when there was only one. Where there was no property, a zero is put down.

	h	c			h	c
Armstrong, James	4		Mann, Moses		7	2
Armstrong, Robert	11	11	Mann, Moses		2	9
Barbery, Thomas	1	1	Massie, Thomas 7S		41	30
Barratt, William	0		McCalister, Garrett		1	
Boller, John	?	?	McCalister, James 2T		7	5
Bullitt, Cuthbert 3S	8	24	McCalister, Thomas ...1S		7	5
Carpenter, Jeremiah	5	6	McClintock, Robert		4	7
Clark, Joseph	2	3	McClintock William		5	5
Corder, William		1	McClintock, William		6	21
Cottle, Benjamin	1	2	McDuff, John		3	5
Craig, James	3	9	McGart, John		3	11
Davis, James		3	Milholland, Thomas		0	
Davis, William	1	3	Morren(?), Bernard		3	4
Dean, John 3S	11	28	Morris, Richard		22	18
Doylton, William	0		Price, Evan		3	
Edwards, Jeremiah	5	4	Price, Zachariah		1	1
Elliott, James	7	20	Robinson, James 3S		5	17
Fitzpatrick, John	0		Robinson, James		5	5
Fitzpatrick, Thomas	0		Robinson, William		3	7
Harvie, Thomas	1		Scott, James		1	3
Jones, Henry	2	3	Scott, John		5	6
Jones, John	1	3	Slath, John		1	
Jones, John	3		Smith, William		4	11
Kender, Peter	0		Sprowl, William		4	7
Kimberlane, Adam	7	5	Thompson, Martha		1	3
Kincade, Andrew	7	17	Trotter, Ezekiel		3	3
Kincade, William	3	9	Wall, Thomas		1	1
Lilley, William	3	4	Ward, William		1	2
Mann, Esau	3	3	Wright, Peter 2S		10	38
Mann, Jean 1S	8	10				

RESIDENTS OF 1840.

FROM THE LIST BY LEE PERSINGER, COMMISSIONER OF THE REVENUE

Allen, John
Anderson, Henry
Andrews, John A., Moses
Aritt, John, Mary, Michael
Armentrout, Abraham, Elizabeth, Jacob, Joel, John, John S., Jones, Joseph
Baker, John T., William
Belcher, Jonathan
Bennet, Henry, Jacob, John, Sampson, Solomon, William
Bess, Alexander, Henry, Nash L., William
Bird, William
Bishop, Jacob
Black, John A.
Boone, George
Boothe, William, Sr., William, Jr.
Boswell, James H., John L., Sr., John L., Jr., William E.
Bowyer, David, John
Boyd, Nathan
Bradley, John
Bratton, Robert
Brosseen (?), John
Brown, Anderson, John J., Samuel, Sr., Samuel, Jr., William B.
Bryan, Hugh, James H.
Burke, James
Bush, Adam, Andrew, Samuel
Butler, Frederick
Byer, David, George, James, Peter, Samuel, William

Callaghan, Charles, John
Carpenter, Samuel, Sr., Samuel, Jr.
Carson, George, James, John, William
Carter, Lemuel
Clark, James B., Joseph B., William
Clarkson, Henry
Cook, John
Cooper, John
Counts, Filander
Cox, Alfred, John, William
Crawford, Owen
Croft, James, John
Crow, John
Cummings, Absalom
Curry, David P.
Dacon, Samuel
Damron, Andrew, Christopher, Isaac P., Joseph, William
Daniels, Joseph
Davis, Andrew, Benjamin J., Leonard H.
Deeds, John, Sr., John, Jr., William
Deloren (?), John
Dempsey, Wesley G.
Dew, Absalom, Achilles, Charles, Mary
Dickson, Joseph, Robert, Samuel, Thomas C., William H.
Douglas, Francis, Harriet
Downey, Archibald

Dressler, Absalom, Adam, Charles, Henry, John, Peter
Dysard, Jacob
Ervin, Joseph, Samuel
Evans, William
Fandree, Richard
Fleet, Alexander
Forbes, George, Sr., Quincy C.
Fridley, Charles, David, George, Gideon, Isaac, James, John, Sr., John, Lewis, Margaret, Nelson, Thomas
Fry, Feagans E., John, Randolph
Fudge, Andrew, Conrad
Gibson, John, Nicholas F.
Gilbert, David A., Nelson L.
Gillespie, Robert, William G., William W.
Gilliland, Nancy G., Samuel
Goldsmith, William
Griffith, Caleb, Jefferson, Wortley
Grose, Samuel
Hamilton, John
Hammer, Francis, John
Hammersley, David J.
Hansbarger, Jacob, John H., Sebastian
Hardbarger, Abraham, Thomas
Hardy, John, John L.
Harmon, Anthony, Barbara, Christopher, George W., Peter, Thomas
Harris, Frederick
Hart, William
Haynes, Henry Y., Joseph, John P., Lemuel W., William H.
Hays, George
Helmintoller, Peter
Hempinstall, Charles
Henderson, William
Hepler, John, Sr., John Jr.
Hill, John
Hinton, William
Holley, William
Holloway, John, John M., William G.
Hood, Edward
Hook, Eli, Elias, James S., John B., Madison
Hoover, George P., Jacob, Madison
Huddleston, Abraham J.
Hull, Joseph
Humphries, Jesse, John, William
Hunley, William
Jackson, Abel, Crawford
Jones, Hannah
Joseph, Alexander, Isaac, Daniel
Karnes, Elizabeth, Harvey, Jacob, Sr., Jacob, Jr., James, Michael, Sampson, William
Kelso, Hugh
Kindle, Jacob M.
Keslin, Samuel
Keyser, Davis A., Fleming, James, James B., Joseph A., Joseph D.
Kimberlin, Charlotte, Joseph, Nancy
Kincaid, Alexander Mc., Alice, Andrew, Andrew K., James

C., James S., John S., Samuel, Thomas McD.

Kindell, James, James W.

King, Absalom, Charles, George, P., John, William F.

Kitinger, Washington

Knox, David, Hannah, Isaac, William, Wilson

Kyle, Galbraith, William

Landers, Jacob, Peter

Larkin, Patrick

Layne, Douglas B.

Lee, Arthur

Leighton, Isaac N., John

Lemon, Conrad

Lewis, John

Linglocker, John

Linkswiler, Adam, Jr., John

Lockhart, David, David B., John L.

Longaker, John

Lowry, Samuel B.

McCallister, Andrew, Barbara, Rufus, William

McClintic, James

McElhenny, S. W.

McGuire, Arthur

McKartney, John

McKenny, Nathaniel

Mallow, John

Mann, Archibald G., Archibald J., John McD., Lewis T., Moses H., William

Marks, Edmund

Mason, Morton

Massie, Henry, Jr.

Massey, Henry

Maston, John

Matheny, William

Matthews, Campbell C.

Meaks, Edmund

Medings, Patrick H.

Milhollen, Andrew

Monroe, John

Morrison, Fountain, James D.

Moser, David

Moss, William

Morgan, Jerrard

Morton, William, William F.

Myers, Augustus, George, Henry

Neel, Hugh, Mary

Nicely, Circle, Elizabeth, George, Jacob, Sr., Jacob, Jr., John, Lewis, Matthew, Peter

Oiler, Henry, John, Sr., John, Jr., Nancy, Stephen

Oliver, James

Paris, Alexander

Patterson, Dion C., Pharr, Sampson D.

Paxton, William

Payne, Charles C., George H.

Pence, John, Peter

Perry, Thomas L.

Persinger, Aaron, Alexander, Alexander B., Andrew, Andrew J., Eli, Henry, Jacob, Sr., Jacob, Jr., John, Joseph H., Lee, Marton, Sampson, William, Sr., William, Jr., Zebedee

Peyton, John H.

Phillips, Jesse

Pinkney, Solomon W.

Pinnell, Joseph

Pitzer, Jane, John, John L., Robert C.
Pleasants, Henry F.
Plymale, William B.
Polk, Joseph
Polock, Samuel
Printz, Cornelius
Pulliam, Sophia
Quickel, Adam, Henry
Ray, William
Rayhill, Alexander
Reynolds, Anderson, Diocletian, Judith, Lewellen J., Lucy W., Thomas
Richardson, Thomas
Rigon, Henson
Roach, John B.
Robeson, Elizabeth, John L., William
Rogers, George W., James, Philip, William C.
Rose, Denison, Jackson, William S., William W.
Ross, James, William
Rucker, James
Samples, John
Sawyers, Alexander, Archer, George, Matthews, Sampson, William
Scott, Elizabeth, Rachel, William
Shumaker, David, John, Nicholas W., William, Sr., William, Jr.
Shumate, John
Simmons, Ephraim, Hugh, Ruth, William M.
Simpson, Alexander, John, Preston, Rezin, Washington

Sively, Andrew J., Elizabeth, Harrison D., Joseph, Mary A.
Skeen, Robert, William
Smith, Henry, Peter, Samuel, Thomas E., Thomas J., Wright
Snead, Elisha, William
Sparks, John
Sprowl, W. B.
Steele, Isaac
Stevens, James, John
Slittings, Joseph
Stone, John, John H., Joseph P., William
Stringer, John
Stull, Daniel, George, Sr., George, Jr., Jacob, Sr., Jacob Jr., John, Samuel
Sullender, William
Tailor, Amandress, James M., John R., Mary
Taylor, William W.
Terry, William
Thomas, John, Wright B.
Tingler, Jacob, John, Michael
Tinnell, Joseph
Tinsley, Bennet, Charles W., Obadiah, Roderick M., William J.
Tolbert, Richard H.
Trailor, Field
Trusler, George W.
Vickers, John
Waltron, James M.
Waren, James, Margaret
Way, John
Whiteside, Hayze
Whitmon, Robert

Whitton, Lewis
Wilson, Andrew
Wininger, John
Wolf, Abraham, Isaac, Jacob, Sr., Jacob, Jr., John, Samp-
son, Sarah
Woods, Robert
Woodson, Zachariah A.
Wright, George W., John, Stephen

MARRIAGES RECORDED IN BOTETOURT

Armstrong, James—Mary Thompson of Martha—1787—by Rev. Edward Crawford.

Arrett, Michael—Mary Woolf of John—1795.

Carpenter, Solomon—Lucretia Prentice of Daniel?—1783.

Clark, Christopher—Agnes Wright of Peter—1789.

Fought, George—Mary Persinger of Christopher—1789.

Downey, Michael—Mary Persinger of Nelly Wells—1789.

Elliott, John—Jane Cross—1785.

Gillespie, William—Sarah Carpenter—1780.

Glassburn, David—Elizabeth Carpenter of Zopher and Mary—1778.

Helmintoller, Peter—Margaret Brennon—1793.

Karnes, George—Elizabeth Persinger—1793.

Kinkead, John—Alcy Elliott—1787—by Rev. Edward Crawford.

McCollister, Garland—Jane Halls—1794.

Moody, Edward—Frances Carter, stepdaughter of John and Sarah Miller.

Morris, William—Margaret McClintock—1788—by Rev. Christopher Clark.

Nox (Knox), William—Anna Reed of William and Ruthy—1789.

Persinger, John—Elizabeth Kimberlane—1778.

Wooley, Michael—Jane Mann—1779.

Wright, John—Catharine Persinger—1785.

MARRIAGES RECORDED IN BATH

Armstrong, Archibald—Nancy Scott—1797.

Armstrong, John—Jane Kincaid of Robert—1797.

Armstrong, John—Polly Crawford—1790.

Garnett, Abraham—Frances Morris—1794.

Gillespie, John—Comfort Griffith—1798.
Griffith, Mary—Peter Flack—1793.
Knox, Elisha—Nancy Parker—1801.
Knox, John—Sarah Robinson of Joseph—1793.
Knox, William—Sarah Acklin of Green of Craig county—1792.
Mann, Thomas—Elizabeth Armstrong of Robert—1792.
McCallister, Garnett—Ann Sprowl—1792.
McCallister, John—Mary Kincaid—1800.
Morris, Edward—Rhoda Jackson—1795.
Payne, Lewis—Nancy Davis—1794.
Scott, Hugh—Betsy Bell—1800.
Simms, Jeremiah—Sarah Milhollen—1800.

MARRIAGES RECORDED IN ALLEGHANY

Andrews, Moses—Catharine Wolf—1826.
Bishop, Abraham—Mary Brennaman—1828.
Bishop, Jacob—Margaret Moyer—1827.
Brown, William—Elizabeth Lemmon—1825.
Brunnewell, Jacob L.—Charlotte Brennaman—1828.
Clark, Joseph B.—Christena Dressler—1828.
Claughton, Richard A.—Susan Printz—1825.
Dressler, George—Malinda Dressler—1827.
Dressler, Peter—Patsy Fleet—1826.
Duke, Hugh—Pauline L. White—1829.
Duke, William—Nancy Glassburn—1829.
Frazer, Henry—Eliza Wright—1825.
Gillispie, Alexander—Patty Wright—1825.
Grass, John—Julia A. Taylor—1827.
Hart, Moses—Margaret Nicely—1825.
Keeble, James—Agnes Oliver—1827.
Kimberlin, Jacob—Nancy Blair—1827.
Lange, David—Gantha A. Walton—1827.
Lemmon, William—Harriet Pitzer—1825.
Morton, William F.—Catharine Mallow—1825.
Pitzer, Duiguid—Sally Mayse—1829.
Rayhill, Alexander—Elizabeth Johnson—1827.
Rush, Hugh B.—Julia McCallister—1827.

Shawver, William—Keziah Ross—1825.
Standley, Francis—Mary C. Massie—1827.
Stull, Jacob—Margaret Bennett—1825.
Williams, John—Abigail Sively—1826.
Wolf, George—Sarah Paxton—1827.
Wolf, Sampson—Elizabeth Nickle—1826.

Allen, Franklin—Nancy Persinger—1831.
Arritt, John—Elizabeth Baugher—1831—by Rev. Joseph Pennell.
Bayed, Porterfield—Rachel Nichol—1831.
Beckner, John A.—Martha I. Lantz—1846.
Brown, Matthew D.—Mary Smith—1850.
Bush, Samuel—Mary Myers—1831.
Bush, Nimrod—Sarah Spencer—1831—by Rev. Joseph Pennell.
McCallister, William H.—Amanda M. Snead—1846.
Carter, James—Mary M. Aritt of John—1855.
Childs, Robert—Sarah E. Harmon—1851.
Clark, William—Elizabeth Morris—1830.
Damron, Isaac—Margaret Bennett of Sampson—1855.
Davies, John B.—Joanna Armentrout—1850.
Douglas—Harriet Morris—1830—by Rev. James Watts.
Duke, John—Judith Humphris—1829.
Fridley, Isaac—Elizabeth Stull—1831.
Fry, Henry—Mary E. Anderson—1851.
Gillespy, Henry—Mildred Handly—1829.
Gilliland, Henry—May I. Hook—1851.
Gallaspie, William H.—Elizabeth A. Gallaspie—1850.
Grady, Hamilton C.—Nancy Fudge—1830—by Rev. James Watts.
Gray, Oliver B.—Rebecca R. Scott—1850.
Knox, John—Synthia McCallister—1829.
Landis, Peter—Rachel Carren—1829—by Rev. Joseph Pennell.
Mann, Lewis.— Sally Cotten—1830.
Pitzer, Duiguid—Sally Mayes—1831.
Persinger, Allen—Paulina Peters—1831—by Rev. Joseph Pennell.

Persinger, James O.—Mariah J. Bennett—1857.

Pleasants, John H.—Mary L. Massie—1829.

Rayhill, Jacob—Rebecca A. King—1851.

Rose, William H.—Jane Persinger—1846.

Sawyers, Alexander—Sarah Stone—1828.

Sawyer, Archer—Susan Lewis—1835.

Simmons, Rolung—Mary Bush—1831.

Smith, William—Cornelia A. Boley—1851.

Surber, Andrew—Caroline Hansbarger—1830—by Rev. John A. Vanlear.

Terry, James—Leah Pinkley—1830.

Wickline, William—Virginia Blaker—1846.

Williams, Erasmus T.—Leah C. Ivnes(?)—1851.

Wood, John C.—Maria S. Gilliland—1850.

Wright, John—Jane Andess—1829.

XIX

LEGISLATORS AND COUNTY OFFICIALS

LEGISLATORS FROM ALLEGHANY

SENATORS

UNTIL 1880, Alleghany was in a senatorial district with Bath, Botetourt, Greenbrier, Monroe, Nicholas, and Pocahontas. Nicholas was then taken out. In 1838, Roanoke was added, and in 1849, Highland. In 1852, Botetourt, Craig, and Roanoke became the other counties of the district. In 1865, the others were Bath, Botetourt, and Highland, and in 1869, Bath and Rockbridge. In 1874 they were Botetourt, Craig, and Roanoke, and in 1879, Bath, Botetourt, Highland, and Rockbridge. Since 1904, the district comprises Alleghany, Bath, Botetourt, and Craig, except that in 1908, Clifton Forge was added. For the sessions in the years mentioned below, the senators have been the following:

John Brown, Jr. ...1822-1826	Joseph H. Sherrard, 1879-1880
Pere B. Wethered ..1826-1830	William A. Glasgow
Charles Beale 1830-1834	1881-1884
John T. Anderson..1834-1842	Charles P. Jones ...1885-1896
John McCauley 1842-1850	S. H. Letcher 1897-1898
Douglas B. Layne ..1850-1861	Charles E. McCorkle (died)
Robert M. Wiley ..1861-1865	1899
W. W. Boyd (died) 1865	A. Nash Johnson ..1899-1900
Fleming B. Miller ..1865-1867	George A. Revercomb
William A. Anderson	1901-1904
1867-1873	Harvey L. Garrett (died) 1906
William H. Lackland	F. W. King 1906-1910
1874-1875	W. A. Rinehart 1912-1918
James W. Marshall, 1875-1879	George W. Layman 1920-1924

DELEGATES

Until 1830, Alleghany was entitled to two delegates, the same as all other counties. From 1830 to 1853, it was a delegate district by itself. Bath was then added, but was taken off in 1865. In 1869 Craig was joined to Alleghany. In 1879, Bath and Highland were substituted for Craig, but since 1904, Alleghany and Craig again comprise one district.

Bryan, Cyrus P. 1863-65
Byrd, John T. 1889-90
Carpenter, Samuel ..1839-40, 1840-41, 1852-53, 1855-56, 1857-58, 1859-61, 1861-63, 1875-77
Damron, Joseph 1833-34
Damron, Andrew 1850-51
Davis, Jesse 1825-26, 1826-27, 1827-28, 1829-30
Garrett, Harvey L. 1901-04
Goodwin, B. C. 1916-18
Holloway, William G. 1839, 1841-42
Jones, Charles P. 1883-84
Layne, Douglas B. ...1834-35, 1835-36, 1836-37, 1843-44, 1844-45, 1845-46, 1846-47, 1847-48, 1848-49, 1849-50
Lee, John A. J. 1874-75
Legrand, Nash 1823-24
McAllister, William M. 1899-1900
McCaleb, T. B. ....1922—
McClintic, Archibald M. 1885-87, 1887-88
McGuffin, Andrew G. 1853-54
Mann, Moses 1822-24
Mann, Moses H. 1842-43
Mann, Lewis T. 1865-67
Merry, James, Jr. 1822-23, 1824-25
Persinger, John ..1824-25, 1825-26, 1826-27, 1827-28, 1828-29, 1831-32, 1832-33
Revercomb, William H. 1879-80, 1881-82
Rinehart, W. A. 1895-96
Robertson, H. H. 1871-73
Robinson, A. A. 1920-22
Spessard, N. E. 1904, 1906, 1907, 1910, 1914-15
Terrill, William H. 1828-29, 1829-30, 1830-31
Withrow, A. F. 1891-92, 1893-94, 1897-98
Woodson, B. L. 1869-71

NOTE:—There were two distinct Samuel Carpenters, but we do not know in what year the term of the second Samuel began.

COUNTY OFFICERS

The lists below are made up from what may be gleaned from the county records. Until 1852 they do not enable one to compile a perfect register, and gaps therefore occur.

County officers did not become elective until 1852, the first election being held May 27th of that year.

The first election for supervisors took place May 26, 1870, the members taking their seats July 1st of the same year.

Until 1852 the sheriff was chosen from among the justices, and his term was little longer than one year. The terms of the other county officers were somewhat indefinite. Since the reconstruction regime of 1866-70, officers are chosen for definite terms.

JUSTICES, 1822-1852

Names followed by a star are of the justices present on the opening day of the first court. Names followed by a date are of those justices who were commissioned later than July, 1823.

Allen, John 1831	Hook, Stephen
Arritt, Michael*	Kean, Samuel, Sr. 1826
Arritt, John	Keyser, Joseph D.*
Bishop, Jacob 1846	Kincaid, Archibald M. ..1831
Boswell, John L.	King, Charles 1839
Bryan, Hugh 1839	Knox, Elisha
Callaghan, John*	Layne, Douglas B. 1831
Callaghan, Charles	Lowry, Samuel B. 1827
Carpenter, Samuel, Jr.	Mallow, George 1826
Crow, John	Mann, Moses H.
Damron, Joseph 1827	Mann, Lewis T. 1849
Damron, Andrew 1838	Massie, Henry—resigns, 1826
Davis, Jesse*	Morton, William F. 1846
Harry, John 1831	Paris, Alexander 1838
Harnsbarger, Sebastian	Pence, Peter
Haynes, William H.	Persinger, John
Herbert, William	Persinger, Peter
Holloway, John	Persinger, Lee 1839
Holloway, William G. ...1839	Pitzer, John L. 1846
Hobbs, James O. 1839	Sancy (?), Harry

Sawyers, Sampson
Skeen, John 1827
Skeen, Robert 1838

Smith, Henry 1831
Steele, Isaac
Warren, James 1839

JUSTICES, 1852-1856

James Mann, president; Peter Helmintoller, William Herbert, John C. Taylor.—District No. 1.

Lewis T. Mann, Samuel Brown, Jr., Jacob Bishop, Thomas Richardson.—No. 2.

John Hansbarger, John J. Paxton, John A. Black, James Shanklin.—No. 3.

William F. Morton, Madison Hook, Charles King, Samuel Carpenter.—No. 4.

JUSTICES

1856

Boswell, John S., Jr.
Brown, Samuel, Jr.
Carpenter, Samuel
Davis, John B.
Hook, Madison
Morton, William F.
Richardson, Thomas
Riggs, Williamson

Scott, W. M.
Shanklin, James
Shumaker, Thomas T.
Sproul, William B.
Stull, George, Jr.
Walthall, Thomas
Waren, James (president)

1860

See Chapter VIII: John Crow died 1863, and William Damron filled the vacancy.

1864

The four districts were now reduced to three.

Bare, S. E.
Byer, D.
Farr, Moses B.
Fudge, Andrew
Hook, Madison
Jones, P. A.
Mann, Lewis F.

Rogers, O. F.
Shirkey, C.
Smith, Andrew S.
Stull, George
Wilson, David
Matheny, Asbury

Justices, 1865, commissioned by the Governor and taking oath August 21st:

Milton Armentrout	Samuel Kincaid
J. E. Bare	A. Adams McAllister
Charlton Shirkey	Alexander McCurdy
George Hull	Lewis T. Mann, president
Beale V. Keyser	Asbury Matheny

Justices, elected July 27, 1865, for three years from August 4th-

Arritt, Michael	Matheny, Asbury
Bowyer, John	Pitzer, John L.
Damron, William	Scott, William M.
Haynes, P. V.	Shirkey, Charlton
McAllister, A. A.	Stull, George
Mann, L. F. (president)	Williamson, David

Justices, 1869—John A. Carson, John R. Hart (1870), Joel Kindell, Edmund P. Tinsley, Samuel Wilson, John M. Woltz.

SUPERVISORS, 1870-1923

Acord, A. J., Jr. 1891-95	Hook, Henry W. 1872-73
Aritt, Michael 1879	Hughes, Dr. J. F. 1882-83
Aritt, John M. 1893-95	Humphreys, William A.
Cabell, E. M. 1897-99	1873-74
Cargill, S. G. 1899-1915	McPherson, William H.
Carson, Henry P. 1889-91	1883-91
1889-91, 1895-97	Mann, John McD. . . .1870-73
Childs, W. A. 1897-99	Nettleton, E. M.
Davis, David M.	1887-89, 1893-1915
1891-1893, 1899-1901	Payne, Lewis 1873-75
Dew, John 1901-03	Persinger, Lee 1874
Dressler, Charles H. . .1875-82	Rose, R. B. . . . . .1903—
Dressler, Lee H. 1916-19	Shelding, James 1887-88
Elwee, C. M. 1895-97	Smith, Ballard J.
Gathright, T. M. . . . . .1920—	1883-87, 1889-91
Haynes, C. L. . . . .(?)	Stull, A. M. 1895
Helmintoller, Peter 1870	Stull, Allen L. . . . . .1918—
Hook, Beale 1872-82	Surber, A. O. 1915-18

CIRCUIT JUDGES

James Anderson	1822-1831
Allan Taylor	1831-1836
John J. Allen	1836-1841
Edward Johnson	1841-1855
Robert M. Hudson (circuit judge only)	1853-1869
W. K. Barnitz (military appointee)	1869-1870
William McLaughlin	1870-1898
S. H. Letcher	1898-1904
George K. Anderson	1904—

COUNTY AND CIRCUIT CLERKS

Oliver Callaghan	1822, 1831
Andrew Fudge	1831-1858
Lewis P. Holloway	1858-1862
William M. Scott	1862-1864
Joseph T. Fudge	1864-1869, 1870
Henry C. Vaughn	1869-1870
John R. Pharr	1870-1875
J. J. Hobbs	1875-1918
Olin J. Payne (appointee)	1918—

(Oliver Callaghan was clerk from the organization of Alleghany until August 15, 1831, when he was succeeded by Andrew Fudge. Lewis P. Holloway qualified July 1, 1858 and died a prisoner of war at Fort Delaware. William M. Scott filled a vacancy until July 1, 1864, when Joseph T. Fudge was elected, serving until November, 1870, except for an interim in the Reconstruction period, when Henry C. Vaughn was a military appointee. John R. Pharr served until January 1, 1875, and was followed by J. J. Hobbs, who died in office.)

SHERIFFS

William Herbert	1822	Stephen Hook	1840
John Holloway	1824-25	Sampson Sawyers	1842
Robert Kincaid	1826-27	Isaac Stull	1842
Michael Aritt	1828-29	James M. Montague	1852-56
John Davis	1830	John D. Sadler	1859-60
John Callaghan	1834	John I. Stuck	1860-64

John R. Pharr 1866-69
C. A. Brockmyer 1868-70
William M. Rose 1870-82
William Helmintoller 1882-87
Samuel G. Byer 1887-1895
F. M. Turner 1895-Jan. 1, 1904

Andrew C. Sizer 1904-20
Edward B. Butler
            1920-Aug. 12, 1922
Robert E. Dyche
    (appointee) 1922

Sheriff Butler was murdered in the discharge of duty.

PROSECUTING ATTORNEYS

William Skeen, 1854, 1856,-60,
    1867(?)-1871
Andrew Damron 1865
Robert L. Parrish ..1871-1883
James Bowler 1883-1887
J. K. Campbell 1887-1891
William E. Allen
        1891-95, 1904-16

George A. Revercomb
                1895-1904
R. B. Stephenson .....1916—
Thompson Crutchfield 1822-27
W. H. Terrill 1827
H. P. Taylor 1828

SURVEYORS

William Herbert ...1822-1824
Joseph Dawron ...1824-1833
Andrew Damron ..1833-1850
William S. Holloway
        1850-1859

Chesley H. Collins
                1865-1870(?)
John A. Carson 1870-1906
C. H. H. Rumbold ....1906—

TREASURERS

William C. Fudge ....1875 (probably from 1870 to about 1879)
John B. Pitzer ....1879 (or earlier)—1883
Joseph F. Fudge 1883-1904
William F. Tinsley ....Jan. 1, 1904-July 1, 1906
J. D. Mustoe ....July 1, 1906—

DIVISION SUPERINTENDENTS

S. F. Chapman
W. W. Pendleton

F. W. King
George O. Green

James G. Jeter

XX

SOLDIERS OF 1861 AND EARLIER WARS

THERE is no means of knowing the full number of the Alleghany pioneers who served in militia companies during the French and Indian war. In 1779 land claims were allowed to the following veterans:

Joseph Carpenter, member of Captain John Dickenson's Rangers in 1759. John Carpenter, son of Thomas, was his heir.

Solomon Carpenter was under Dickenson, 1757-8. His sons, John and Thomas, were his heirs.

Thomas Carpenter served under William Preston in 1759.

Thomas Carpenter, Jr., served under Dickenson, 1757-8. His heir was John Carpenter.

Zopher Carpenter was a drummer in Dickenson's Rangers.

John Mann was in Captain Cunningham's company, a part of the force under Colonel Bouquet in 1764.

Thomas Mann was in Dickenson's Rangers in 1756. His heir was Moses Mann, son of John.

William Mann was a sergeant in Colonel Peachy's Battalion in 1759. His heir and oldest son was Moses Mann.

Jacob Persinger was under Dickenson in 1757. The claim was proved by his sons, Abraham and Philip.

Peter Wright was a sergeant in Dickenson's Rangers in 1759.

Some other members of Dickenson's Rangers were Patrick Carrigan, David Galloway, Sergeant Robert Gillespie, Sr., William Hamilton, Ensign Humphrey Madison, Edward McMullen, John McMullin, Abraham Persinger, and Philip Persinger.

Neither are there any known rosters of the soldiers of the Point Pleasant expedition who came from the Alleghany area. But some of the men who served in that campaign were Jeremiah Carpenter, John Carpenter, Solomon Carpenter, George Carpenter, Thomas Gillespie, James Mann, John Mann, William Mann, Jacob Persinger, James Scott, and William Scott.

During the war for American independence, the population of the Alleghany area was very small; probably decidedly less than 1,000. It is almost certain that nearly all the able-bodied men performed more or less militia service, especially against the Indians. But the lists of Revolutionary soldiers are generally unsatisfcatory, in that they do not clearly point out the county or town where the soldier belonged. The only Alleghany men who served in that war, of whom we are certain, are those named in the next paragraph, and it is probable that several of them settled in this county after the Revolution.

John Kincaid, Charles King, Thomas Landes, Jacob Persinger, Adam Quickle, John Richardson, and William Smith.

The only Alleghanian whom we know to have been in the war of 1812 was David Bowyer. But there were probably others.

The Alleghany soldiers serving in the war with Mexico were Alexander Taylor, George Craft, William Craft, Reuben Ball, and George W. Hayes. Mr. Hayes was also in the Confederate army.

The only native and resident of Alleghany named to us as in the Union army in the war of 1861 was John A. Carson.

We now turn to the Alleghany men in the Confederate army. Rosters of Company D, 60th Virginia Infantry, and Company C, 27th Virginia Infantry, were compiled from memory, the first by W. A. Matheny, the second by D. N. Gilbert, and in both instances were revised and enlarged by Mrs. A. M. Evans. As the book was going to press lists of five commands were received from the Virginia State Library. These were copied with great care from the Confederate records, and it has been thought best to present them as given to us, although the names are not in full alphabetic order. Appended to the roster of Company D, 60th Virginia, is a list of the names given by Mr. Matheny as do not appear to be in, or to agree with, the official list.

*   *   *   *   *   *   *   *   *   *

Bryan's Battery: A. A. McAllister (sergeant), James Clark.

SECOND VIRGINIA CALVARY

Dungan, Robert K.
Pharr, Dion C., wounded at Philippi
Pharr, John R.
Pitzer, Henry C.
Rocke, William

COMPANY I 10TH REGIMENT VIRGINIA INFANTRY
COVINGTON

Covington, William D. C.—Enlisted April 18, 1861, Conrad's Store—Capt.

Sellers, Samuel A.—1st Lt.—Capt.

Miller, J. George H.—Enlisted April 23, 1862—2d Lt.—Surr'd at Appomattox C. H. '65.

Miller, Hiram H.—Enlisted June 17, 1861—Bvt. 2d Lt.—Resigned Sept. 22, 1864, G. O. 79.

Sellers, James M.—Enlisted August 12, F. Station—1st Sgt..

Secrist, Philip A. (Secrist Philip M.?)—Enlisted May 25, H. Ferry—2d Sgt.—Wounded August 9, 1862, 4 years. Page.

Monger, Joseph F.—Enlisted Apr. 18, C. Store—3d Sgt.—Rockingham, p. 1.
Wolfe, Jas. H.—Enlisted June 17,—4th Sgt.—To May '64—Captured.
Philips, James M.—Enlisted April 18—1st Corpl.
Crickenberger, Benj. F.—2d Corpl.
Secrist, Daniel W.—Enlisted June 17—3d Corpl.—Died in Elmira and buried in Woodlawn National Cemetery, N. Y.
Smith, John Jeff—4th Corpl.
Caton, Richard H.—Enlisted Oct. 18, Centerville—Private—4 years.
Cook, Jeremiah—Enlisted June 17, C. Store Rockingham pl.—Absent without leave June 15 to Sept. 1, '62, and still absent. Comr. Rept. Rockingham Co. gives this man as having served through the war.
Coffman, William T.—Enlisted April 18—Private.
Carrier, Henry F.—Wagoner.
Davis, William H.—Enlisted June 17—Private—Absent without leave July 26 to Sept. 1, '62, and still absent.
Essard, Jos. C. (Espard, Jos. C.?)
Eddins, William A.—Enlisted April 18—Private.
Elliott, Francis W.—Private—Discharged Aug. 4, '62, Gordonsville.
Frazier, Noah W.—Private—Wounded Aug. 9, '62.
Glenn, Geo. H.—Private—Absent without leave June 19 to Sept. 1, '62, and still absent.
Grove, John W.
Grove, Miles McG.—Private—Wounded Aug. 9, '62.
Grove, Joel R. (Grove Jacob R.?)—Enlisted May 5, 1862—Private.
Goodwin, Geo. H.—Enlisted Aug. 10—Private.
Harnsberger, Robert—April 18, 1861—Private.
Hall, Christian—Private—Absent without leave April 18 to Sept. 1, '62, and still absent.
Hitt, Silas B.
Ham, J. W.—1 year.
Huffman, James—Enlisted June 17.
Huffman, David—Private—Nurse in hospital.
Harris, William E.—Private—Absent without leave June 18 to Sept. 1, '62, and still absent.
Harris, James R.—Private—Absent without leave April 20 to Sept. 1, '62, and still absent.
Harmsberger, Charles W.—Enlisted April 25, 1862—Private.
Jennings, William K.—Enlisted May 25, 1861, H. Ferry—Wounded Aug. — 30, '62.
Killinger, William C.—Enlisted April 18, 1861, C. Store—4 years Louisa pl.
Lane, Lewis Z.—Wounded Aug. 9, '62.
Lamb, E. Alexander—Absent without leave June 15 to Sept. 1, '62, and still absent.
Louderlack, John P.—Enlisted June 17, 1861—4 years.
Long, Thomas L.
Long, William C.—Enlisted April 25, 1862, Elk Run—To 1864—Captured.
Marshall, John H.—Enlisted April 18, C. Store—Died in prison Rocking-

ham pl. (Absent without leave May 1 to Sept. 1, '62, and still absent.)

Marshall, William H.—Enlisted 1861—Through war. Wounded twice.

Murray, Francis H.—Nurse in hospital.

Monger, John B.—Enlisted June 17, 1861, C. Store—Private.

Marica, George S.—Enlisted 1861—4 years.

Powell, Moses—Enlisted April 18—Absent without leave June 18 to Sept. 1, and still absent.

Price, John Henry—Enlisted June 7—Killed 2d Manassas.

Shiflett, Samson (Sampson)—Enlisted April 18, Rockingham p. l.—Absent without leave July 1 to Sept. 1, '62, and still absent.

Shiflett, Jos. N.—Ambulance driver.

Shiflett, Divis—Enlisted April 25, 1862, E. Run—Absent without leave June 19 to Sept 1, '62, and still absent.

Stanley, Isaac—Enlisted June 17, C. Store—Absent without leave June 20 to Sept. 1, '62, and still absent.

Suthard, John—Nurse in hospital.

Shepp, Charles N.

Shiflett, George W.—Enlisted April 18, 1861—Killed 2d Manassas.

Tidler, George W.—Enlisted June 17, 1862—Absent without leave May 1 to Sept 1, '62, and still absent.

Weekley, Newman W.—Enlisted April 18—Absent without leave June 15 to Sept. 1, 1862, and still absent.

Wimbigler, George H. (or Wirbigler)—Sur—Appo.

Wyant, Alexander—Absent without leave Aug. 1 to Sept. 1, '62, and still absent.

Wolfe, Thurston P.—Enlisted April 25, 1862—Sur. Appo.

Walker, John C.—Commissary clerk.

Wilson, M. A.—Enlisted 1861—4 years.

Wingfield, C. H.—1½ years Campbell p. l.

ADDENDUM

Bridges, A. P.—7 months Rockingham p. l.

Chandler, Jno. B.—Enlisted Sept., 1864—To end of war.

Courtney, W. C.—Died in Elmira and buried in Woodlawn National Cemetery, N. Y.

Davis, George W.—Enlisted 1861—Through the war.

Glenn, Geo. H.—Rockingham p. l.

Hammer, J. A.—Enlisted 1865—2 months.

Huffman, Jno. P.—Enlisted 1861—1 year.

Hammer, H. C.—7 months.

Jefferson—Died at Ft. Delaware and buried in Finns Pt. National Cemetery, N. J.

   Louker, William P., or Lusker, or Locker—Enlisted May, 1861—To close of war.

Lewis, Ellis—Died in hospital, Rockingham p. l.

McDowell, Arch—Enlisted 1861—3 years Greene.

McCauley, D.—Rockingham p. l.

Marshall, J. N.—Died in Elmira and buried in Woodlawn National Cemetery, N. Y.
Mong, J. F.—Private.
Powell, M. F.—Enlisted 1861—To 1865.
Propst, H. F. (Propst, H. T.?)—4 years, Augusta p. l.
Rhine, J. D.—Rockingham, p. l.
Sellers, J. P.—Enlisted 1862—To 1865, Captured Petersburg.
Shiflett, T.—4 years Rockingham p. l.
Shipp, C. M.—4 years Rockingham p. l.
Stover, W. H.—2 years Rockingham p. l.
Shipley, J. N.—4 years Rockingham p. l.
Stanley, I. H.—Page p. l.
Slemp, S. S.—Private.

COMPANY K 11TH REGIMENT VIRGINIA INFANTRY
VALLEY REGULATORS ROCKBRIDGE AND ALLEGHANY CO.

Yeatman, Robert—Capt.—Resigned.
Houston, Andrew M.—Capt.—Wounded and captured Gettysburg; Fort Delaware till near close of the war.
Houston, Thomas D.—Capt.—Wounded and captured Gettysburg; Johnson's Island till end of war.
Dix, Edward T.—Lt.—Killed, Frazier's Farm.
Gilmore, Thomas R.—Lt.—Wounded Strausburg, '63. Transferred to Co. H 14th Va. Cav.
Hardy, James T.—Lt.—Killed Drewry's Bluff.
Walkup, William M—Lt.
Martin, James W.—Enlisted May 25, 1861—2d Sgt.—Pro. to Lt. Killed May 5, '62.
Ayers, George—Private.
Brown, William—Died disease Amelia Springs '62.
Bradford, Marcellus—Prisoner Ft. Delaware and Point Lookout from July 3, '63, till end of war.
Boggs, Daniel.
Cash, James—Killed Drewry's Bluff.
Campbell, Robert—Killed 2d Manassas. Capt. in command at the time of his death.
Crawford, W. T.—Captured April, 1865.
Campbell, William—Killed Drainsville, 1863.
Dass, James—Killed Frazier's Farm.
Ferguson, James W. (or M.)—Enlisted 1861—4 years—Wounded and captured Gettysburg, prisoner Point Lookout.
Ferguson, Eldred—Captured Gettysburg, died at Point Lookout.
Ferguson, William C.
Hunt, Barnet—Killed Gettysburg.
Houston, Edward M.—Courier to Genl. Terry; sur. at Appox. C. H.
Hardy, William—Killed Gettysburg.
Isaac, George—Killed Drewy's Bluff.

Isaac, John R.—Prisoner Point Lookout.
Johnson, Luther—Died, disease, Fairfax C. H., '61.
Kidd, John W.—Enlisted May 25, 1861—5th Sgt.
McClelland, William—Trans. Anderson's Battery, captured at Vicksburg.
Mayo, James H.—Enlisted 1861—3 years.
McClelland, George—Private—Died, disease, Feb., 1862.
McClelland, Alfred—Sur. Appox. C. H.
McClelland, Joseph E.
McCullough, Eli P.—Enlisted 1861—Captured Frazier's Farm; Pt. Lookout.
McCullough, John—Wounded and captured Williamsburg.
McCullough, William—Killed Frazier's Farm.
Powers, James—Died disease, Amelia Springs, Sept., '62.
Powers, John—Captured near Farmville April, '65.
Rice, Benjamin—Died of disease Centreville, Feb., '62.
Ray, James H.
Silers, Jacob—Sur. Appo. C. H.
Spindle, Samuel P.—As Corpl. commanded the Co. at Sharpsburg, Md.
Spindle, John H.—Lost his foot accidentally.
Walkup, Houston, or S. H.—Enlisted 1861—Wounded Williamsburg May 5, '62.
Walkup, James—Wounded 2d Manassas, disabled.
Walkup, Matthew.
Witcher, James—Captured at Gettysburg, prisoner at Point Lookout.
Bowyer, Jno. D.—Enlisted 1862—3 years, wounded 2d Manassas p. l.
Bowyer, D. W.—Rocky p. l.
Brown, J. N.—4 years, Rockbg. p. l.
Campbell, J. W.—Enlisted 1861—2½ years.
Cash, Thomas—Killed on R. & P. R. R., Amherst p. l.
Crawford, W. S.—Private—Wounded at 2d Manassas, Roanoke City p. l.
Depriest, F.—Sur. Appo. C. H.
Daniel, T. E.—Campbell, p. l.
Falls, B. S.—3 years, p. l.
Grymes, J. W.—Fauquier p. l.
Hardbarger, George W.—Enlisted 1862—1 2-3 years.
Heslip, T. N.—Enlisted 1861—4 years Giles p. l.
Johnson, J. B.—Died Ft. Delaware, buried at Finn's Pt. National Cemetery, N. J.
Knapp, William—Rocking Co. p. l.
Markham, Wm. T.—Sur. at App. C. H.
Oyler, J. M.—Enlisted 1861—4 years.
Poague, J. W.—Detailed nitre M bureau Oct. 9, '63, spec. order S. O. 240.
Painter, J. M.—Botetourt p. l.
Parks, Charles S.—Enlisted July 1, 1861—Private—Killed at Gettysburg July 3, '63 (Bedford History).
Painter, J. J.—Private—Died in prison Rockbg p. l.
Paynter, J. M.—Private—3 years Rockbg p. l.

Reynolds, T. E.—Enlisted 1861—4 years.

Sharer, Jas. E.—Sur. Appo.

Unrew, Henry—Bath p. c.

Wright, W. D.—Private—Prisoner at Newport News 1865; died there June 4 and buried in West Farm.

Zimmerman, W.—Botetourt p. l.

COMPANY G 22D REGIMENT
"ROCKY POINT GRAYS" ALLEGHANY COUNTY

Cook, James A.—Enlisted May, 1861, Kanawha Co.—Capt.—Resigned 1864, at Staunton.

Roach, M. P.—Enlisted May, 1861, Kanawha Co.—1st Lt.

Gore, Floyd S.—Enlisted May, 1861, Kanawha Co.—2d Lt.—Wounded Burgess Mill 1863; arm and leg broken; discharged Staunton 1864.

Bailey, Theodore F.—Enlisted May, 1861, Kanawha Co.—3d Lt.—Trans. to Thurman's Co. 1863. Resigned April 1, '64, G. O. 51.

Johnson, John—Enlisted March, 1862, Lewisburg—3d Lt.

Cook, Irvine—Enlisted May, 1861, Kanawha Co.—1st Sgt.—Captured New Market.

Cook, Kemper—Enlisted May—2d Sgt.

McDevitt, John H.—Enlisted March, 1862, Lewisburg—3d Sgt.

Cooper, Thomas—Enlisted May, 1861, Kanawha Co.—Corpl.

Aritt, Michael J.—Enlisted March, 1862, Lewisburg—Private.

Aritt, John M.

Allen, Amon—Enlisted May, 1861, Kanawha Co.

Allen, Albert.

Allen, John (A.)—Died Ft. McHenry and buried in London Park National Cemetery.

Acord, William.

Barly, Alexander (Barley, Alexander?)—Private.

Bowyer, David—Enlisted March, 1862—Lewisburg—Prisoner Camp Chase 9 months, died disease.

Bridgett, Jacob H.—Enlisted Oct., 1864, New Market.

Bess, John L.—Enlisted March, 1862, Lewisburg—Wounded.

Bowyer, Benton.

Bush, Alchany A.—Private.

Baily, Miles (Bailey, Miles?)

Baily, Lucian (Bailey, Lucian?)—Private.

Bailey, James O.

Cook, R. E.—Enlisted May, 1861, Kanawha Co.

Cook, Harry.

Clendenon, James, or Clendenen.

Damron, Henry C.—Enlisted March, 1862, Lewisburg—Died disease.

Damron, Stannard—Discharged 1863.

Damron, William.

Damron, Samuel A.

Evans, Patrick.

Fridley, William A. (Fridly, William H.?)—Private.
Gadd, Sanford—Enlisted May, 186-, Kanawha Co.—Private—Killed New Market.
Gadd, Andrew.
Gleason, Paul—Enlisted March, 1862, Lewisburg.
Harvey, William—Captured Winchester 1864.
Hall, Henry.
Hall, L. A. (or Hale)—Enlisted March, 1862, Lewisburg.
Jackson, Samuel W.
Jackson, George W.—Enlisted 1863—2 years.
Kean, Alfred H.—Died disease.
Kean, Lewis—Died disease.
Kincaid, William A.—Alleghany pension list wounded.
Kincaid, Andrew B.—Alleghany pension list wounded.
Keyser, William H.
Leighton, John R.—Enlisted Oct., 1864, New Market.
Massie, H. W.
McPherson, James R.
McCaleb, Bruce.
Mann, James W.—Enlisted March, 1862—Lewisburg.
Mann, John.
Mann, A. H.
McPherson, William H.
Oliver, John H.—Enlisted Oct., 1864—New Market.
Oiler, John.
Roach, William—Enlisted May, 1861, Kanawha Co.
Smoot, Creed F.
Smith, Peter—Enlisted March, 1862, Lewisburg.
Smith, William.
Smith, James W.
Sawyers, Alfred C.
Smith, Sampson.
Smith, Richard—Captured, Dry Creek.
Smith, Ballard J.
Smiley, James.
Sawyers, Wellington—Enlisted March, 1862.
Tyree, William, or W. W.—Bath p. l.
Tyree, John R.
Tyree, James.
Tyree, Alexander.
Toler, James—Enlisted May, 1861—Kanawha Co.
Toler, Wyatt.
Terry, Joseph P.—Enlisted March, 1862, Lewisburg.
Vowels, James N.—Private.
Witzell, James.
Wallace, R. W.—Private—Died and buried at Pt. Lookout, Md.
Vowells, James N.

ADDENDUM

Baily, Theodore F.—Private.

Burke, W. H.—Alleghany p. l.

Brown, James M.—Enlisted 1863—2 years (promoted Sgt. Cav.)

Clendenon, A. H.

Clendemon, M.—Enlisted 1862—Private—3 years, wounded Strasburg, Washington Co.

Carneal, W. P.—Enlisted 1862—3 years, wounded.

Clark, V. F.—Enlisted 1861—4 years Lunenburg.

Chapman, J. W.—Amelia p. l.

Clendenon, A. H.—Private—Died and buried at Pt. Lookout, Md.

Holman, J. T.—Private—Wounded at Cold Harbor, Nottaway p. l.

Hamilton, J. P.—Died in service.

Huppman, H.—Craig p. e.

Harris, William—Discharged Surgeon cft. S. O. 257 Aug. 21, 1861.

Holt, R. C.—Wounded at Gaines Mill, Amelia p. l.

Kerr, B. H.—Enlisted 1864—1 year.

Mann, H. C.—Enlisted Feb., 1862—4 months, wounded at Gaines Mill, Amelia p. l.

Moore, Thomas—Wythe p. l.

Myers, A. G.—Killed Winchester, Giles p. l.

Oliver, J. F. (Oliver, J. T.?)—Enlisted Feb., 1862—Private to close of war —Nottaway.

Oliver, T. J.—Enlisted Aug., 1864—8 months Nottaway, wounded at 5 Forks.

Puckett, J. A.—Enlisted 1864—1 year.

Sarver, M. Jackson—Enlisted 1864, Craig—1 year.

Sloan, M.—Buchanan p. l.

Thompson, C. B.—Enlisted 1862—3 years, wounded Winchester, Alleghany p. l.

Taylor, C.—Enlisted 1861—4 years.

Tyree, I. H. (Tyree, J. H?.)—Private—Alleghany p. l.

Causeling, Samuel.

COMPANY D 60TH REGT. VA. INFANTRY ALLEGHANY CO.

Hammond, Geo. W.—Enlisted June 26, 1861, Lewisburg—Capt., Major, Lt.-Col. Killed.

Given, Adam—Enlisted June 26, 1861, Lewisburg—Capt.—Wounded, Valley, Oct. 19, 1864; captured, prisoner Fort Delaware.

Gross, Henry—Enlisted June 26, 1861, Lewisburg—1st Lt.—Wounded Fishersville, May 9—? Captured, prisoner Fort Delaware.

Johnson, Allen—Enlisted June 26, 1861, Lewisburg—2d Lt.—Killed May 5, '64, Cloyd's Farm.

Boswell, John L.—Enlisted June 26, 1861, Lewisburg—2d Lt.—Wounded near Rd. June 26, 62.

Given, George—Enlisted June 26, 1861—2d Lt.

Thompson, Philip A.—Enlisted June 26, 1861, Lewisburg—1st Sgt.

Johnson, Lee—2d Sgt.—Wounded 3 times, killed New Hope, June 9th?

Hepler, Arch S.—3d Sgt.—Wounded; killed New Hope.

Shanklen, Henry D.—Enlisted June 26, 1861—4th Sgt.—Wounded twice, prisoner Johnson's Island 8 months.

McCallister, John A.—Enlisted June 26, 1861, Lewisburg—1st Corpl—Wounded Malvern Hill 1862; prisoner Pt. Lookout 8 months.

Hook, Edwin E.—Enlisted June 26, 1861, Lewisburg—2d Sgt.—Wounded Cold Harbor June 27, '62, prisoner Elmira, N. Y.

Stull, George F.—Enlisted June 26, 1861, Lewisburg—3d Corpl.—Wounded near Rd. 1862; prisoner Ft. Delaware 12 months.

Oilier, Alexander S.—Enlisted June 26, 1861, Lewisburg—4th Corpl.—Wounded Cloyd's Farm, May; died from wounds in hosp. May 15, '64.

Anderson, John—Enlisted Feb. 15, 1863, Princeton—Wounded Cloyd's Farm May, '64; prisoner Ft. Delaware.

Bowen, William—Enlisted June 26, 1861, Lewisburg—Wounded Cloyd's Farm; 4 years.

Boley, William O.—Enlisted June 26, 1861, Lewisburg—Wounded Cedar Creek Sept. 19, '64.

Burger, Martin—Enlisted 1861, Botetourt Co.—Killed Winchester 1864.

Bess, Charles J.—Enlisted 1861, Lewisburg—Wounded near Rd. 1862; prisoner Point Lookout 7 months.

Bess, C. L. (Bess, Charles L.?)Enlisted 1861, Lewisburg—Wounded near Richmond 1862.

Bess, William H.—Enlisted Sept. 15, 1863, Princeton—Wounded near Richmond 1862.

Bess, Alexander (L.)—Enlisted June 26, 1861, Lewisburg.

Bess, Allen—Enlisted June 26, Lewisburg—Wounded near Richmond June 26, '62.

Bess, Charles H.—Enlisted Sept. 10, 1863—Wounded 3 times.

Bess, "Kagie" G.—Enlisted Feb. 29, Covington—Wounded Valley (prisoner Ft. Delaware?)

Bennett, J. L. (Bennett, John L.?)—Enlisted June 26, 1861, Lewisburg—Private—Wounded 4 times; lost left arm; prisoner Ft. Delaware.

Bennett, Jackson—Enlisted June 26, 1861, Lewisburg.

Bush, Jacob H.—Enlisted June 26, 1861, Lewisburg—Private—Wounded Malvern Hill 1862.

Bush, David N.—Enlisted Feb. 15, 1863, Princeton—Wounded Fayettsville, 1864; killed May, '64, Cloyd's Farm.

Bowyer, David N.—Enlisted Dec. 15, 1862, Narrows—Private.

Bowen, Erastus—Enlisted June 15, 1862—Wounded New Hope, June 9, '64; lost right leg.

Brown, James—Deserted prison.

Bugg, J. L.—Died in prison.

Brown, William—Enlisted June 26, 1861, Lewisburg—Wounded Mechanicsville, 1862.

Boyd, J. L.—Detailed as gunsmith Sept. 4, '62.

Craft, J. W. (Craft I. W.?)—Private—Teamster Sept., 1862.

Craft, George W.—Enlisted June 26, 1861, Lewisburg—4 years.

Craft, John H.

Craft, Hulth J., or J. H.—Enlisted June 26, 1861, Lewisburg—Died in prison and buried at Pt. Lookout, Md., 1865.

Copley, William T.—Enlisted June 26, 1861, Lewisburg—Wounded Cedar Creek, 1862.

Clarkson, Henry—Enlisted Feb. 20, 1863, Covington—Prisoner Johnson's Island 8 months; wounded Perry, W. Va., 1863; died.

Crawford, George W.—Enlisted Feb. 20, 1863, Covington—Wounded Piedmont, 1864.

Crawford, John J.—Enlisted July 3, 1863, Lewisburg

Carson, William T.—Enlisted Feb. 28, 1863, Giles C. H.—Mortally wounded May, 1864.

Crossley, William M.—Enlisted March 26, 1864, Alleghany—Wounded.

Cosby, Henry Preston—Private—3 years Bath p. l.

Diggs, Abner—Enlisted June 26, 1861, Lewisburg—Wounded Malvern Hill, 1862; captured; died in prison.

Dickson, George W.—Enlisted Feb. 1, 1863, Princeton.

Dressler, Alex. P. (or P. A.)—Enlisted June 26, 1861, Lewisburg—Wounded Narrows 1862.

Dressler, Geo. W.—Enlisted June 26, 1861, Lewisburg.

Engaret, Otis—Enlisted June 26, 1861, Lewisburg—Wounded Winchester; prisoner Point Lookout.

Fridley, W. H. (Fridley, William H.?)—Enlisted 1861—Private—4 years.

Fridley, George—Enlisted June 26, 1861, Lewisburg—Killed near Richmond June 27, 1862.

Frear, Henry H.—Enlisted June 26, 1861, Lewisburg—Hospital steward.

Frear, Henry—Enlisted March 8, 1862, Covington—Wounded 5 times.

Franklin, Valentine—Enlisted 1863—Wounded.

Fridley, John L.—Enlisted April 15, 1863, Union

Fridley, James—Deserted.

Fridley, C. (Fridley, Charles O.?)—Private.

Fry, Wm. H.—Enlisted Covington—Pension List Alleghany.

Gillispie, James P.—Enlisted Feb. 1, 1865, Fishersville.

Given, Lewis C.—Enlisted Jan. 1, 1864, Princeton—Mortally wounded May 5, '64.

Gilleland, Shepard (Y.)—Enlisted June 26, 1861, Lewisburg—Wounded New Hope June '64—Sgt.

Gilleland, John—Enlisted June 26, 1861, Lewisburg—Private.

Gilbert, Wyete R.—Enlisted June 26, 1861—Lewisburg—Wounded near Richmond, '62, died.

Gilleland, J. J. (Gilleland, I. I.?)—Enlisted June 26, 1861, Lewisburg—Color Corpl.

Hepler, Lewis—Enlisted June 26, 1861, Lewisburg—Wounded Cold Harbor '62, died.

Hepler, Robert—Wounded Cold Harbor, 1862; died.

Hepler, E. (Hepler, Elias?)—Enlisted June 26, 1861, Lewisburg—Wounded Malvern Hill.

Hepler, Archer S.—Enlisted June 26, 1861, Lewisburg—Killed.

Hudson, J. T.—Enlisted June 26, 1861, Lewisburg—4 years Lynchburg p. 1.

Isenhower, J. S.—Enlisted June 26, 1861, Lewisburg—Killed.

Johnson, Barned—Enlisted Aug. 15, 1862, Covington—Wounded New Market 1864.

Johnson, Lee (W.)—Enlisted Aug. 15, 1862—Covington—Wounded twice, died in prison.

Kelley, Abe—Deserted.

Kelley, James or Jno.—Enlisted Sept. 10, 1863, Princeton—Wounded Mechanicsville 1864.

Leighton, James E.—Enlisted Aug., 1862, Covington—Private—Wounded Fayettsville 1862.

Leighton, "Merricon"—Enlisted 1861, Lewisburg—Wounded Gaines Mill, died in prison, '62.

Lockhart, John G.—Enlisted 1864—Served 1 year.

Mussulman, James—Deserted.

Myers, John W.—Enlisted June 26, 1861, Lewisburg—Wounded Malvern Hill; prison 10 months.

McCallister, James R.Enlisted June 26, 1861, Lewisburg.

Matheny, William D.—Enlisted Sept. 20, 1862, Covington—Died in prison.

Matheny, W. A.—Enlisted Sept 20, 1862, Covington.

Matheny, Loransie—Enlisted Sept. 25, Charleston.

McMahan, John J.—Enlisted Sept., 1863, Covington—Detailed on signal corps Washington, D. C. (N. C.)?, March 31, '64.

Nida, Chapmond J.—Enlisted June 26, 1861, Lewisburg—Wounded Seven Pines 1862, killed at Cloyd's Farm, May 5, '64.

Nida, James A.—Enlisted June 26, 1861, Lewisburg—Wounded New Hope June 9, '64, in head; demented from wound.

Oiler, William H.—Enlisted Aug. 15, 1862, Covington—Private—Wounded Ganley River Oct., 1862.

Plymale, William C.—Enlisted June 26, 1861, Lewisburg—Wounded Gaines Mill 1862.

Pharr, James E.—Enlisted June 26, 1861, Lewisburg—Private, Teamster— Detailed as Teamster Sept. 20, '62.

Paxton, Clifton J.—Enlisted Aug. 15, 1863, Covington—Died in prison.

Persinger, W. J. (Persinger, William J.?)—Enlisted Aug. 15, Covington— Private.

Pruett, N.—Private—Danville p. 1.

Reynolds, John O.—Enlisted June 26, 1861, Lewisburg—Wounded 1861; killed Fishersville March 5, 1865.

Richardson, Thomas W.—Enlisted Aug. 15, 1862, Covington—Wounded New Hope 1864.

Rose, William W.

Rogus, Charles—Enlisted June 26, 1861, Lewisburg.

Robinson, William—Enlisted Feb. 1, 1865, Fishersville.

Rogers, Jas. A. (or J. L.)—Enlisted June 26, 1861, Lewisburg.

Rogers, Clifton—Enlisted June 26, 1861, Lewisburg—Wounded New River May, '64; died.

Riddesbarger, F. (Riddleberger, Fred?)—Private—Deserted.

Riddleberger, Sam—Deserted May 26, '62, at Hanover Junction.

Stull, George W. (or Geo. F.)—Enlisted June 26, 1861, Lewisburg—Wounded Malvern Hill, 1862.

Simms, J. H. (Simes, J. H., or J. A.?)—Enlisted July 1, 1861, Covington—Private—Wounded Seven Pines; deserted.

Simmons, James A.—Enlisted July 1, 1861, Covington—Deserted.

Stull, D. L. (Stull, Daniel L.?)—Enlisted June 26, 1861, Lewisburg—Private—Wounded Fayettsville, '62; deserted.

Stull, Mead (T.)—Enlisted Sept., 1862, Princeton.

Simmons, William M.—Enlisted June 26, 1861, Lewisburg—Killed Winchester.

Simmons, William R.—Enlisted June 26, 1861, Lewisburg—Died in Camp Morton, Ind., and buried in Green Lawn Cemetery.

Shumaker, Chas. W.—Enlisted Sept. 25, Narrows—Wounded New Hope June 9, '64; wounded Kernstown, 1864.

Smith, Richard—Enlisted Sept. 25, 1862, Covington.

Smith, William—Enlisted Sept. 25, 1862, Covington.

Stuard (or Stuart), John W.—Enlisted Sept 25, 1862, Covington—Wounded June 9, 1864.

Simmons, J. C.—Wounded Piedmont; pension list Alleghany Co.

Shanklin, H. D.—Private.

Taylor, John—Enlisted June 26, 1861, Lewisburg—Died March, '64, Princeton.

Thompson, John R.—Enlisted June 26, 1861, Lewisburg—Wounded Seven Pines 1862.

Thomas, Charles—Enlisted June 26, 1861—Wounded Winchester, 1864.

Terry, Henry—Died in prison.

Taylor, William—Died in prison.

Thompson, P. A.—Private.

Willard, Sam—Private.

Wright, George L.—Enlisted June 26, 1861, Lewisburg—Wounded Gaines Mill; prisoner 8 months Elmira.

NAMES IN MATHENY-EVANS LIST

Arritt, John	Cooke, John
Arritt, Michael	Cooke, W. A.
Bess, Donohue	Crossley, Charles
Bess, Nash	Crow, John
Brown, Joseph	Damron, Henry
Burger, Martin	Damron, Samuel
Burns, Bird	Dickson, Washington
Carter, James	Dressler, Harrison
Carter, John	Franklin, Pine
Clarkson, George	Fridley, Lewis
Clarkson, Henry—died at Camp	Fudge, Kester
Douglas	Hamilton, Samuel

Hughes, J. W.
Kelley, Dennis
Kyle, Robert—killed
McGiven, John
Matheny, George
Matheny, Michael
Pobe, Wat

Rogers, Cooper—lost at Dry Creek
Shanklin, Andrew
Sizemore, Owen
Vance, J. R.
Vance, Rice
Wade, Luke

Captain George W. Hammond was promoted to lieutenant-colonel, and was killed at Cloyd's Mountain, May 9, 1864.

Captain Addison Givens was promoted to major.

CARPENTER'S BATTERY—BRAXTON'S BATT.—VA. ARTILLERY

Company A, 27th Virginia Regiment, was enlisted at Covington, Va., on April 22, 1861, and was attached to General (then Colonel) Thomas J. Jackson's Brigade at Harper's Ferry, Va., in May, 1861, and served as infantry in said brigade from that time until the 12th of November, 1861, at which time it was, by a special order from General Jackson, converted into an Artillery Company, and from thence to the close of the war continued to serve in the Artillery.

McAllister, Thompson—Enlisted April 22, 1861, Covington—1st Capt—Resigned, ill health.

Carpenter, Joseph H.—Enlisted April 22, 1861, Covington—2d Capt—Died from wounds received at Cedar Run and was succeeded by his brother, Jno. C. Carpenter, who retained the command until the close of the war.

Carpenter, Jno. C.—Enlisted April 22, 1861, Covington—3d Capt.—Lost arm.

McKendree, George—Enlisted April 22, 1861, Covington—Lieut.

Dunott, Henry H.—Enlisted April 22, 1861, Covington—Lieut.

Carpenter, Benj.—Lieut.

Barton, D. R.—Lieut.

Anthony, Robert I.—Enlisted April 22, 1861, Covington—1st Sgt.—Promoted from 2d Sgt. May 15, 1861; wounded Winchester Sept. 13, 1864, and died.

Karnes, Benami—Enlisted April 22, 1861, Covington—2d Sergeant.

Dickey, Littleton T.—Enlisted April 22, 1861, Covington—3d Sgt.

Rixey, Jno. G.—Enlisted April 22, 1861, Covington—4th Sgt.

Jordan, Charles O.—Enlisted April 22, 1861, Covington—5th Sgt.—Promoted Lieut.

Vowels, Philip D.—Enlisted April 22, 1861, Covington—1st Corpl.

Hammond, James M.—Enlisted April 22, 1861, Covington—2d Corpl.

Carpenter, Samuel S.—Enlisted April 22, 1861, Covington—3d Corpl—Promoted Lieut.; wounded in arm June, 1862.

Thompson, J. H.—Enlisted April 22, 1861, Covington—4th Sgt.

Alford, Marion—Enlisted April 22, 1861, Covington—Private.

Arey, W. S.—Private—Killed at Fisher's Hill, 1864, Sept.; Rock p. 1.

Argenbright, M. W. D.—3 years Buena Vista p. 1.

Bacon, Stephen—Enlisted April 22, 1861, Covington—Private.

Baker, James T., Jr.—Enlisted April 22, 1861, Covington—Private.

Bauker, Van. R.—Enlisted April 22, 1861, Covington—Private.

Baggage, William W.—Enlisted April 22, 1861, Covington—Private.

Branham, James W.—Enlisted April 22, 1861, Covington—Private.

Byrd, George T.—Enlisted April 22, 1861, Covington—Private—Wounded in 1862.

Boswell, Joseph M.—Enlisted April 22, 1861, Covington—Private.

Barrett, Charles W.—Private—Jno. W. Rowan Camp C. V.

Baker, J. P.—Private—Wounded 1st Manassas, Alleghany p. l.

Blake, A. P.—Private—Died in prison, Brooklyn, N.Y.

Canty, Patrick—Enlisted April 22, 1861, Covington—Private.

Clark, James P.—Enlisted April 22, 1861, Covington—Private.

Core, Patrick—Enlisted April 22, 1861, Covington—Private.

Carpenter, Tobe—Private—Killed at Wades Depot.

Chipley, R.—Private—4 years, Frederick p. l.

Dressler, Joseph S.—Enlisted April 22, 1861, Covington—Private.

Dyke, J. W.—Private—4 years, Frederick p. l.

Everett, George E.—Private—Jno W. Rowan Camp.

Evans, H. L.—Enlisted Augusta—Private—Private.

Edmondson, S. J.—Frederick Co. p. l.

Foster, Hopkins B.—Enlisted April 22, 1861, Covington—Private.

Fudge, William C.—Enlisted April 22, 1861, Covington—Private.

Fudge, Jos. T.—Enlisted April 22, 1861, Covington—Private—Corpl., until 1 May 19, 1861.

Flinn, Timothy—Enlisted April 22, 1861, Covington—Private.

Fonerden, Clarence A.—Enlisted April 22, 1961—Private

Glenn, James—April 22, 1861, Covington—Private.

Grady, James—Enlisted April 22, 1861, Covington—Private.

Gaines, J. W.—Enlisted 1861, Richmond City—Private—To end of war.

Holmes, James P.—Enlisted April 22, 1861, Covington—Private.

Humphries, Wm. H.—Enlisted April 22, 1861—Private.

Hastings, Thomas—Enlisted April 22, 1861, Covington——Private.

Hite, William B.—Enlisted April 22, 1861, Covington—Private.

Hicks, W. F.—Private—Jno. W. Rowan Camp.

Hosey, Robert F.—2d Corpl. Co. C, Capt. Grove (1st Pendleton's) known as Newtown Artillery. This company was disbanded. He is shown to have enlisted as 2d Corpl. Capt. Cutshaw's Co. Va. Light Artillery March 10, 1862; to have been trans. to Capt. Carpenter's Co. Va. Artillery Sept. 23, 1862; present with that Co. April 30, 1864 on roll dated August 31, 1864, was reported absent in hands of the enemy; no later record found. (War Dept., May 20, 1916.)

Jordan, James A.—Enlisted April 22, 1861, Covington—Private.

Jordan, Edwin W.—Enlisted April 22, 1861, Covington—Private.

Jones, Peter—Enlisted April 22, 1861, Covington.

Jones, Jno. W.—Enlisted April 22, 1861, Frederick Co.—Private—To 1865.

Jordan, Thomas—Private—Wounded in head.

Jones, William—Private—Killed at Winchester.

Kearnes, Patrick—Enlisted April 22, 1861, Covington—Private.

Karnes, John—Enlisted April 22, 1861, Covington—Private.

Karnes, Francis L.—Enlisted April 22, 1861, Covington—Private—Promoted to Sergeant.

King, John—Enlisted April 22, 1861, Covington—Private.

Kimberlin, Joseph—Enlisted April 22, 1861, Covington—Private.

Knight, Jno. M.—April 22, 1861, Covington—Wounded at Malvern Hill.

Kupp, B. H.—Enlisted May 18, 1861, Harper's Ferry—Private.

Kirkpatrick, Geo. R.—Enlisted 1862, Rockbridge—Private—Served 3 years.

Keyser, Joseph—Private—Jefferson Co. Camp No. 123 C. V.

Kline, Daniel W.—Enlisted 1861, Winchester—Private—4 years.

Low, Samuel—April 22, 1861, Covington—Private.

Lambie, William T.—Enlisted April 22, 1861, Covington—Private—Promoted to Lieut.; lost eye.

Lafferty, Charles—Enlisted April 22, 1861, Covington—Private.

Lampkins, John—Enlisted April 22, 1861, Covington—Private—In arrest.

Lotts, J. S.—Private—3 years; Rockbridge p. 1.

Moran, William—Enlisted April 22, 1861, Covington—Private—Surrendered at Appomattox C. H.

Montague, James R.—Enlisted April 22, 1861, Covington.

Milligan, John—Enlisted April 22, 1861, Covington—Private.

Murrill, William W.—Enlisted April 22, 1861, Covington—Private.

Matheney, John G.—Enlisted April 22, 1861, Covington—Private—Lost an arm.

McGowan, Andrew—Enlisted April 22, 1861, Covington—Died and buried at Pt. Lookout, Md.

McMahan, Patrick—Enlisted April 22, 1861, Covington—Private.

McCarnan, Thomas—Enlisted April 22, 1861, Covington—Private.

McCullough, John—Enlisted April 22, 1861, Covington—Private.

McKnight, George R.—Enlisted April 22, 1861, Covington—Private.

Moyers, Jacob L.—Enlisted April 22, 1861, Covington—Private.

McDonald, Gabriel—Enlisted April 22, 1861, Covington—Private.

McAllister, Wm. M.—Enlisted April 22, 1861, Covington—Private—Promoted Sgt.; wounded in thigh June, 1862.

Mackay, John.

Michael, Clem—Private—Killed at Gettysburg; Clarke p. 1.

Newcomer, W. K.—Private—4 years; Frederick p. 1.

Ogden, T. A.—Private—4 years; Frederick p. 1.

Otey, Virginius B.—Enlisted April 22, 1861, Covington—Private.

Omdorf, J. J.—Private—Wounded at Paynes Farm; Shen. Co. p. 1.

O'Neil, John—Enlisted March 10, 1862—Private.

Pence, Peter M.—Enlisted April 22, 1861, Covington—Private.

Pitzer, William D.—Enlisted April 22, 1861, Covington—Private—Wounded 1st Manassas; Nelson p. 1.

Plumb, Alfred—Enlisted March, 1862, Augusta—Private—Served to June, 1862.

Quinlin, Michael—Enlisted April 22, 1861, Covington—Private.
Rose, James E.—Enlisted April 22, 1861, Covington—Private.
Rosser, Thomas W.—Enlisted April 22, 1861, Covington—Private.
Ray, Henry B.—Enlisted April 22, 1861, Covington.
Rogers, James A.—Enlisted April 22, 1861—Private.
Read, Alexander H.—Enlisted April 22, 1861, Covington—Private.
Riley, James—Enlisted April 22, 1861, Covington—Private.
Read, James W.—Enlisted April 22, 1861, Covington—Private—Wounded at Malvern Hill (Rockingham p. l.)
Ritenour, Hampson—Enlisted 1862, Shenandoah—Private—Served to '65.
Read, C. P.—Private—Served 1½ years; Roanoke City p. l.
Rushbrook, J. W.—Private—Prisoner at Newport News 1865, and died there May 29; buried at West Farm.
Sawyers, John S.—Enlisted April 22, Covington—Private—Lost arm.
Scott, Kyle C.—Enlisted April 22, Covington—Private.
Stewart, John W.—Enlisted April 22, 1861, Covington—Private.
Stewart, Benjamin P.—Enlisted April 22, 1861—Covington.
Steel, William—Enlisted April 22, 1861—Private.
Smith, Patrick—Enlisted May 18, Harper's Ferry—Private.
Smith, John—Enlisted May 18, 1861, Harper's Ferry—Private.
Swindell, Isaac—Private—3 years; Alleghany Co. p. l.
Simmons, J. W.—Private—Wounded at Kearneys Mill; Frederick p. l.
Sitlington—Private—Living in Bath Co.
Tabler, Geo. F.—Enlisted 1862, Frederick—Private—1 year.
Thompson, Inman—Enlisted Warren—Private.
Via, Chesley C.—Enlisted May 1, 1862—Private—Wounded at Appomattox April 8, 1865; "Bedford History."
Walker, J. L.—Private—Wounded at Winchester; Alleghany p. l.
Walker, James S.—Private—Wounded at Winchester; Alleghany p. l.
Wilkinson, J. M.—Private—3 years; Frederick p. l.
Willey, J. W.—Private—4 years; Frederick p. l.
Whitlocke, M.—Private—Died in Savannah, Ga.; Augusta Co. p. l.
Woodson, P. T.—Augusta Co. p. l.
Woodward, Samuel M.—Enlisted March, 1862—In Co. "L" 5th Infty.; trans. Aug. 1, '62; wounded Sept. 17, '62, at Sharpsburg; appointed hospital steward April 7, '63; ordered to report to the 62d Reg.; paroled at Staunton April 30, '65.
Weddows, T. S.—Private.

ROSTER OF COMPANY C, 27TH VIRGINIA INFANTRY

OFFICERS

Lewis P. Holloway, captain—died at Fort Delaware, prisoner of war.
Charles Haynes, first lieutenant.
George P. Persinger, second lieutenant—promoted to captain.
Samuel Lowery, third lieutenant.
Joseph Haynes, first sergeant—promoted to lieutenant—killed at Second Manassas.

John Stull, second sergeant—promoted to lieutenant—killed at Second Manassas.

PRIVATES

Arrington, Thomas
Baker, John
Buckley, William—missing at Spottsylvania
Clark, William
Dee, Michael—killed?
Deeds, Haynes—died of measles at Winchester
Deeds, William
Dodd, Floyd
Emgarett, Otis
Evans, William—killed at Chancellorsville
Garibaldi, John
Gibson, Scott
Gilbert, Charles—killed at Gettysburg
Gilbert, David N.—wounded at Second Manassas and Gettysburg
Gilbert, George—younded at Port Republic
Gilbert, James C.
Gilliland, Charles
Gilliland, Hazael
Gilliland, Henry—killed at Gettysburg
Ham, Mark
Hepler, John
Hepler, William
Holmes, Martin
Humphries, Henry—wounded at Winchester
Jackson, Peter
James, Robert
Joyce, John—captured at Kernstown

Kennedy, James
Keyser, James
Kincaid, Andrew
Kincaid, Archibald
Kincaid, James
Leighton, Daniel
Logan, Patrick
Lossan, William—killed
Lounsbury, James—wounded at Gettysburg and Spottsylvania
McDonald, John
Mann, Augustus
Mann, James—wounded at Gettysburg
Miles, Michael
Moore, Robert
Murray, Patrick
O'Conner, Patrick—wounded at Gettysburg
Nicely, Jacob
Nowell, George—killed
Peters, Neal
Porter, Thomas
Reynolds, Isaac
Reynolds, James
Rocke, James
Rodgers, George
Rollins, James—killed
Rose, Thomas
Ross, Edward
Simpson, Hezekiah
Stanley, William—killed
Steers, William
Terry, Allen
Tingler, George W.
Wilcher, George

XXI

ALLEGHANY SOLDIERS IN THE WORLD WAR

ROSTER OF THE SELECTIVE DRAFT

NOTE:—The name of each draftee is followed by age, date of enlistment, camp, serial number, army number (in brackets), and home address. C'ton is an abbreviation for Covington, CF for Clifton Forge.

LIST A WHITE

Adkins, James Robert—21—Mar. 28, 1918—Lee (died Aug. 28, 1918)—18 (7,467,344)—C'ton.

Alexander, James Robinson—21—Dec. 14, 1917—Ft. Thomas, Ky.—16—C'ton.

Allen, George Hunter—21—June 3, 1917—150 Inf., W. Va.—12—150 (in draft)—C'ton.

Anderson, Charles Bert—21—Mar. 25, 1918—Lee—15—(3,467,240)—C'ton.

Anderson, John Emel—25—June 24, 1918—Lee (rej. July 1, 1918)—9—(3,640,109)—C'ton.

Armstrong, Herbert Lee—21—June 24, 1918—Lee—14—(3,633,145)—C'ton.

Barger, Walter Lee—25—Aug. 24, 1918—Lee—32—(3,171,306)—C'ton.

Barkley, Alexander Newton—27—June 24, 1918—Lee—24—(3,637,857)—C'ton.

Berry, Cary R.—22—Aug. 28, 1918—Lee—56—(2,467,218)—C'ton.

Bickers, James Allen—23—May 24, 1918—Lee—48—(3,171,518)—C'ton.

Blankenship, Charles—22—July 17, 1918—Humphreys—57—C'ton.

Bookman, George Meredith—23—Oct. 5, 1917—Lee—46—Mallow.

Bosserman, William Ernest—21—June 28, 1918—Navy—60—C'ton.

Bowling, Cloid Linzy—23—June 24, 1918—Lee—45—(3,633,138)—C'ton.

Breeden, Charles Lester—21—June 24, 1918—Lee—57—(3,625,868)—C'ton.

Brisendine, Stephen—23—Sept. 3, 1918—Humphreys—41—C'ton.

Brooks, George Walter—30—May 22, 1918—U'y of Va.—23—C'ton.

Brown, Marshall—24—June 24, 1918—Lee—44—(3,633,162)—C'ton.

Burns, Henry Lacy—24—June 24, 1918—Lee—42—(3,625,884)—C'ton.

Burns, John Wilson—23—June 24, 1918—Lee—50—(3,625,855)—C'ton.

Byer, Charles Walter—21—July 17, 1918—Humphreys—58—Barber.

Campbell, Lonnie Preston—26—June 24, 1918—Lee—88—(3,633,147)—C'ton.

Coffey, Willie W.—24—May 24, 1918—Lee—86—(3,171,284)—C'ton.

Colley, Lawrence W.—27—June 24, 1918—Lee—94—(3,633,159)—C'ton.

Collins, Cecil Cornelius—22—Oct. 3, 1917—B. Hospital, No. 41—118—C'ton.

Cook, Connie Lee—25—May 24, 1918—Lee (rej. June 7, 1918)—90—C'ton.

Cook, Edward Ellsworth—21—May 24, 1918—Lee 124—(3,171,304)—C'ton.

Cook, Oliver—23—July 17, 1918—Humphreys—112—C'ton.

Cox, Hubert Erskin—22—Sept. 6, 1918—Lee—119—(4,632,638)—C'ton.

Crowder, Robert Ryan—24—Sept. 19, 1917—Lee—107—C'ton.

Dickson, Harry Wilson—25—May 24, 1918—Lee—150—(3,171,283)—C'ton.

Donovan, Stephen Lanier—22—June 24, 1918—Lee—160—(3,633,131)—C'ton.

Downey, Walter Lloyd—26—June 1, 1918—Lee—151—(3,175,455)—C'ton.

Dressler, Charles Kyle—29—Sept. 19, 1917—Lee—140—C'ton.

Dressler, Will Chester—21—July 17, 1918—Humphreys—162—C'ton.

Driscoll, Patrick C.—22—May 24, 1918—Lee—156—(3,171,274)—C'ton.

Ealy, Robert Henry—29—Sept. 3, 1918—Humphreys—176—C'ton.

Elliott, Samuel Pilson—23—June 24, 1918—Lee—180—(3,633,105)—C'ton.

Flippen, Clarence Jackson—26—July 23, 1918—Humphreys—192—C'ton.

Foster, Guy Burney—23—May 22, 1918—U'y of Va.—195—C'ton.

Fridley, William Carl—21—May 12, 1917—Co. L., 157th Inf.—201—C'ton.

Friend, William B.—July 17, 1918—Humphreys—204—C'ton.

Furry, Holmes Fordora—29—Mar. 28, 1918—Lee—183—(2,467,243)—C'ton.

Gardner, Francis Philip—24—Dec. 21, 1917—Med. Res. C—214—C'ton.

Golden, Arnold Bennett—21—May 9, 1918—Ft. Thomas, Ky.—221—C'ton.

Goodbar, Cecil Graham—27—June 24, 1918—Lee—205—(3,625,885)—C'ton.

Harlow, Isaac Franklin—23—Oct. 1, 9117—B. Hospital, 41—263—C'ton.

Harrington, John L.—21—July 17, 1918—Humphreys—273—C'ton.

Harrington, Michael—30—June 24, 1918—Lee—228—C'ton.

Hawkins, Jesse James—21—June 24, 1918—Lee—299—(3,625,912)—C'ton.

Heintz, Esther Other—21—May 24, 1918—dis. Aug. 10, 1918—272—(3,171,504)—C'ton.

Herron, Aristides Montero—27—June 24, 1918—Lee (rej. July 1, 1918)—239—(3,640,107)—C'ton.

Hess, John Abraham—27—May 16, 1918—Sevier, S. C.—240—C'ton.

Hill, Clarence F.—28—June 24, 1918—Lee—244—(3,633,642)—C'ton

Hooper, Benjamin R.—28—Sept. 6, 1918—Lee—242—(4,632,642)—C'ton.

Hubank, Milner—22—June 18, 1918—Lee—285—(3,176,792)—C'ton.

Hubbard, Charles Robert—27—Sept. 19, 1917—Lee—258—C'ton.

Hubard, McKinley—21—July 13, 1917—2d Va. Inf.—276—C'ton.

Hubbard, Withrow Sutton—24—July 23, 1918—Humphreys—264—C'ton.

Hughes, John Wesley—30—Sept. 3, 1918—Humphreys—228—C'ton.

Irvine, William Oscar—25—July 25, 1917—McClellan—298—C'ton.

Jackson, Marshall—24—June 24, 1918—Lee—310—(3,625,892)—C'ton.

Jones, Cecil G. M.—21—July 17, 1918—Humphreys—313—C'ton.

Jones, Gordon Fergusson—22—May 22, 1918—U'y of Va.—311—C'ton.

Jordan, Clarence Herbert—21—June 19, 1918—Lee—315—(3,176,861)—C'ton.

Joseph, Clarence Entsler—21—Mar. 28, 1918—Lee—312—(2,467,226)—C'ton.

Kaufman, Martin A.—23—Nov. 5, 1918—Garden City, N. Y.—Aviation service—344—C'ton.

Kelly, Mordaunt, B.—22—Mar. 28, 1918—Lee—350—(3,467,229)—C'ton.
Keyser, Edward Arnold—26—June 24, 1918—Lee—339—(3,625,828)—
    C'ton.
Keyser, Garnett K.—21—Oct. 12, 1917—Navy—352—C'ton.
Knighton, Emory Luther—24—June 24, 1918—Lee—341—Mallow—
    (3,633,164).
Knighton, Lewis Edward—21—Mar. 28, 1918—Lee—353—(2,467,230)—
    Mallow.
Knighton, Wilbur Benson—23—Sept. 3, 1918—Humphries—342—Mallow.
Lavender, Benjamin F.—21—Sept. 3, 1918—Humphreys—375—C'ton.
Lawrence, Ethan Russell—25—June 24, 1918—Lee—361—(3,525,865)—
    C'ton.
Leffel, Arthur James—21—June 18, 1918—Navy—376—C'ton.
Leftwich, Joseph S.—26—June 21, 1917—Lee—360—C'ton.
Lockard, John William—25—May 22, 1918—U'y of Va.—362—C'ton.
Loving, Kyter Anderson—24—June 8, 1918—Navy—365—C'ton.
McConihay, John Merry—24—July 30, 1918—Lee—432—(4,086,820)—C'ton.
McCormick, Harlow—21—Sept. 19, 1917—Lee—437—C'ton.
Markham, Arthur C.—26—June 24, 1918—Lee—395—(3,625,861)—C'ton.
Martin, Gonlay—26—1917—Inf.—396—C'ton.
Mays, Harry Alexander—22—Dec. 12, 1917—Ft. Thomas, Ky.—405—C'ton.
Morgan, Pinckney Davis—22—Mar. 28, 1918—Lee—406—(2,457,235)—
    C'ton.
Morris, Burnette More—27—Mar. 28, 1918—Lee—388—(2,665,876)—Mal-
    low.
Myers, James—21—May 22, 1918—U'y of Va.—409—C'ton.
Myers, Oliver Wilbur—27—June 24, 1918—Lee—389—(3,630,215)—C'ton.
Nichols, Belton Baker—29—May 24, 1918—Lee—449—(3,171,314)—Mal-
    low.
O'Brien, Michael Lawrence—25—Oct. 9, 1917—Base Hospital 41—461—
    C'ton.
O'Brien, Patrick J.—29—Oct. 17, 1917—Base Hospital, 41—455—C'ton.
Oliver, Oren Austin—29—Nov. 27, 1917—M. R. C.—456—C'ton.
Otten, Edward Miller—22—May 22, 1918—U'y of Va.—463—C'ton.
Parker, William C.—30—May 9, 1918—Ft. Thomas—470—C'ton.
Persinger, Andrew Jackson—23—June 24, 1918—Lee—476—(3,633,183)—
    Mallow.
Pierce, Elmore Roy—27—Oct. 5, 1917—Base Hospital, 41—471—C'ton.
Pierce, Filmore J.—30—Oct. 5, 1917—Base Hospital, 41—466—C'ton.
Pryor, H. C.—23—July 1, 1918—Lee—474—(3,637,656)—C'ton.
Rauch, Emmett Frank—28—July 1, 1918—Lee—518—(3,639,646)—C'ton.
Reeves, Jesse A.—30—May 16, 1918—U'y of Va.—503—C'ton.
Reid, Lawrence E.—30—May '16, 1918—Camp Sevier, S. C.—504—C'ton.
Revercomb, William Chapman—21—July 17, 1918—Coast Artillery—531—
    C'ton.
Rhea, Shaw Caldwell—21—July 17, 1918—Humphreys—532—C'ton.
Rice, Howard C.—26—July 17, 1918—Humphreys—535—C'ton.

Richardson, Charles E.—22—Oct. 5, 1917—Lee—530—C'ton.
Robinson, Beard G.—28—June 24, 1918—Lee—516—(3,625,856)—Lexington.
Scott, Howard Cecil—25—Aug. 12, 1918—Lee—569—(4,087,480)—C'ton.
Scott, M. C.—23—June 24, 1918—Lee—579—(3,633,118)—C'ton.
Shirley, Paul Clark—21—May 22, 1918—U'y of Va.—599—C'ton.
Simmons, Abraham J.—21—May 24, 1918—Lee (rej. June 9, 1918)—593—C'ton.
Simpson, Grover Cleveland—24—Dec. 12, 1917—Ft. Thomas—Dec. 12, 1917—C'ton.
Sizer, Gordon—26—Sept. 28, 1917—Lee—570—C'ton.
Sizer, Richter—26—Sept. 28, 1917—Lee—564—(550,739)—C'ton.
Spiller, Ernest McComas—29—July 18, 1918—Engineers—551—C'ton.
Sprouse, Stephen Edward—21—Dec. 4, 1917—Navy—595—C'ton.
Stewardson, Calavah H.—21—Sept. 19, 1917—596—C'ton.
Taylor, John Bunyan—23—July 17, 1918—Humphreys—626—C'ton.
Thomas, George Graham—24—June 24, 1918—Lee—625—(3,640,109)—(rej. July 1, 1918)—C'ton.
Tolley, Harry Budd—25—May 24, 1918—Wadsworth—622—C'ton.
Vance, Ira—21—July 22, 1918—U'y of Va.—644—C'ton.
Walker, Gilbert C.—22—June 8, 1918—Lee—674—(3,176,111)—C'ton.
Wickline, Leonard—22—July 22, 1918—U'y of Va.—673—C'ton.
Wightman, Landon Leeper—29—Oct. 5, 1917—Lee—645—C'ton.
Wilson, Robert Lee—25—Sept. 29, 1918—Col. Barracks (rej. Oct. 1, 1918)—655—C'ton.
Witt, Otis Earl—21—June 6, 1918—Humphreys—666—C'ton.
Worley, Fred Wilton—23—Sept. 19, 1918—Lee—676—C'ton.
Wright, Esther Wiley—21—May 22, 1918—U'y of Va.—668—C'ton.
Young, Joseph B.—28—June 24, 1918—Lee—699—(3,633,181)—C'ton.

COLORED

Bailey, Charles—30—Aug. 7, 1918—Meade—82—(4,016,850)—C'ton.
Banks, William—31—June 18, 1918—Lee—83—(3,176,836)—C'ton.
Beauregard, Lewis—21—April 25, 1918—Lee—70—(2,667,084)—C'ton.
Beverly, Henry—22—April 25, 1918—Lee—72—(2,667,111)—C'ton.
Brown, Denny—22—July 27, 1918—Meade—74—(4,011,474)—C'ton.
Brown, George—22—July 16, 1918—Lee—73—(3,631,179)—C'ton.
Brown, John—23—July 16, 1917—Lee—81—(4,086,411)—C'ton.
Brown, Otis—24—July 18, 1918—Lee—80—(3,631,176)—C'ton.
Bumpass, Shaley—21—July 16, 1918—Lee—68—(4,086,414)—C'ton.
Calloway, Pleasants—25—July 16, 1918—125—(3,631,185)—C'ton.
Carter, John Loid—27—July 17, 1917—Ft. Thomas, Ky.—97—Greenfield.
Clark, George Gilbert—23—April 25, 1918—Lee—128—(2,667,045)—Greenfield.
Coleman, Spencer—29—June 18, 1918—Lee—133—(3,176,794)—C'ton.
Codwell, Thomas—24—July 16, 1918—Lee—131—(3,631,168)—C'ton.
Crenshaw, Frederick—27—June, 18, 1918—Lee—127—(3,176,837)—C'ton.

Davis, Lapralla—21—July 16, 1918—Lee—165—(3,631,197)—C'ton.
Dickerson, James Lewis—25—July 18, 1918—Dix, N. J.—168—C'ton.
Douglas, Lonie—24—July 18, 1918—Lee—170—(3,631,183)—C'ton.
Goodall, Daniel—21—Oct. 26, 1917—Lee—223—C'ton.
Halloway, Donald—29—July 16, 1918—Lee—295—(3,631,186)—Mallow.
Harris, Fred Douglas—25—June 18, 1918—Lee—(3,176,874)—C'ton.
Harrison, Newman Sellar—24—May 24, 1918—Lee—265—(3,171,302)—
C'ton.
Hicks, Edward Lewis—21—July 27, 1918—Meade—281—C'ton.
Hilton, Harry—23—July 16, 1918—Lee (rej. July 21, 1918)—289—
(3,631,173)—C'ton.
Holland, Thomas—21—July 18, 1918—Lee—292—(3,631,151)—C'ton.
Hooker, Curtis—21—June 18, 1918—Lee—284—(3,176,797)—C'ton.
Hubank, Milner—22—June 18, 1918—Lee—285—(3,176,792)—C'ton.
Hunter, Cluster Earthard—23—July 16, 1918—Lee (rej. July 23, 1918)—
291—C'ton.
Jackson, Harry—22—June 18, 1918—Lee—(3,196,810)—C'ton.
Jackson, Lorain P.—22—April 25, 1918—Lee—320—(2,669,120)—C'ton.
Jackson, Sylvester E.—24—April 25, 1918—Lee (rej. April 29, 1918)—
C'ton.
James, Cæsar—24—July 15, 1918—Lee—330—(3,631,184)—C'ton.
Jeter, Stephen—21—June 18, 1918—Lee—316—(3,176,826)—C'ton.
Jordan, Harry F.—21—July 16, 1918—Lee—318—(3,631,169)—C'ton.
Jordan, Will—24—June 18, 1918—Lee (rej. June 28, 1918)—326—C'ton.
Leftwich, Moses Lee—24—June 18, 1918—Lee—281—(3,196,836)—C'ton.
Leftwich, William S.—25—June 18, 1918—Lee—379—C'ton.
Lowery, Samuel—21—June 18, 1918—Lee (rej. June 25, 1918)—378—
C'ton.
McDonald, Edward—28—July 18, 1918—Lee—445—(4,086,413)—C'ton.
McDowell, Addie—24—June 14, 1918—Hampton Institute—466—C'ton.
McDowell, Commis—22—June 18, 1918—Lee—442—(3,176,802)—C'ton.
McDowell, James—21—May 1, 1918—Fort Wayne, Ind.—441—(2,680,169)
—C'ton.
McDowell, James Lincoln—24—June 18, 1918—Lee—447—(3,176,831)—
C'ton.
McDowell, Joseph Frank—26—June 18, 1918—Lee—446—(3,176,828)—
C'ton.
McDowell, Julian Gray—22—July 16, 1918—443—(3,631,174)—C'ton.
Massie, Charles—28—June 18, 1918—Lee—422—(3,196,820)—C'ton.
Matthews, Eugene—24—July 16, 1918—Lee—(3,631,162)—C'ton.
Matthews, Russell B.—26—June 18, 1918—Lee—417—(3,176,834)—C'ton.
Mills, Thomas Jerome—30—July 16, 1918—Lee (rej. July 21, 1918)—428—
(3,631,164)—C'ton.
Minor, Boyd—23—Oct. 26, 1917—Lee—420—C'ton.
Morris, Windell—21—July 16, 1918—Lee—413—(3,631,170)—C'ton.
Owens, James Coleman—21—July 27, 1918—Meade—464—(4,011,468)—
C'ton.

Pegram, Bishop—21—July 16, 1918—Lee—(3,631,152)—C'ton.
Pegram, William—23—May 1, 1918—Fort Wayne, Ind.—492—(2,680,167)
    C'ton.
Pollard, Edgar Douglas—21—July 27, 1918—Meade—485—(4,011,467)—
    C'ton.
Quarles, Allen—22—June 18, 1918—Lee—488—(3,176,833)—C'ton.
Quarles, Fred—25—June 18, 1918—Lee—499—(3,176,809)—Mallow.
Reed, Moses Wesley—22—July 16, 1918—Lee—537—(3,639,646)—C'ton.
Reynolds, James Harry—30—Oct. 28, 1917—Lee—550—C'ton.
Rose, William Luther—21—Oct. 26, 1917—Lee—536—C'ton.
Ross, Lewis—26—April 25, 1918—Lee—542—C'ton.
Rucker, Emmett Dee—22—June 19, 1918—Lee—541—(3,176,805)—C'ton.
Scruggs, James—24—Aug. 21, 1918—Upton—610—(4,153,784)—C'ton.
Sims, Benjamin—24—June 18, 1918—609—(3,176,806)—C'ton.
Smith, Robert Nelson—27—June 14, 1918—Hampton Institute—605—C'ton.
Stokes, Warren—22—Oct. 28, 1917—Lee—604—C'ton.
Stone, Charles—21—Aug. 2, 1918—Meade—599—C'ton.
Taylor, Charles Henry—21—July 16, 1918—Lee—628—(3,631,161)—C'ton.
Taylor, William—25—June 18, 1918—Lee (rej. June 25, 1918)—633—C'ton.
Tinsley, Charles Scott—22—July 21, 1918—Lee—632—C'ton.
Tinsley, Philip—25—July 16, 1918—631—C'ton.
Traynham, James—22—Aug. 1, 1918—Meade (rej. Aug. 23, 1918)—630—
    (4,013,661)—C'ton.
Turner, Charles—24—June 27, 1918—Lee—637—(3,630,567)—C'ton.
Wallace, Richard—22—July 16, 1918—Lee—696—(2,627,106)—C'ton.
Watson, Charles—25—July 16, 1918—Lee—682—(3,631,163)—C'ton.
Watson, Robert Allen—25—June 14, 1918—Hampton Institute—683—C'ton.
Wilkerson, Della—25—April 25, 1918—Lee—685—(2,667,106)—C'ton.
Winston, Ralph—24—July 16, 1918—Lee—(3,631,172)—C'ton.
Wood, Chunk—21—July 27, 1918—Meade—678—(4,011,465)—C'ton.
Woods, John William—27—July 17, 1918—Lee—688—(3,631,180)—C'ton.
Wright, Henry Wise—27—June 14, 1918—Hampton Institute—697—C'ton.
Wright, Richard—23—Jan. 15, 1918—Meade—692—C'ton.
Wyatt, Roy—21—July 27, 1918—Meade—679—(4,011,466)—C'ton.

LIST B—WHITE

Alfred, Andrew Jackson—26—June 24, 1918—Lee (disch. Dec. 7, 1918)—
    1301—(3,633,133)—CF.
Anderson, George Cline—26—June 24, 1918—Lee—1540—(3,625,910)—CF.
Anderson, George K.—24—Dec. 1, 1917—Rock Island, Ill.—1741—CF.
Anderson, Henry Watkins—19—Oct. 18, 1918—U'y of Va.—134—C'ton.
Angell, Howard Webb—21—Dec. 12, 1917—Ft. Thomas, Ky.—1296—CF.
Armistead, Charles Edward—24—July 17, 1918—Humphreys—1541—CF.
Baker, George Frank—24—June 24, 1918—Lee—1312—(3,633,132)—CF.
Baker, William George—21—Sept. 6, 1918—Lee—708—(4,634,999)—Potts
    Creek.
Ball, Alfred —22—June 24, 1918—Lee—115—(3,633,178)—Callaghan.

Bates, John Henry—21—July 17, 1918—Humphreys—796—Sweet Chaly-
beate.
Bazzarea, Roy A.—24—May 24, 1918—Lee—866—(3,175,339)—Low Moor.
Beale, Frank D.—26—Mar. 28, 1918—Lee—1305—(2,467,222)—CF.
Bean, Harry Earl—21—July 24, 1918—Navy—75—CF.
Beasley, Grover C.—24—July 7, 1918—Ft. Thomas—1553—CF.
Beasley, John—29—June 24, 1918—Lee—1311—(3,633,153)—CF.
Bell, Nathan Stuart—21—May 25, 1918—Navy—1316—CF.
Bess, James Raymond—22—May 9, 1918—Ft. Thomas, Ky.—709—Jordan
Mines.
Blachwelder, Oswald M.—21—June 9, 1917—Ft. Thomas, Ky.—1744—CF.
Bolt, Green Simon—22—July 17, 1918—Humphreys—794—Sweet Chaly-
beate.
Bolt, Posey Jason—21—Sept. 19, 1917—Lee—797—Sweet Chalybeate.
Boswell, Ocie Bennett—24—June 24, 1918—Lee—1552—(3,633,182)—CF.
Brimen, Philip Haney—22—May 24, 1918—Lee—1556—(3,170,592)—CF.
Broughman, Lacey N.—21—June 24, 1918—Lee—1315—(3,633,175)—CF.
Broughman, Melvin C.—23—May 22, 1918—1315—CF.—U'y of Va.
Broughman, Elmer—30—Sept. 29, 1918—Col. Barracks—1551—(3,376,413)
—CF.
Brown, Clarence—21—Aug. 6, 1918—Lee—13—(4,087,342)—Callaghan.
Burch, Jack Thomas—30—Oct. 5, 1917—Lee—867—Low Moor.
Bush, Harry Payne—21—June 24, 1918—Lee—1252—(3,633,250)—Rich
Patch.
Bush, Lonnie Stanford—24—July 17, 1918—Humphreys—1254—Rich Patch.
Cahoon, Cecil Luther—23—Mar. 28, 1918—Lee—1574—(2,467,224)—CF.
Cahoon, Jesse Norman—29—Dec. 12, 1917—Ft. Thomas, Ky.—1571—CF.
Callaghan, Charles C.—26—June 22, 1918—U'y of Va.—804—Sweet Chaly-
beate.
Callaghan, Howard—22—July 17, 1918—Humphreys—876—CF.
Callaghan, Walter Cleveland—30—July 17, 1918—Humphreys—880—Low
Moor.
Campbell, Oliver Jacob—22—Aug. 6, 1918—Lee—718—Potts Creek—
(4,087,369).
Camper, James Jefferson—21—Sept. 19, 1917—Lee—1572—CF.
Carper, Charles Henry—23—May 24, 1918—Lee—802—(3,171,305)—Alle-
ghany.
Carter, Beaudrich—24—May 16, 1918—Sevier, S. C.—799—Earlhurst.
Carter, Claude Marion—22—May 21, 1918—Meade—1576—(3,115,265)—
—CF.
Carter, Harvey Coles—23—May 24, 1918—Lee—1326—(3,171,300)—CF.
Carter, Ray Kevil—21—Mar. 28, 1918—Lee—805—(2,476,215)—Earlhurst.
Cave, Casper Lee—26—Mar. 28, 1918—Lee—1221—(2,467,221)—Rich
Patch.
Chapman, Mansfield S.—25—Oct. 5, 1917—Lee—721—Jordan Mines.
Chongas, Victor George—26—Mar. 28, 1918—Lee—1565—(2,467,206)—CF.
Chrisman, Edward E.—22—Oct. 5, 1917—Lee—874—Low Moor.

Clarkson, Leonard Anderson—24—Sept. 4, 1917—Lee—1752—CF.

Cline, George Robert—22—June 24, 1918—Lee—116—(3,633,203)—Callagh.

Cline, John Adam—21—Aug. 6, 1918—Lee (rej. Aug. 11, 1918)—88—
    (4,087,344)—Callaghan.

Clough, Stewart Lynn—30—Sept. 4, 1917—Lee—1748—CF.

Collins, John McGuire—21—June 7, 1918—Navy—65—C'ton.

Colvin, Robert Lee—30—Dec. 14, 1917—Ft. Thomas, Ky.—1749—CF.

Counts, Andrew Paul—25—May 24, 1918—Lee—806—(3,171,316)—Earle-
    hurst.

Craft, Thomas Earle—24—June 24, 1918—Lee—1573—(3,633,161)—CF.

Crouse, John Lee—21—Aug. 6, 1918—Lee—117*—(4,087,365)—Ollie.

Crutchfield, Graham Dold—22—Oct. 10, 1917—Lee—1020—Iron Gate.

Curtis, Edgar Lee—26—July 17, 1918—Humphreys—1190—Longdale.

Damewood, Osie Carl—21—Sept. 17, 1917—Col. Barracks—1596—CF.

Davidson, Francis A.—21—Dec. 12, 1917—Ft. Thomas, Ky.—961—Ollie.

Davies, Frank Wesley—21—Jan. 19, 1918—Cornell—25*—CF.

Davis, Hansford H.—25—July 23, 1918—Humphreys—884—Selma.

Davis, Kenneth E.—21—July 23, 1918—Humphreys—886—Selma.

Davis, Richard Jackson—28—June 24, 1918—Lee (rej. July 1, 1918)—
    1594—(3,640,106)—CF.

Dawson, Thomas—21—Aug. 6, 1918—Lee—79*—(4,087,356)—C'ton.

Deaton, Charles Pollard—21—June 24, 1918—Lee—1589—(3,633,152)—CF.

Deeds, Russell Joseph—21—Aug. 6, 1918—Lee—55*—(4,087,339)—CF.

Dehart, Claude Henry—21—Aug. 6, 1918—Lee (rej. Aug. 11, 1918)—90*—
    (4,087,335)—Earlehurst.

Dehart, John Robert—23—July 23, 1918—Humphreys—815—Earlhurst.

Depriest, John Allen—22—June 24, 1918—Lee—950—(3,625,893)—Ollie.

Desper, David Austin—23—July 1, 1918—Lee—1344—(3,637,655)—CF.

Desper, Robert Powell—30—July 22, 1918—U'y of Virginia.—1590—
    (2,747,890)—CF.

Dew, Almer Ray—22—July 23, 1917—Humphreys—1027—Iron Gate.

Dew, Ira Allen—23—July 17, 1918—Humphreys—1028—Iron Gate.

Dodd, John Lithel—29—May 24, 1918—Lee—1591—(3,171,546)—CF.

Dodson, Owen W.—23—Aug. 1, 1917—?—1191—Longdale.

Downey, Captain M.—22—May 23, 1918—Lee—1160—(3,171,363)—Long-
    dale.

Downey, William McClung—21—Aug. 6, 1918—Lee—40*—(4,087,345)—
    Goshen.

Downey, Warren Price—21—May 24, 1918—Lee (disch. Aug. 8, 1918)—
    1159—(3,171,617)—Kerr's Cr.

Dressler, John William—21—Aug. 6, 1918—Lee—76*—(4,087,330)—C'ton.

Dryden, Fred Bruce—24—Sept. 3, 1918—Humphreys (rej. Sept. 19, 1918)
    —Sweet Chalybeate.

Dudding, Kent—27—Sept. 29, 1918—Lee—722—(3,376,444)—Potts Cr.

Duggar, Roy Rainey—25—May 24, 1918 (rej. June 7, 1918)—1760—CF.

Duke, James Fletcher—27—Sept. 19, 1917—Lee—1763—CF.

Duval, Harry Gordon—24—Sept. 7, 1918—Lee—1593—(4,637,535)—CF.

Eakle, Emory Brooke—29—July 8, 1918—Washington Barracks—817—
Sweet Chalybeate.
Elmore, Chapman Harrison—28—June 24, 1918—Lee—1224—(3,633,134)—
Rich Patch.
Eton, Russell Leswig—22—Dec. 4, 1917—Ft. Thomas—1759—CF.
Farrow, Aubrey James—26—Oct. 10, 1917—Coast Artillery—892—Low
Moor.
Feury, Hice Martin—29—June 8, 1918—Navy—821—Alleghany.
Fitzgerald, Ashby J.—28—Mar. 29, 1918—Navy—1355—CF.
Foster, Lewis Coe—27—May 22, 1918—U'y of Va.—1604—CF.
Fout, Charles Emery—24—May 24, 1918—Lee—1357—(3,171,280)—CF.
Fox, Charles Franklin—23—Oct. 29, 1917—Col. Barracks—1603—CF.
Fridley, Ernest Lee—22—July 22, 1918—U'y of Va.—1352—CF.
Fridley, John Loyd—23—July 17, 1918—Humphreys—820—Alleghany.
Fry, Pleasant—21—Aug. 6, 1918—Lee—17*—(4,087,331)—Hot Springs.
Frye, Calvin—22—June 24, 1918—Lee—963—(3,625,898)—Hot Springs.
Gallagher, Earl Hughes—21—June 24, 1918—Lee—1770—(3,633,143)—CF.
Gibbs, Herbert Ryland—24—Mar. 28, 1918—Lee—1369—(2,467,233)—CF.
Gilbert, Jacob David—30—Aug. 6, 1918—Lee—1082—(4,087,368)—Selma.
Gladwell, Calvin M.—21—June 24, 1918—Lee—1120—(3,633,199)—C'ton.
Glass, John Linwood—28—Sept. 3, 1918—1614—CF.—Humphreys.
Gleason, Michael Emmett—24—June 24, 1918—Lee—1612—(3,625,871)—
CF.
Glover, Clyde Merritt—21—Aug. 2, 1918—Navy—45*—CF.
Golden, William Roy—21—June 27, 1918—Navy—93*—C'ton.
Gooch, Harry Gordon—24—July 17, 1918—Humphreys—1081—Selma.
Goolsby, Lewis Edward—23—May 24, 1918—Lee—1370—(3,171,300)—CF.
Gordon, Albert Howard—22—June 24, 1918—Sherman—1368—CF.
Green, Edwin Carter—24—Oct. 5, 1917—Lee—1769—CF.
Griffith, Dennis Richter—30—June 24, 1918—Lee—822—(3,625,874)—Earle-
hurst.
Griffith, William Stanley—25—July 23, 1918—Humphreys—825—Earle-
hurst.
Groves, William B.—21—Aug. 6, 1918—Lee (rej. Aug. 11, 1918)—104*—
(4,087,359)—CF.
Haley, William Argyle—21—Aug. 15, 1917—Lee—1780—CF.
Hamilton, Warren Paul—22—May 24, 1918—Lee—1227—(3,171,307)—
Rich Patch.
Haner, Edward Raymond—24—Dec. 12, 1917—Coast Artillery—1775—CF.
Harris, Harry Yost—23—Mar. 28, 1918—Lee—1625—(2,467,200)—CF.
Harris, Joseph Walker—24—June 24, 1918—Lee—1392—(3,633,144)—CF.
Harrison, Ollie Alexander—21—June 27, 1918—Navy—91*—C'ton.
Haskins, Harry Tucker—23—May 22, 1918—U'y of Va.—1776—CF.
Hawkins, John Simpson—18—Oct. 26, 1918—W. and L.—906—CF.
Hawkins, Robert Preston—23—July 3, 1918—Navy—1391—CF.
Helmintoller, William L.—21—Oct. 5, 1917—Lee—1294—Callaghan.
Higgens, Lawrence F.—21—July 23, 1918—Navy—74*—CF.

Hill, Edward Nettleton—19—Oct. 17, 1918—V. P. I.—131*—C'ton.

Hippert, William Leon—22—Mar. 27, 1918—Lee—1376—(1,849,073)—CF.

Hoke, William C. C.—22—June 24, 1918—Lee—1125—(3,625,890)—Alleghany.

Holland, Lewis Earle—24—June 14, 1918—Lee—1377—(3,633,157)—CF.

Hornbarger, William Henry—26—May 24, 1918—Lee—1390—(3,171,632) —CF.

Howard, Rupert Ezra—21—Mar. 28, 1918—Lee—1779—(2,467,209)—CF.

Hubbard, Clinton H.—26—July 17, 1918—Humphreys—730—Callaghan.

Hubbard, Grover C.—30—July 17, 1918—Humphreys (rej. July 31, 1918) —1124—C'ton.

Huffman, Albert Early—30—Sept. 3, 1918—Humphreys—1389—CF.

Huffman, Roy Lewis—May 24, 1918—Lee—1255—(3,171,297)—Rich Patch.

Huggard, William E.—21—July 3, 1918—Navy—95*—Selma.

Hughes, Thomas—23—July 16, 1918—Lee (rej. July 22, 1918)—896—Low Moor.

Humphris, Reginald R.—21—Mar. 28, 1918—Lee—1256—(2,467,274)—CF.

Hyler, William—22—July 17, 1918—Humphreys—1165—Longdale.

Hylton, John H. W.—21—June 24, 1918—Lee—834—(3,625,916)—Earlehurst.

Ingledew, Jesse—23—June 24, 1918—Lee (disch. Aug. 30, 1918)—1399— CF.

Ingledew, Raymond E.—25—May 24, 1918—Lee—1398—(3,171,296)—CF.

Irvine, William Baxter—25—May 24, 1918—Lee—1086—(3,171,321)—CF.

Jackson, Lonnie Parrish—23—June 28, 1918—Navy—971—Ollie.

Jamison, Alvin Denton—21—July 26, 1918—Navy—21*—Potts Cr.

Jamison, George Lewis—24—Sept. 19, 1917—Lee—739—Potts Cr.

Jamison, George Vernor—21—July 17, 1918—Humphreys—1261—Clift.

Jamison, Henry Parker—22—July 22, 1918—U'y of Va.—737—Potts Cr.

Jenkins, Henry Percy—24—Oct. 5, 1917—Lee (disch. June 15, 1918)—972 Hot Springs.

Johnson, Grover C.—24—May 9, 1918—Ft. Thomas—738—Blue Spring Run.

Johnson, John Earl—26—May 22, 1918—U'y of Va.—742—Blue Spring Run.

Johnson, John Wilson—24—July 17, 1918—Humphreys—1402—(3,633,191) —CF.

Johnson, Munford—22—May 24, 1918—Lee—1034—(3,191,285)—Iron Gate.

Johnson, Robert Cline—21—Oct. 19, 1918—?—48*—CF.

Jones, John Irvin—18—Oct. 23, 1918—W. and L.—1544—CF.

Jordan, Eugene J.—July 13, 1917—Ft. Thomas, Ky.—1408—CF.

Karnes, Claude Everett—21—Aug. 6, 1918—Lee—68*—(4,087,353)—C'ton.

Kelley, Peter Anthony—26—June 24, 1918—Lee (disch. Aug. 8, 1918)—902 Low Moor.

Kelly, Harry Monroe—26—June 24, 1918—Lee—1037—Iron Gate.

King, Robert Hezekiah—21—Aug. 2, 1918—Meade—67*—Barber.

Landrum, William Clyde—22—June 24, 1918—Lee—976—(3,633,174)— Barber.

Larman, Emmett Edward—21—July 1, 1918—Lee—1039—(3,637,645)—
Iron Gate.

Lawhorn, John Douglas—21—July 22, 1918—U'y of Va.—1038—Iron Gate.

Laurence, Jesse Cameron—22—Sept. 29, 1918—Col. Barracks—1415—
(3,376,414)—CF.

Leslie, William Lee—30—Nov. 22, 1918—Ft. Thomas, Ky.—1789—CF.

Lewis, Lee Ander—22—May 23, 1918—Lee—838—Alleghany—(3,171,293)

Lewis, James Warner—21—Dec. 12, 1917—Ft. Thomas, Ky.—1797—CF.

Lewis, Luther—21—Aug. 6, 1918—Lee—52*—(4,087,350)—Alleghany.

Lewis, Meriwether—23—July 7, 1917—Ft. Thomas, Ky.—1791—CF.

Lipes, Walter William—24—Nov. 14, 1917—Lee—1417—CF.

Lockhart, Pleasant Carl—21—May 24, 1918—Lee—1265—(3,171,328)—Blue
Spring Run.

Lumsden, Lyle Edward—23—Feb. 16, 1918—Fort Leavenworth—1793—CF.

Lyle, Clyde Cecil—21—May 24, 1918—Lee—1794—CF.

McAllister, Frank Adams—21—Aug. 2, 1918—Navy—49*—C'ton.

McCallister, Frank Renick—23—July 17, 1918—Humphreys—988—Hot
Springs.

McCallister, Wilbert—30—June 24, 1918—Lee (rej. July 1, 1918)—1138—
Callaghan.

McCray, William Diamond—

McCune, Thomas Fritz—21—Aug. 6, 1918—Lee—42*—(4,087,329)—C'ton.

McKinley, William P.—21—Aug. 6, 1918—Lee—18*—(4,087,343)—CF.

Markli, Lewis Rawdon—28—Dec. 13, 1917—Ft. Thomas, Ky.—1798—CF.

Martin, James—21—Nov. 1, 1917—Lee—1266—Clift.

Mason, Lawrence Herbert—21—Oct. 5, 1917—Lee—CF.

Mason, William—24—July 30, 1918—Lee—1041—(4,086,821)—Iron Gate.

Matheny, Arden Roy—21—Aug. 8, 1918—Lee—71*—(4,087,352)—Callaghan.

Matheny, James Edward—23—June 24, 1918—Lee—1134—(3,625,874)—
Callaghan.

Matthews, Joseph Irvine—21—Sept. 8, 1918—Meade—77*—Washington,
D. C.

Mawyer, Robert Lee—22—June 24, 1918—Lee—1093—(3,625,870)—Selma.

May, Samuel Byrd—29—Nov. 28, 1917—M. R. C.—1649—CF.

Mays, Clarence V.—21—June 24, 1918—Lee—912—(3,633,131)—Low
Moor.

Mays, Frank James—24—June 24, 1918—Lee—980—(3,633,154)—Barber.

Mays, Millard—22—June 24, 1918—Lee—1231—(3,625,883)—Low Moor.

Meadows, Guy Degar—26—June 24, 1918—Lee—1092—(3,725,905)—Selma.

Meadows, Isaac Jacob—22—Oct. 5, 1917—Lee—981—Ollie.

Meeshler, Alva Edison—23—May 22, 1918—U'y of Va.—1800—CF.

Miller, Emmett Aubray—21—May 22, 1918—U'y of Va.—1433—CF.

Miller, Everett Lynn—21—May 24, 1918—Lee—1652—(3,172,887)—CF.

Miller, Henry Gilmore—28—Aug. 6, 1918—Lee—1045—(4,087,371)—Iron
Gate.

Miller, John Henry—22—Aug. 6, 1918—Lee (rej. Aug. 20, 1918)—745—
(4,087,367)—Jordan Mines.

Milton, Luther Graham—26—May 16, 1918—Humphreys—1045—Iron Gate.
Milton, Pollard Ezra—24—Oct. 10, 1917—Lee—1651—CF.
Moneymaker, Joseph A.—21—Aug. 6, 1918—Lee—78*—(4,087,333)—Selma.
Montgomery, Clayton—21—July 22, 1918—U'y of Va.—1434—CF.
Montgomery, Samuel Luck—30—Dec. 14, 1917—Newport News—1648—CF.
Moomaw, John Clayton—30—June 24, 1918—Lee—984—Barber.
Morris, Cecil Van Horn—21—Oct. 16, 1918—S. A. T. C.—26*—CF.
Moyers, Warren Philip—21—Aug. 6, 1918—Lee (rej. Aug. 11, 1918)—7*—
    (4,087,347)—C'ton.
Myers, Jesse F.—22—Sept. 3, 1918—Humphreys—845—Alleghany.
Nair, William Burger—26—Oct. 5, 1917—Lee—1454—CF.
Nelson, Harry E.—23—Oct. 5, 1917—Lee—1456—CF.
Nicely, James M.—22—June 24, 1918—Lee—1202—(3,625,899)—Longdale.
Nicely, Jesse Jackson—21—July 17, 1918—Humphreys—1203—Longdale.
Nicely, Jacob Price—29—April 26, 1918—Laurel, Md.—1808—(2,547,012)
    CF.
Nicely, Lee Washington—28—June 24, 1918—Lee—1809—(3,633,185)—CF.
Nicely, Lenwood Houston—21—Aug. 6, 1918—Lee—83*—(4,087,354)—
    Longdale.
Nicely, Sharrach Marion—22—May 24, 1918—Lee—1810—(3,633,157)—CF.
Nicely, Thomas L.—25—May 24, 1918—Lee—1198—(3,176,317)—Longdale.
Nuchols, Herbert Washington—21—Aug. 6, 1918—Lee—27*—(4,087,348)
    —C'ton.
Nuchols, Robert Wilson—24—July 17, 1917—Ft. Thomas, Ky.—1096—
    Selma.
Obenchain, Emmett—22—July 17, 1918—Humphreys—1664—CF.
Oiler, George Washington—21—Aug. 6, 1918—Lee (rej. Aug. 11, 1918)—
    4,087,364)—Low Moor.
Oiler, Leslie Irvine—21—Aug. 6, 1918—Lee (rej. Aug. 11, 1918)—115*—
    (4,087,372)—Low Moor.
Owens, John Jefferson—24—July 22, 1918—U'y of Va.—846—Sweet Chaly-
    beate.
Oyler, William Philip—21—July 6, 1918—Navy—32*—Selma.
Pace, Percy James—30—June 24, 1918—Lee—991—(3,633,160)—C'ton.
Painter, Robert E. L.—24—May 24, 1918—Lee—1048—(3,171,744)—Iron
    Gate.
Patterson, Charles William—21—May 24, 1918—Lee (disch. Aug. 20, 1918)
    —1667—(3,171,401)—CF.
Paxton, Dewey Lee—21—July 17, 1918—Humphreys—1293—Callaghan.
Payne, Paul Jennings—22—Dec. 12, 1917—Ft. Thomas—1667—CF.
Pendleton, Littleton Flippo—28—Sept. 4, 1917—Lee—1813—CF.
Plunkett, Thomas Joseph—29—July 22, 1918—U'y of Va.—1668—CF.
Powell, Walter Forest—23—May 22, 1918—U'y of Va.—1464—CF.
Powers, John Joseph—22—Sept. 10, 1918—Meade (deserted, Sept. 13,
    1918)—23*—C'ton.
Revercomb, George A., Jr.—21—July 6, 1918—Navy—12*—C'ton.
Rhodes, Forest Ware—21—Aug. 6, 1918—Lee—14*—(4,987,351)—C'ton.

Rhodes, Herman Gill—22—Oct. 5, 1917—Lee—1476—CF.
Riddlebarger, Cecil A.—25—Mar. 28, 1918—Lee—1674—CF.
Roadcap, Russell Robert—21—Aug. 6, 1918—Lee—103*—CF.
Robbins, John J.—24—Sept. 6, 1918—Lee—993—(4,632,635)—Barber.
Rogers, George Lewis—23—June 24, 1918—Lee—1471—(3,625,876)—CF.
Rose, Floyd Ernest—22—June 24, 1918—Lee—1144—(3,633,155)—Callaghan.
Rose, Jesse Allen—25—Sept. 3, 1918—Humphreys—755—Blue Spring Run.
Rose, Wilbur McKinley—21—Sept. 19, 1917—Lee—1237—Rich Patch.
Ross, Blane W. C.—26—May 1, 1918—Lee—926—Low Moor.
Rule, Raymond Jennings—21—July 2, 1918—Navy—46*—CF.
Samples, Fife Hugh—23—June 18, 1917—Navy—1698—CF.
Sanders, Raymond E.—21—Dec. 12, 1917—Ft. Thomas, Ky.—1701—CF.
Saunders, Cecil Wellington—18—Oct. 19, 1918—W. and L.—1199—CF.
Saunders, Curtis Preston—23—Sept. 6, 1918—Lee—1697—(4,632,637)—CF.
Savage, Francis Dicken—18—Oct. 30, 1918—W. and L.—1550—CF.
Savage, Walter Henry—20—Oct. 15, 1918—W. and L.—1567—CF.
Scruggs, Harry Preston—24—Aug. 6, 1918—Lee (rej. Aug. 11, 1918)—1146—Callaghan.
Scruggs, Jesse J.—23—May 22, 1918—U'y of Va.—1689—CF.
Scruggs, Warren B.—21—Dec. 12, 1917—Ft. Thomas, Ky.—1700—CF.
Sharp, Wallace W.—22—June 24, 1918—Lee—1482—(3,633,163)—CF.
Shelton, Oscar Norman—19—Oct. 29, 1918—Manassas—1220—CF.
Shue, Clyde W. O.—22—July 17, 1918—Humphreys—1147—Callaghan.
Simmons, Charles—28—June 24, 1918—Lee (rej. July 1, 1918)—1208—Longdale.
Simpson, Homer Edgar—23—May 22, 1918—U'y of Va.—1699—CF.
Sloan, Silas Oby—21—Aug. 8, 1918—Lee—80*—(4,087,360)—CF.
Sloane, Robert Lee—29—Sept. 3, 1918—Humphreys—1490—CF.
Sloane, William E.—22—June 24, 1918—Lee—1481—CF.
Slusser, Frank M.—25—June 24, 1918—Lee—1494—(3,633,168)—CF.
Smith, Charles E.—21—Sept. 3, 1918—Humphreys—1692—CF.
Smith, Ernest Lawrence—21—Aug. 6, 1918—Lee—70*—(4,087,337)—C'ton.
Smith, Elmo McCarty—26—Sept. 6, 1918—Lee—1694—(4,632,636)—CF.
Smith, Jasper M.—26—June 24, 1918—Lee (disch. Aug. 29, 1918)—998—(3,626,047)—C'ton.
Smith, Lester Joseph—27—June 24, 1918—Lee—995—(3,633,124)—C'ton.
Smith, Russell—23—June 24, 1918—Lee—997—(3,633,136)—C'ton.
Smith, Walter Keeble—18—Oct. 26, 1918—W. and L.—1205—CF.
Snead, Thomas Eugene—21—Sept. 29, 1918—Col. Barracks—11*—(3,376,415)—C'ton.
Snider, Albert Elmer—21—Aug. 6, 1918—Lee—82*—(4,087,338)—CF.
Snyder, Luther Wheeler—22—June 24, 1918—Lee—1497—(3,633,149)—CF.
Sorrels, Sterling—21—Aug. 6, 1918—Lee—60*—(4,087,362)—Longdale
Staley, Frank Spiller—28—Mar. 28, 1918—Lee—1102—(2,467,213)—CF.
Staley, James Garland—27—May 22, 1918—U'y of Va.—1492—CF.
Steele, Oscar Lee—23—June 24, 1918—Lee (rej. July 9, 1918)—1239—(3,641,492)—Rich Patch.

Stinnett, Aubrey Neff—21—Aug. 6, 1918—Lee—112—(4,087,363)—C'ton.

Stinnett, Charles O.—25—Dec. 5, 1917—Navy—1695—CF.

Stock, Cecil Fred—21—July 2, 1918—Navy—54*—CF.

Stratton, Leslie Michie—21—Nov. 27, 1917—Ft. Thomas, Ky.—1824—CF.

Straub, Robert Eten—21—July 20, 1918—Navy—47*—CF.

Strauss, William Frank—21—Aug. 6, 1918—Lee (disch. Sept. 13, 1918)—
    84*—(4,087,336)—Cincinnati, O.

Stull, Chester James—23—Aug. 30, 1918—Lee—929—(4,627,271)—Low
    Moor.

Stull, Harry Richard—28—Dec. 13, 1917—Ft. Oglethorpe—1241—Rich
    Patch.

Sussman, Louis Frank—21—Aug. 6, 1918—Lee—108*—(4,087,334)—C'ton.

Switzer, Harry Lee—24—Nov. 11, 1917—Ft. Thomas, Ky.—1696—CF.

Taylor, Harry E.—23—Nov. 21, 1917—Ft. Thomas—1709—CF.

Terry, Clyde Wesley—23—May 19, 1918—Ft. Thomas—856—Earlehurst.

Thomas, Denton Elmer—21—June 24, 1918—Lee—1243—(3,637,957)—Rich
    Patch.

Thomas, Floyd Mason—25—May 24, 1918—Lee—1831—(3,171,545)—CF.

Thurston, Charles F.—23—Sept. 29, 1918—Columbus Barracks—1830—
    (3,376,445)—CF.

Tingler, Richard James—21—Dec. 12, 1917—Navy—1242—Rich Patch.

Tribbett, Frank M.—28—Dec. 13, 1917—Ft. Thomas, Ky.—1508—CF.

Tucker, James A.—23—Nov. 14, 1917—Lee—1509—CF.

Turpin, Lambert M.—23—May 9, 1918—Ft. Thomas, Ky.—1507—CF.

Tyree, Charles Meredith—25—June 24, 1918—Lee—1000—(3,633,166)—
    Barber.

Tyree, John David—23—May 9, 1918—Ft. Thomas, Ky.—1002—Ollie.

Tyree, Achilles D.—26—Dec. 8, 1917—M. R. C.—1056—Iron Gate.

Tyree, Silas Oby—21—Aug. 6, 1918—Lee (rej. Aug. 11, 1918)—81*—
    (4,087,346)—CF.

Van Fossen, Mason Patterson—24—May 24, 1918—Lee—1767—(3,171,444)
    —CF.

Vanscoy, Ernest E.—21—Dec. 12, 1917—Navy—1712—CF.

Vess, Lonnie Mason—28—June 24, 1918—Lee—1210—(3,625,904)—Long-
    dale.

Vess, Ora L.—21—Aug. 6, 1918—Lee—111*—(4,087,608)—CF.

Vest, William Taylor—22—May 9, 1918—Ft. Thomas, Ky.—1064—Iron
    Gate.

Vint, George William Alvin—21—Sept. 29, 1918—Col. Barracks—8*—
    (3,376,409)—Jordan Mines.

Wade, Lewis Mowyer—23—June 28, 1918—Sherman—1732—CF.

Waldrop, Thomas G.—27—Dec. 13, 1917—Navy—1728—CF.

Walker, Frank Well—23—June 24, 1918—Lee—779—(3,625,882)—Jordan
    Mines.

Walker, French B.—25—May 24, 1918—Lee (disch. Nov. 21, 1918)—1525
    CF.

Waldrop, Walter William—18—Oct. 16, 1918—Randolph-Macon—1201—
CF.

Wallace, Russell Newman—25—May 22, 1918—U'y of Va.—944—Low
Moor.

Walton, Jesse James—23—July 23, 1918—Ft. Thomas, Ky.—1528—CF.

Wamsley, Charles—22—May 24, 1918—Lee—1735—(3,171,288)—CF.

Wamsley, James Hubert—20—Oct. 15, 1918—W. and L.—1211—CF.

Waskey, William B.—21—Aug. 6, 1918—Lee—1*—(4,087,349)—CF.

Weaver, Embrey Clark—21—June 24, 1918—Lee—1009—(3,633,102)—
C'ton.

Weber, Charles Harne—26—May 24, 1918—Lee—1109—(3,171,287)—
Selma.

Weller, Erskin Melvin—25—Jan. 29, 1918—Princeton, N. J.—1005—Barber.

Westerman, Dewey Everett—20—Oct. 25, 1918—Richmond College—1233
CF.

Westerman, Elmer C.—21—Dec. 13, 1917—Ft. Thomas, Ky.—1737—CF.

Whanger, Leighton Emmitt—25—Sept. 3, 1918—Humphreys—962—Alleghany.

Wheeler, James Brice—21—Aug. 6, 1918—Lee—15*—(4,087,357)—Hematite.

White, George Franklin—21—June 24, 1918—Lee—1246—(3,633,188)—
Low Moor.

White,.William Sherman—23—May 24, 1918—Lee (disch. Aug. 29, 1918)
—1527—(3,171,313)—CF.

Wickline, Staley Otto—25—July 25, 1918—Washington Barracks—859—
Sweet Chalybeate.

Wilcher, Gilbert Clyde—21—Sept. 29, 1918—Col. Barracks—1110—
(3,376,412)—Selma.

Williams, Carl Richter—27—June 24, 1918—Lee—1004—(3,633,156)—Barber.

Williams, Roland Albert—22—July 6, 1917—Ft. Thomas, Ky.—1734—CF.

Williams, Raymond Edison—21—July 7, 1917—Ft. Thomas, Ky.—1738—
CF.

Williams, James Neil—29—Oct. 7, 1917—M. R. C.—1815—CF.

Williamson, John Matheny—23—July 17, 1918—Humphreys—1733—CF.

Withrow, Charles A.—22—May 6, 1918—Lehigh U'y—1736—CF.

Wolfe, David Pearl—23—May 24, 1918—Lee—1008—(3,171,295)—Barber.

Wolfe, John Luther—21—Aug. 6, 1918—Lee (rej. Aug. 11, 1918)—102*—
(4,087,340)—Barber.

Wolfe, Otto Jacob—25—Sept. 19, 1917—Lee—786—Potts Cr.

Wood, Owen Morris—21—Aug. 6, 1918—Lee—110*—(4,087,358)—C'ton.

Woods, Harvey Drewry—21—Dec. 13, 1917—Ft. Thomas, Ky.—1837—CF.

Worley, James Wiley—21—Aug. 6, 1918—Lee—119*—(4,087,366)—C'ton.

Worsham, Charles Edward—21—June 24, 1918—Navy—106*—C'ton.

Wright, Robert Lee—22—Sept. 29, 1918—Col. Barracks—778—(3,376,411)
—Jordan Mines.

Wysor, Frank Laird—25—Oct. 10, 1917—Ft. Oglethorpe—1834—CF.
Young, John G.—21—Aug. 6, 1918—Lee (rej. Aug. 11, 1918)—87*—
   (4,087,332)—Alleghany.

COLORED

Allen, Daniel—27—June 18, 1918—Lee (June 25, 1918)—1013—Iron Gate.
Allen, George Alexander—22—Oct. 26, 1917—Lee—1014—Iron Gate.
Anderson, Oscar—25—Nov. 7, 1917—Lee—792—Charlottesville.
Anderson, Oscar L. B.—21—June 18, 1918—Lee—1304—(3,176,838)—CF.
Anderson, Frank Lee—23—July 16, 1918—Lee—1302—CF.
Austin, Harry—22—June 18, 1918—Lee—864—(3,176,827)—Low Moor.
Carter, Lawrence E.—24—Oct. 10, 1917—Lee—1329—CF.
Calender, Munford—21—May 1, 1918—Ft. Wayne, Ind.—1024—(2,680,175)
   Iron Gate.
Calloway, James—23—July 17, 1918—Camp Gordon, Ga.—1222—Low Moor.
Crawford, Hugh—24—Oct. 26, 1917—Lee—1329—CF.
Davis, James Blaine—22—July 26, 1917—Meade—120*—(4,011,472)—C'ton.
Dickerson, Oliver B.—27—June 18, 1918—Lee—1348—(3,624,155)—CF.
Doss, Charles F.—21—May 1, 1918—Wayne—1348—(2,680,168)—CF.
Hill, George—27—Nov. 11, 1917—Lee—1395—CF.
Hunter, Bolivia E.—21—Aug. 2, 1918—Meade—94*—(4,019,192)—C'ton.
Jackson, Asey—21—Aug. 2, 1918—Meade—3*—(4,013,185)—CF.
Jackson, Lacy—21—July 16, 1918—Lee—1036—(3,631,158)—Iron Gate.
Leftwich, Redwood—21—July 27, 1918—Lee—1854—(4,011,469)—C'ton.
Lee, Frank A.—22—July 27, 1918—Meade—1418—(4,011,470)—CF.
Lemon, Russell—25—Dec. 1, 1917—Col. Barracks (stevedore)—1642—CF.
Lewis, Elmore—30—June 7, 1918—Lee (rej. June 16, 1918)—1419—CF.
Lewis, John—25—July 16, 1918—Lee (rej. Aug. 4, 1918)—910—Low Moor.
McCray, William Diamond—21—Aug. 2, 1918—Meade—2*—(4,011,079)—
   CF.
Marks, Charles—21—Aug. 10, 1918—Lee—1438—(4,087,826)—CF.
Maryland, Elick—25—June 18, 1918—Lee (rej. June 28, 1918)—985—Bar-
   ber.
Massey, Albert—22—July 16, 1918—Lee—1445—(3,631,165)—CF.
Moore, Alphonso—21—May 1, 1918—Lee—1447—(3,176,155)—CF.
Moore, Branch Cecil—25—Oct. 26, 1917—Lee—1436—CF.
Moore, Theodore H.—24—June 14, 1918—Hampton Institute—1437—CF.
Nelson, Gratton Andrew—21—June 18, 1918—Lee (rej. June 24, 1918)—
   990—Barber.
Nelson, Gratton George—21—June 18, 1918—Lee—989—(3,176,878)—Bar-
   ber.
Phelps, Nathan—23—April 25, 1918—753—(2,667,113)—Jordan Mines.
Pryor, John—23—July 16, 1918—Lee—922—(3,631,175)—Low Moor.
Reed, Howard—21—Aug. 1, 1918—Fort Wayne—1478—(2,680,174)—CF.
Reynolds, Boise—27—July 16, 1918—Grant—1479—(3,745,997)—CF.
Reynolds, John Daniel—30—June 18, 1918—Lee—1477—(3,176,810)—CF.
Shelton, Leonard—21—June 18, 1918—Lee—1500—(3,176,832)—CF.

Smith, Jerry—21—Aug. 2, 1918—Meade—97*—(4,019,190)—C'ton.
Smith, Stenson—22—July 16, 1918—Lee—938—(3,631,156)—Low Moor.
Smith, Thomas—27—June 18, 1918—Lee—1827—(3,176,801)—CF.
Spencer, Clarence—21—Aug. 2, 1918—Meade—98—(4,011,085)—C'ton.
Taylor, Clayborne—24—July 16, 1918—Lee—1514—(3,631,159)—CF.
Thomas, Harrison—21—July 16, 1918—Lee—1245—(3,631,167)—Low
    Moor.
Thompson, George—22—July 26, 1918—Lee—942—Low Moor.
Tinsley, Charles Lee—25—July 16, 1918—Lee—1710—(3,631,178)—CF.
Tinsley, Walter—21—Mar. 24, 1918—Lee (rej. Oct. 1, 1918)—152*—C'ton.
Tucker, Isaac—21—July 16, 1918—Lee—1003—(3,631,155)—C'ton.
Tyler, Raymond L.—22—April 25, 1918—Lee—1510—(2,667,085)—CF.
Waller, Payton—22—Nov. 14, 1917—Lee—1536—CF.
Ware, Emmanuel—30—May 18, 1918—Lee—1844—(3,176,803)—CF.
Washington, Steward Elvert—21—Aug. 2, 1918—Meade—19*—(4,011,078)
    —Iron Gate.
Wilson, David, Jr.—21—July 16, 1918—Lee—947—(3,631,152)—Low Moor.
Woodfork, Chester—21—Aug. Aug. 2, 1918—Meade—99*—(4,011,084)—
    Low Moor.
Wright, Bridgett—26—July 16, 1918—Lee—1739—(3,631,171)—CF.
Yancey, Edward—27—Aug. 2, 1918—Meade—113*—(4,011,082)—C'ton.

LIST C—WHITE

Anderson, John Robert—21—Sept. 29, 1918—C'ton.
Aquor, Ricie D.—22—Alleghany Co.
Bass, William E.—21—Oct. 29, 1918—C'ton.
Biggs, Roy Carson—23—June 24, 1918—Longdale.
Brown, Dunlap Emesh—21—Oct. 5, 1917—Callaghan.
Brown, Frank Conway—21—Aug. 7, 1918—Mallow.
Brown, Harry A.—21—Sept. 24, 1918—C'ton.
Brown, James—21—Aug. 2, 1918—C'ton.
Carter, Briscoe E.—23—Sept. 19, 1917—CF.
Coffman, Daniel Luther—36—Nov. 14, 1918—C'ton.
Dame, Harry—23—June 24, 1918—Low Moor.
Deweese, William A.—Supply Company, 2d Va., Roanoke.
Dickenson, Arthur—22—Headquarters Company, Staunton.
Dodd, Edward T.—18—March 25, 1917—Company E, 2d Va., Chase City.
Doyle, Henry W.—March 25, 1917—Company E, 2d Va., Chase City.
Hoke, Archibald—21—August 6, 1918—Lee—White Sulphur Springs.
Humphreys, Lacy E.—24—July 23, 1918—Humphreys—Rich Patch.
Humphries, Lewis B.—23—May 24, 1918—Lee—Clift.
McConnell, Lee—19—Oct. 30, 1918—Pack—C'ton.
McCoy, Thomas Floyd—25—March 28, 1918—Lee—CF.
McCoy, Wayman Busby—26—Sept. 3, 1918—Humphreys—Iron Gate.
McGowan, Leitch Bunk—28—June 24, 1918—Lee—C'ton.
McNeer, Seldon S.—23—Oct. 1, 1917—Base Hospital 41—C'ton.
Merriman, Garnett Lee—22—July 17, 1918—CF.

Mowyer, Robert Lee—26—June 24, 1918—Selma.
Nicely, Homer W.—22—May 24, 1918—Lee—Longdale.
Painter, Lawrence Michael—22—Sept. 29, 1918—University of Va.—CF.
Slaugh, Franklyn Bruce—21—May 24, 1918—Lee—Iron Gate.
Smith, Hubert M.—24—May 1, 1918—Bristol, Va.—Alleghany Co.
Thompson, Emmett—28—July 17, 1918—Humphreys—Low Moor.
Terry, Franklin E.—25—March 28, 1918—Lee—Clift.
Tyler, Frank A.—18—March 25, 1917—Chase City—Alleghany Co.
Tyler, Ray C.—19—March 25, 1917—Chase City—Alleghany Co.

COLORED

Blakey, Adolphus—21—April 25, 1918—CF.
Brown, Frank Conway—21—August 7, 1918—Mallow.
Brown, Harry A.—21—Sept. 24, 1918—C'ton.
Brown, James—21—August 2, 1918—C'ton.
Brown, Standford—21—April 25, 1918—C'ton.
Cash, Ernest—23—May 1, 1918—Iron Gate.
Fleshman, Joseph G.—22—July 16, 1918—Longdale.
Galston, Judge William—21—July 16, 1918—Low Moor.
King ,Robert Hezekiah—21—August 2, 1918—Meade—Barber.
Leftwich, Ernest Samuel—21—August 2, 1918—Meade—C'ton.
Martin, John—21—June 16, 1918—Dix—Callaghan.
Morris, William—23—July 16, 1918—Lee—CF.
Mosby, Harvey—23—June 16, 1918—Lee—CF.—rej.
Ross, Blaine W. G.—26—May 1, 1918—Lee—Low Moor.
Reed, Howard—21—May 1, 1918—Fort Wayne—CF.
Smith, Percy Alfred—21—August 2, 1918—Meade—C'ton.
Thomas, John M.—21—Oct. 3, 1917—Columbus Barracks—CF.

LIST D

COMPANY H, 116TH VIRGINIA INFANTRY—ALL WHITE

Alderman, Oscar W.
Allen, John W.—29
Anderson, McKinley
Arbogast, Mead
Archondithis, Achileas G.—cook
Armstrong, Lubie L.
Bass, Thomas R.
Bayne, Mack C.
Beckner, John L.
Blake, Luther J.
Blakey, Adolphus
Bowling, Braxton W.
Bray, Russell L.
Breeden, Claude—corporal
Brinkley, George G.—sergeant
Brisendine, Nokomus

Bryant, Charles P.
Bunch, Clarence L.
Byers, Henry Douglas—26—June 4, 1917—31
Byers, Hobson A.
Byers, Kenneth Roy—21—July 27, 1917—63
Callaghan, Wamer J.
Campbell, Benton K.
Carson, Charles L.
Carson, Elmer L.
Carson, George F.
Carter, John L.—27
Chambers, John M.
Chames, Lewis B.—cook.
Chaplin, Malcolm T.

Clark, Charles L.
Clifford, Leo M.
Coleman, Charles A.
Collins, John V.
Cooke, Horace G.
Crawford, Harvey T.
Crowder, Jack.
Crowder, McKinley S.—21
Dame, Earl—21—Sept. 20, 1917—885 —Low Moor
Damewood, Osie Carl—21—Sept. 17, 1917—Col. Barracks—1596 —CF.
Deaner, George E.—22—June 17, 1917—158
Deeds, Acil A.
Dinges, Lester L.
Donovan, Harry S.
Doyle, Garnett L.
Dressler, Benjamin E.—24—Sept. 21, 1917—957—Barber
Dunlap, Morris J., Jr.—mess sgt.
Eades, Roy G.
Edwards, Osborne Y.—19
Ehrhart, George—corporal
Ewell, Nathaniel M. G.—1st Lt.
Ferrell, Albert M.
Fisher, Hansford
Flippo, Walter A.—corporal
Ford, William G.
Fridley, Wilbur G.—18
Fridley, Osborn Y.
Gibson, William L.—18
Gilbert, Carl Roger—29—July 27, 1917—205
Grayson, Merlin F.—18
Greene, William M.
Grubert, Reese T.—2d lt.
Haner, Edward R.
Harman, Lester M.
Helmintoller, Henry W.
Hepler, Lewis P.—21
Hinkle, Leonard H.—18
Hinty, Cecil G.
Hippe, Lewis P.
Hooke, John J.—20
Holbert, Zachariah
Hood, Ernest E.
Hope, Lyell A.

Hudlow, Russell W.
Hyler, Harvey Marion—22—June 29, 1917—1167—Longdale
Ingledew, John I.—19
Irvin, William O.
Johnson, Cary B.
Johnson, Clarence L.
Johnson, Gordon P.
Johnson, William L.
Kelly, Alexander H.
Kemper, Everett C.
Kerns, William E.
Keyser, Garnett K.—19
Keyser, Virgil Lefridge—23—July 28, 1917—343
Kimberlin, George D.
Kimberlin, Jesse R.—21—July 7, 1917—351
Kimberlin, Robert—Sgt.—22— July 7, 1917—347
Kincaid, Edwin
Kincaid, Ernest
Lam, Bedford C.—supply sgt.
Lam, Edgar
Lavender, Clyde S.—18
Lawrence, Milton D.—corporal
Layne, Bernard V.—22—July 25, 1917—1414—CF.
Leffel, Alvey R.
Leffel, George D.
Leffel, John H.
Lester, Henry H.
Lindsay, James N.
Linkenhoker, Charles E.
Lobban, Harry E.
Long, James F.—21
Loving, Vernon W.
Lowman, John H.
Lugar, Frank J.
Lynch, Luther L.
McCaleb, Thomas B.
McCormack, Glen William—22— June 24, 1917—438
McSherry, Robert J.—26—April 20, 1917—1807—CF.
Mahaney, Howell H.
Markham, Joseph A.
Matheny, James Oliver—21—April 24, 1917—410

Matthews, James Oliver—21—April 24, 1917—410—C'ton.

Martin, Broadus—22—July 28, 1917—407

Meadows, Charles Franklin—21—July 27, 1917—1430—CF.

Miller, Cletus

Mitchell, Roy L.

Montgomery, William R.—27

Newcomb, Cecil Q.

Obenchain, William R.

Painter, Lawrence M.

Pattterson, Lincoln

Patton, Basil H.

Paxton, Alvah

Paxton, Noah Carter—21—July 26, 1917—749—Jordan Mines

Paxton, William M.

Persinger, Earl

Phillips, Raymond V.

Proffit, Melvin B.

Quater, Joseph W.

Reynolds, Charles E.

Reynolds, Lewis Franklin—30—July 7, 1917—759—Jordan Mines

Richter, Simpson J.—sgt.

Rickett, Harry H.

Richmond, Frederick S.

Rush, Russell

Rutherford, Emory P.

Samdle, Ralph L.—20

Sartain, Dessie C.—18

Scott, Clarence L.

Scott, Henry L.

Scott, Hubert—18

Seldomridge, Archibald D.

Seldomridge, Charles L.

Shackford, Samuel Bunham—27 June 24, 1917—562

Shellhass, Welford D.

Sizer, Harry C.

Stinespring, William P.

Stone, Hollie D.

Sweet, Graham C.

Terry, Joseph F.—1st sgt.

Thompson, Frank J.

Traft, Nevin

Tucker, Robert W.

Tyree, Berlin A.—corporal

Tyree, Lonnie E.

Vandevander, Lechard A.

Vess, Malcolm H.—24

Vess, Rex.

Via, Bulah W.

Webb, Harry E.

Wheeler, Mallon C.

Whitlock, Benjamin Jeater—27—July 17, 1917—1524—CF.

Winchester, Baxter L.

Withrow, Carl W.

Wood, Ora

Worsham, John D.

Worsham, William E.—24—July 29, 1917—662

APPENDIX

PARAGRAPHS FROM THE WEST

IN THE VALLEY OF VIRGINIA and the Alleghany Belt, the pioneer settlers were not the same kind of people as those of the section of the state lying east of the Blue Ridge. It is true that the assimilating influence that began at once to penetrate the transmontane country has in our time measurably succeeded in moulding to the "Tuckahoe" pattern the Valley region as far as North Mountain. But on the other hand, the Valley people began at once to move on to the Great West. They began the settlement of Kentucky only forty-three years after the settlement of Augusta. The Augusta people and the early settlers of the West were of the same stock; a stock that was very largely Scotch-Irish.

Until 1850, the social and economic history of Kentucky, and the older communities in the states to the north and west, was much the same as that of the Alleghany valleys. Herein lies the explanation of what would otherwise be a curious fact. Very much of the history of the old Augusta is to be found in the West rather than in Virginia. In that section the local historian has been more alert than in the East. He has rescued from oblivion many of the reminiscences, traditions, and documents that were carried West by the early settlers, who, as a rule, stood high in intelligence and enterprise.

The author of this book has received from Boutwell Dunlap, the historian, valuable transalleghany and local biographical and genealogical notes on sixty prominent families, and data on early Indian history. From out of this material he has written the sketches that appear in this article.

Some of the paragraphs may seem to have little or no bearing on the Alleghany area, yet the basins of the upper James and the upper South Branch of the Potomac constitute a region by itself, and the county lines crossing from east to west are not natural boundaries. Mr. Dunlap found it best to treat this great valley as a geographic unit. He has made prodigious researches in all the territory from the Blue Ridge to the Pacific, and in this broad field he is a recognized authority. A statement is never given out by him until all doubt in the matter has been settled.

*   *   *   *   *   *   *   *   *

FAMILY AND BIOGRAPHIC SKETCHES

Thomas Adams was born in New Kent county, 1730, spent several years in England prior to the Revolution, was clerk of Henrico county, member of the House of Burgesses, chairman of the New Kent Committee of 1774, delegate to the Continental Congress, 1778-80, and in 1774 signed the "Articles of Association." He finally settled on the Calfpasture, buying land from John Carlisle as early as 1766. In 1783-86 he was senator from Augusta, Rockbridge, Rockingham, and Shenandoah. Mr. Adams died without issue in 1788.

Robert Armstrong of Jackson's River was a brother to Archibald of the Calfpasture. Near relatives were John and Lanty (Lancelot) of Botetourt. Major Lanty Armstrong, hero of Slaughter's Kentucky regiment in the battle of New Orleans, 1815, was of the Botetourt branch. The wife of Robert was Betsy, daughter of John Graham of the Calfpasture. His children were Elizabeth, Thomas, Archibald, Robert, and Margaret. The first husband of Elizabeth was Thomas Mann, the second was James Steele. The wife of Thomas was Isabella Armstrong, his first cousin. Archibald marrried Nancy Scott, and the Rogers and Keeney families of Greenbrier are his descendants. Margaret married Joel Walker, a land surveyor, and went to Ohio in 1803. Her daughter Margaret A. married Adley Gregory, pioneer settler of Des Moines, Iowa. Two daughters of Mrs. Gregory, Ann W. and Emma G., married, respectively, Major General J. A. Williamson of the Union army and Congressman J. A. T. Hull. A daughter of Mrs. Williamson married Rear Admiral Warner B. Bayley. J. A., son of Congressman Hall, is Judge Advocate General of the National Army. Thomas Armstrong Walker, son of Joel, was colonel of Iowa territorial troops and register of the United States land office of Iowa.

The children of Archibald, who owned land on Jackson's River as well as the Calfpasture, and who gave his name to Archie's Peak were these: Robert, Ann, Thomas, Isabella, Jane, and William. Ann married Captain James Elliott, Isabella married Thomas Armstrong, Jane married Samuel McCray, William, born 1759, married Peggy Jameson, and his son Archibald, who married Elizabeth McCutchen, was the father of A. T. Armstrong, a notable horticulturist of Orange county, California.

James Henry Banks, a colored man from Alleghany, has been forty-seven years on the payroll of Harvard University. He is there known as General Banks and is a table waiter. He receives $44 a month and his meals.

George, the first Benson in Highland, married a Hamilton.

William and Alexander Black of the Cowpasture just above the Bath line were the sons of an immigrant who was born at sea. William went to Clarke county, Ky., in 1792. Alexander and many families from Bath settled near Pisgah church in Woodford county of the same state. The rest of the family remained on the Cowpasture. Major Black, a son of William, born July 5, 1775, made the following statement to John D. Shane:

"Thomas Feamster, who had a son named John, had a fort, just below my father's in Virginia, down on the Cowpasture. Some of the picketing stood there yet, when I left that country. One morning I heard my father say he went out to get his horses, and fell in with some Indians. It was then peace with the whites. They were going his direction, and he kept along with them. As they went, some wild turkeys called 'tuck.' He said the Indians were all down in the grass in an instant, as if shot. He told them it was nothing but turkeys, and started his dog in and chased them up. When he had done so, they got up and went along. There was a high knob on the Cowpasture, from which you could see up and down a long ways. I had a crab orchard on it. Here a party of Indians lay two or three days, watching. At length they saw the smoke of some Indian fires in a bottom some distance off, and told a man that lived in a cabin on a rise near by if he wanted to see them surprise the others, he might get up a little before day, and just as day was breaking, watch, but not to come too near. At about daybreak an Indian was rising and one shot killed him; and as the rest sprang up, they all fired and nearly all were killed. The Indians had come to the man and asked him if there was not a camp there. He said there was. He (Indian) then told him if he would get up he would see some fun, but not to come too nigh. This knob was not far from Windy Cove meeting house below Shaw's—on the right going down, on the left coming up to my father's. Francisco, McRoberts, and Shaw lived higher up the Cowpasture above Windy Cove. H. Rafferty (Laverty) lived near the meeting house. My father lived say eight (?) miles from the meeting house, still above Francisco's. John Montgomery, Thomas Feamster that had the station, and then came the McRory's (Mc-Creery), John and Robert. There was a meeting house on John's land, about two and a half miles down the Cowpasture, that we used to go to. James, a son of Robert, and William Potts' oldest son, lived up here in Montgomery's—William some time—. They both moved away and their wives with them. This same John McRory, where the meeting house was, had his house plundered and burned by the Indians. My father was in that country then, and nearly the first that came there. Ewings, Grays, Hodges, Brattons, and Mateers lived on the Calfpasture. About 1790 my uncle moved his cattle out (to Kentucky), and my father came with him to help him, and brought out some of his own. I think uncle Evans was one that was along at that time." (Major Black goes on to describe a fight on the Wilderness Road.)

Of the two children of the Brown in charge of the Carpenter stockade, one returned and became Colonel Samuel Brown of Greenbrier. The other took an Indian wife, remained with the red people, and was conspicuous in Michigan, where he founded Brownstown. He served in the war of 1812.

Major John Brown, born 1743, married Mary Donally, commanded a company in the Yorktown campaign, and was taken prisoner at Green Spring. He lived in Bath on the Cowpasture, and was sheriff, justice, and representative. His children were Charles (died young), Joseph, Margaret, John, and Rosannah. Joseph, born 1780, married Nancy Smith; Margaret, born 1784, married Joseph Wallace; John, born 1787, married Adelaide Kyle. Rosannah married Gerard Morgan.

Cuthbert Bullitt was living in Alleghany on Jackson's River in 1783. Colonel Thomas Bullitt distinguished himself in the campaigns against Fort Duquesne in 1754 and 1755. In 1764 he joined Andrew and Thomas Lewis in acquiring ownership of Hot Springs, and lived there a while. In 1773 he took up the land where the capital of West Virginia now stands, but sold it to a brother who was president of the Court of Appeals of Virginia. From him it was purchased in 1785 by Charles Clendenin, then in Richmond as a commissioner to construct the first Lewisburg and New River wagon road. Cuthbert, Jr., a son of Thomas, was a judge in Maryland, and Alexander Scott Bullitt, another son, was a state senator in Kentucky and lieutenant governor. While at the Kanawha, Colonel Bullitt visited Kentucky and surveyed the site of Louisville, his companions surveying the site of Frankfort.

Daniel Capito, a merchant of Franklin about 1828, was of a family from the province of Lorraine in France.

Joseph Carpenter, Sr., had a brother Solomon. They were of English descent. John and Joseph, and their sister, who married Jeremiah Seeley, were children of Joseph, Sr. Children of Solomon were Jeremiah, Thomas, and Benjamin. Jeremiah, a doctor, born in 1755, was captured by Indians, exchanged, married on Jackson's River, and was the first white settler of what is now Braxton county. His brothers were killed by Indians on Elk River. The Carpenter stockade was on Solomon's land. Samuel Carpenter* was in the Virginia Assembly. Samuel, Jr., represented Craig and Alleghany, 1875-77.

John Craven was born in Ireland in 1735 and died in Rockingham about 1777. He married Margaret, the widow of William Dyer. In company with other people of the South Fork, at the time of the Indian raid in 1758, she fled to a fort on Beaver Creek, and afterward to one where the town of Dayton now stands. John Craven had several children, one of whom was Joseph, born 1769. In 1830-33 he represented Rockingham and Pendleton in the Virginia Senate. His wife was Polly, daughter of John and Sallie (Raybourn) Nichols, and his two sons lived some time in Franklin, W. Va. One of these was John, a physician and surgeon of Pendleton in 1827-37, and later a surgeon in the Confederate army. He married Ruhannah Chapline and moved to Cravensville, Davis county, Mo. A son of his, born in Pendleton, was Judge Robert O. Craven, an early pioneer of Placer county, Cal. He became state librarian, and much of the fine collection of Americana in the large state library of California is attributed to his good judgment.

Another son of Joseph Craven was James H., who practiced law at Franklin from 1823 to 1829, where he married Sophia Capito in 1824, the marriage being an elopement. He became a prominent lawyer and

---

*See chapter XIX for the years of service.

politician of Indiana, being a representative in 1831-3, state senator, 1839-40, and as a presidential elector helped to make General W. H. Harrison president in 1840. He was in Congress, 1841-43, but was defeated as a Free Soil candidate for governor of Indiana. He was again a state representative, and in 1863 was lieutenant-colonel of the 83d Indiana Volunteers.

Dr. James W. Craven, son of James H., born in Franklin, 1827, served in the war with Mexico, and was a surgeon in the 6th Indiana Cavalry in the war of 1861. Major James O., another son, was three terms prosecuting attorney of Ripley county, Ind., but on account of the large Democratic majority in his district was three times defeated for Congress. However, he was presidential elector in 1888, collector of internal revenue for the sixth district, and in the civil war was on the staff of General Milroy. Still another son was John K. Craven, an eminent lawyer of Kansas City, Mo.

Four descendants of John Craven, all bearing his surname, have been members of the National House of Representatives.

Captain Robert Crockett, first of the name in the Pastures, is said to have been born in 1707. It is further said that he was a brother to John, an ancestor of Crocketts of southwest Virginia. The survey that Robert took up at the mouth of Falling Spring Run was patented by his son Samuel. John, another son, married Margaret McClanahan, and moved to Mecklenburg county, North Carolina. If it be true that a John Crockett and Margaret McClanahan were the grandparents of Davy Crockett of Texas, as the descendants of the latter assert, then the above mentioned Robert was his great grandfather. Andrew Crockett of Sullivan county, Tennessee, sold his interest in the Crocket land on the Calfpasture in Rockbridge, in 1791. Robert Crockett, a pioneer of Montgomery county, Kentucky, was a grandson of the above Captain Robert, and probably the Carlyles of Woodford county, Kentucky, are among his descendants.

John Crow, first colonel of the Alleghany militia, married Amanda F., daughter of Richard Shanklin, and had eleven children. James, Edward, William, Beale, John, and Charles went to Texas. Catharine and Elizabeth died single in Alleghany. Amanda went to Denver, and Fannie married George W. Hutchinson, clerk of Monroe county. John appears to be a descendant of Captain William Crow, a merchant and tavern keeper of Staunton, who married Margaret, only daughter of Colonel John Lewis.

William Cunningham came to the South Branch about 1750. His sons were Robert, John, and William, the last being known as "Irish Billy."

The children of John were John, William, Robert, Isaac, Mary (married William Grimes of Kentucky), Jemima (married William Shok), and Elizabeth (married Samuel Scott of Preston county, Ky.) John, Jr., married Rebecca Harness and died in Hardy county. William married

Jemima Harness, and lived near the family homestead. Robert married Polly Robinson, and in 1792 settled near Winchester, Ky. John, a son of this Robert, was a soldier in 1813, and served in both branches of the Kentucky legislature. Other children were Isaac (married Millie Donaldson), Abner (married Pamelia Clarkson), Jesse (married a Wood), Lucinda (single), Jemina (single), Elizabeth (married John T. Carney of Scott county, Ky.), Maria (married Matthew D. Hume of same county), Belinda (married Nimrod Hutchcroft, Bourbon county, Ky.) Capt. Isaac Cunningham married Sarah, twin sister of the Hannah Harness who married Henry Hull. He went to Clark county, Ky., in 1802, served in both houses of the state legislature, and commanded a company in the battle of the Raisin. A grandson was Benjamin F. Van Meter, author of *Genealogies and Sketches of Some Old Families, Who Have Taken Prominent Part in the Development of Virginia and Kentucky.*

"Irish Billy" married Phœbe Scott and lived on the South Branch. His children were William (married Jemima Harness), James (married a Hutton), Hannah, Ann.

William, son of Irish Billy, had these children: William (married Sallie, daughter of Isaac Van Meter of Old Fields), John (married Rebecca Lauck of Winchester), Solomon (married Kitty Seymour), George (married Rebecca Seymour), Hannah (married David Van Meter, son of Isaac), Sadie C. (married Garrett Van Meter, also of Isaac.)

The last William Cunningham had these children: Isaac (married Catharine Harness), Jesse (married Betsy Ann Williams), Lizzie (married Garrett Van Meter of Jacob), Jemima (married J. Hanson McNeill, captain of McNeill's rangers), Rebecca (married Rev. N. Fish), David (married Lizzie Vance), Mary (married Rev. William Champion), Hannah (married A. J. Fisher), Sallie (married R. J. Silden).

John, brother to the last William, was father of William S., who married Sallie Van Meter, and was great grandfather to Mary Johnston, the novelist; Charles L., who married Mary J. Walton; Hannah, who married Andrew Dyer of Pendleton county; Susan, who married George Shultz of Winchester, Va .

Solomon, son of the third William, had George S. (married Jane Ann Harness), Seymour (married Martha McGreer), William H. (single), Garrett, Jane (married Felix B. Welton), Ann J. (married Charles Green), Phœbe (single).

Captain Isaac, who married Catharine Harness, purchased after 1803 the Matthew Patton farm in Kentucky and made it his home.

Joseph and Andrew Damron, delegates* from Alleghany, were of an old family in the east of Virginia.

Colonel Alexander, son of Captain Alexander Dunlap, first settler on the Calfpasture, was born near Goshen in 1743. He built Clover Lick fort on the Greenbrier, but sold it to Major Jacob Warwick, his cousin. His children were James, Ann, William, Mary, Agnes, Sarah, and Alexander. The first, who settled in Ohio, was colonel in the war of 1812, state senator, presidential elector, and Whig candidate for governor. Ann married William Kinkead. William was an anti-slavery leader and father of Dr. William Dunlap, who shares with Dr. Ephraim McDowell the honor of being the first ovariotomist in the modern world. Mary married James Stevenson, clerk of Woodford county, Kentucky. Agnes married Dr. Alexander Campbell, United States senator from Ohio. Sarah married Thomas Dickings, member of the Lake expedition in the war of 1812. Margaret married Samuel T. Scott, D. D., founder of the first Presbyterian church in Indiana and first president of Vincennes University. Colonel Alexander Dunlap sat in the Kentucky legislature.

Robert, son of the pioneer, married Mary Gay and lived at Aspen Grove on the Calfpasture. His children were Ann (born 1765), William, Alexander (born 1768), Margaret (born 1770), Robert (born 1772), John, and Agnes (born 1779). The first married David McKee, founder of Clear Creek Presbyterian Church, Jessamine county, Kentucky. Major William remained on the homestead and married a daughter of Captain Coursey, who came from Orange to the Calfpasture, and whose wife, Winifred Riddle, was a blood relative of William L. Yancey, the secession orator. Alexander was a delegate from Monroe county 1823-27, and was followed as such in 1839 by his son, James A. John H. Vawter, a son-in-law, was also a delegate from Monroe, as was likewise Alexander Dunlap Haynes, a grandson. Margaret married William Dennison for whom a township in Lawrence county, Illinois, is named. Robert, who married Martha Graham, was father of M. D. Dunlap and father-in-law of James Templeton, both ministers of the Presbyterian Church. John married a Hickman from Bath. Agnes married Samuel McCutchen.

James Dunlap, killed at Fort Upper Tract in 1758, bought in 1753, 875 acres on Meadow (now Dunlap) Creek, a few miles from Covington, Va. He commanded a company in the Sandy Creek expedition. December 21, 1779, the Augusta court granted land certificates to James Brown and Adam Guthrie, heirs-at-law and nephews of Captain James, and "the only legal heirs now in this state." This Guthrie seems identical with General Adam Guthrie of Kentucky, who married Hannah Polk, and whose son James was a Secretary of the Treasury of the United States. The administrator of the estate of Captain Dunlap was Captain Robert Bratton, who married Anne (McFarland) Dunlap, widow of Captain Alexander Dunlap, first settler on the Calfpasture and ancestor of a noted Dunlap family. Alexander and James were near relatives.

James W. Bashford, author, bishop, and president of Ohio Wesleyan College; Robert M. Bashford, dean of the Law School of the University of Wisconsin, and secretary of the State Historical Society of Wisconsin; and James Gilmer McMurtry, dean of Colorado College, are all descendants of Ann Dunlap of the Calfpasture and David McKee. She was a daughter of Robert and Mary Gay.

Two descendants of Roger, father of William Dyer, were wives of United States senators. One was Sarah Dyer, wife of Isaac S. Pennybacker of Virginia. The other was Ann Harrison, who married John S. Williams, a colonel in the war with Mexico, where he became known to fame as Cerro Gordo Williams. He was afterward a general in the Confederate army. His wife Ann was a daughter of Patton D. and Ann (Elgin) Harrison, and a granddaughter of Daniel Harrison, whose wife Ann was a daughter of Matthew Patton by his wife Hester, a daughter of Roger Dyer.

There is some ground for thinking Roger Dyer was also a Quaker. His wife's name was Hannah.

As early as 1525 the Estills were a Protestant family of Provence, France. Just after the massacre of 1572, Belthazer d'Estelle fled to Holland. Thence his family went to England and America. In the fall of 1664, three brothers—William, Daniel, and Thomas Estell landed on the Neversink Highlands, New Jersey, and the same day there was born to the wife of William a son, said to be the first white child native to New Jersey. Thomas married a Wallace in 1670. His son John was the father of Wallace Estill, born in New Jersey in 1698. Wallace settled on the Bullpasture about 1746, but in 1773 moved to Indian Creek, Monroe county, W. Va., where he died in 1792. His first wife was childless. By his second, Mary Boude, he had six children—Boude, Benjamin, Rebecca, John, Susannah, and Mary—the last being born on the Bullpasture. The third wife, whom he married in 1748, was Mary Ann, a daughter of John Campbell. This marriage was an elopement, her parents objecting on the ground that he was fifty years of age and with a family, and she but seventeen. By the third wife there were nine more children.

Boude Estill, born May 15, 1733, moved to Indian Creek, and finally to Madison county, Ky. His children were Samuel and Nancy.

Benjamin, born Sept. 20, 1735, was a justice of Botetourt, but moved to the Holston River after the Revolution. Estillville, Russell county, received its name from his son, Judge Benjamin Estill. The wife of Benjamin, Sr., was Kitty Moffett. Another son was John.

Rebecca, born March 15, 1739, married Thomas Hughart. Her one child, Agnes, married the Rev. John Montgomery, of Deerfield, Va., and was the mother of eleven children.

John, born June 5, 1741, was murdered on Indian Creek about 1781. He married Rebecca Christian, and his one child was William.

Susannah, born March 5, 1744, married John McCreery and died in Virginia, leaving two sons and one daughter.

Mary, born January 4, 1747, married James Gwin.

Sarah, born January 4, 1749, married Col. James Henderson and went to Shelbyville, Ky.

James, born November 9, 1750, married Rachel Wright, and had five children. He built a fort in Kentucky about 1779, was a captain, and fell in a battle with the Indians in 1781. A county in Kentucky is named for him.

William, born November 14, 1752, died in infancy.

Samuel, born September 10, 1755, married Jane Teas and had nine children. He located at Estill's Station, Kentucky, and in 1791 was in the Legislature from Madison county.

Wallace, Jr., born March 5, 1758, married Jennie Wright, had eight children, and settled in Franklin county, Tenn. He was a militia officer in the Revolution.

William (2) born June 16, 1760, married Mattie Wright, had three children, and settled at Winchester, Tenn.

Abigail, born November 22, 1762, married James Woods and went to Franklin county, Tenn.

Isaac, born April 8, 1766, was a justice and sheriff of Monroe and a major of its militia. He at length went South, but finally returned, and appears to have died at Lewisburg, W. Va. He married Elizabeth S. Frogg in 1788, and had twelve children. His wife was a granddaughter of Thomas Lewis, surveyor of Augusta. Floyd, the youngest but one of his children, married Susan B. Kincaid, in 1847, and died at Lewisburg in 1876. The children of Floyd Estill are Elizabeth, wife of Thomas W. McClung of Greenbrier; John F., lately of Covington, Va., and Agatha E.

Ruth, born 1768, was twice married.

As may be imagined, there have been numerous descendants of Wallace Estill, and a number of them attained eminence in professional careers. George S. Nixon, United States senator from Nevada, is a descendant of the Estills of Tennessee.

Edward Webster Felt, born in Alleghany, February 7, 1859, is a son of Sylvester Wakefield and Rebecca Jane Felt. He is a judge of the Appellate Court of Indiana, and is widely known as a speaker on moral, religious, and fraternal themes.

The pioneer Frame was of English descent. He settled first on the Cowpasture. His sons James and David settled on Elk River below Sutton, and gave their name to Frametown. The first wife of James was a daughter of Charles Boggs.

Andrew Pendleton Friend, born in Pendleton county, 1785, was a son of Jacob, an immigrant from England. The son married Elizabeth Skidmore, also from England. A relationship is claimed between the Friends and the Lincolns.

Robert Gay, one of the brothers who came to the Calfpasture, owned land in Highland and probably lived there at times. He married Sarah Johnson in 1750. His second wife was another Sarah, the widow of William Jameson. His son Robert was an organizer of Pocahontas, and one of its first justices. John, a son of Robert, Jr., represented that county in the Virginia Legislature between 1838 and 1845. Jennie, a sister to John, married Captain William Cackley, frequently a representative from the same county between 1832 and 1851. The Gays were prominent among the early settlers of Kentucky.

John, one of the brothers in the Pastures, married Jean Ramsay and died about 1776, one of the largest slaveholders of his time in the Valley of Virginia. A daughter of Major John, one of his four children, married James Brown Ray, governor of Indiana. Jean, another of the four, married Humphrey Montgomery, her first cousin, and was the mother of Robert Johnston, Confederate Congressman from Virginia.

After going back to Ireland three times, William Given settled permanently in Bath, a little south of the Highland line, where it crosses Jackson's River. He married Agnes, daughter of Captain Robert Bratton, the maiden name of whose wife was Ann McFarland. Her first husband was Captain Alexander Dunlap. The children of William and Agnes Given were these: Robert (born 1756); Sarah (born 1766); Jennett (born 1770); Mary (born 1771); William (born 1773); Isabel (born 1775); Samuel (born 1776); Adam (born 1778).

Between 1805 and 1816, Robert Given represented Bath in seven sessions of the Legislature of Virginia. His wife was Margaret Elliott, and his children were as follows: 1. Colonel Samuel, twenty-five years sheriff and clerk of Webster county, W. Va.; 2. William, who also lived in Webster, and whose son Adam was many years a presiding elder of the Methodist Episcopal Church in West Virginia; 3. Adam, who lived in Kanawha county, W. Va.; 4. Mary, who married James McAvoy, of Upshur county, W. Va.

Col. Samuel Given married Mary Gibson. Their daughter Catharine married James E. A. Gibbs, eminent as a sewing machine inventor. Their son, Samuel, Jr., was a sheriff of Webster.

Mary (born 1771) married Colonel Isaac Gregory of Nicholas county, W. Va. The Rev. Adam Gregory, their son, was in the West Virginia Legislature. William J. (born 1773) was a sheriff of Nicholas. He married Virginia Frame of Bath. Some of their many children were these: 1. David (born 1793), was a soldier of the war of 1812 who died in Braxton; William (born 1785) lived in Nicholas. The day before the notification of peace was received in 1815, he was at Fort Meigs, Ohio, ready to enter the army. His son Theodore was a Baptist minister. 3. James F. (born 1808) represented Braxton and Lewis in the Legislature of 1853-54, and afterward sat in the West Virginia Legislature. He married Ruth Duffield. His son Henry was in the 36th and 60th Virginia Infantry, C. S. A. Hamilton, another son, served under Stonewall Jackson. 4. Betsy Ann married Jonathan Pierson, and had a son William G., who married Julia Friend. This son was shot to death in his home at Jane Lew, during the civil war. His own sons were Henry H., who died in the Confederate service, and W. F., lieutenant in the Confederate army and a merchant of Lexington, Va., of which town he was a mayor. His son, Dr. James H., of Daytona, Florida, married Eleanor Gates of New York, a niece of Henry M. Flagler, who was a partner of John D. Rockefeller in establishing the Standard Oil Company.

Adam Given (born 1778) represented Bath in the Legislatures of 1825-26 and 1828-29.

Jennet Given (born 1770) married John Berry, delegate from Bath 1801-05 and 1811-12.

There were other Confederate soldiers in the Given connection.

John Graham of the Calfpasture was the father of Lancelot Graham, who in turn was the father-in-law of John Bell, one of the early Methodist ministers of Augusta. Lancelot G. Bell, son of John, was the first Presbyterian minister west of the Mississippi. Beginning in 1836, he established thirty-three Presbyterian churches in Iowa and Illinois. Lancelot Graham was the brother of Jane, wife of Major Andrew Lockridge of Highland.

William, Alexander, and Andrew Hamilton were very early settlers on the Calfpasture. It is not certainly known whether they were related. William is supposed to be the man of that name whose daughters married into the Mann, Byrd, and other families, and whose son Andrew was a wealthy pioneer of Greenbrier.

Two sons of Alexander were Charles, a captain of militia in the Revolution, and James, who married a daughter of Samuel Vance of Back Creek. Among the children of James were Samuel V., member of the Legislature from Bath; Mary, who married Gawin Hamilton; Rachel, who married a Dr. Scott and afterward Colonel W. H. Terrell. Gawin Hamilton was not related to his wife, but was a grandson of Osborn Hamilton of Back Creek.

There are reasons for believing that Andrew Hamilton married Martha Kinkead. His son Andrew was an ensign in the Revolution, joined the Pisgah settlement in Kentucky, and was the ancestor of the wife of the late John S. Wise. John, another son, was killed by Indians. William, a third son, was a major and one of the first settlers of Greenbrier. He was the ancestor of John M. Hamilton, Congressman from West Virginia. Sarah, a daughter of Andrew, was born in 1746, married William Renick, of Greenbrier. Jane, another daughter, married John A., a son of Samuel Hodge of the Calfpasture. Mary, a third daughter, married James, another son of Samuel Hodge. Martha, a fourth daughter, was born in 1755, and married Captain James Wright, of Bourbon county, Ky. Margaret, the youngest daughter, married George Benson of Highland.

The aforesaid Osborne Hamilton was born in Scotland in 1750, and married in Frederick county, Maryland, Mary Davis, a sister to the wife of Colonel William Poague. About 1772 he settled on Back Creek. His children were Johp (born 1788); Gawin (born 1783) died of fever on the Mississippi; Andrew (born 1784) married a Mann; James (born 1786) married first an Erwin of Long Glade in Augusta, and afterward Hannah Bird; Charles (born 1787) married Elizabeth K. Erwin and reared a large family; William (born 1791); Anna (born 1794) married Pressley Moore of Back Creek.

Gawin Hamilton, first clerk of Pendleton county, was not related to the above family. He went to Georgia.

In Augusta were two families of Hamiltons, and in Rockbridge was another.

John Hamilton, born 1713,, was the ancestor of the Hamiltons of Mount Sterling, Ky., who have long been famous for their blooded cattle. He married Mary Stuart. His descendant, Archibald, born 1774, went to Kentucky.

Michael Harness, born January 1, 1700, built a fort in 1744, three and one-half miles above Moorefield. This was just before Isaac Van Meter built his own fort. Michael's daughter Elizabeth was in advance of the wagons while going up the South Branch, and with punk, steel, and tomahawk helped clear the way. She was thus the first white woman to enter this valley. Her father married Elizabeth Jephete (?) and had the following children: 1. Elizabeth (married Philip Y. Yocom; 2. Rebecca (married Michael Sea); 3. Kate (married Andrew Trumbo); John (married Elizabeth Yocom); Adam (wife unknown) who was killed and scalped by Indians; Leonard (married a Hatch), who went to Illinois, and whose daughter was killed and scalped; Jacob, who first married Unice Peeters and later a Roaber; Michael, Jr., who was killed and scalped.

The children of Michael, the oldest son of John, were Jemima, who married William Cunningham; Elizabeth, who married Michael Welton and went to Missouri; Rebecca, who married Henry Hull.

Children of Isaac Haynes were Charles, who married Mary Dickson in Greenbrier, 1781; Benjamin, a soldier in Lee's Legion of 1781, and who died twelve miles below Covington; Joseph, of Jackson's River, who married Barbara Riffe of Greenbrier; Moses, who went to Tennessee; William, born 1763, delegate from Monroe, 1800-01. Colonel Charles Haynes of the Stonewall Brigade was a grandson of Joseph. James M., a son of William, married Isabella Dunlap. Children of his were James, a Confederate chaplain; Alexander Dunlap, in Virginia Legislature, 1855-56; William, state senator in West Virginia and member of constitutional convention. John, probably a relative to Isaac, moved to Kentucky, 1779. His sons were John and James, the latter a preacher, born 1760.

Paul Henkel, a Lutheran minister, was born 1754 in Rowan county, N. C. Catawba Indians caused the family to seek refuge in Virginia, where a new home was found at New Market. He established churches in Shenandoah and Augusta counties, and also in his native county, being one of the founders of the Lutheran synod of North Carolina. He made missionary tours into Kentucky, Tennessee, Ohio, and Indiana. Paul Henkel was an eloquent preacher in both English and German. In 1809 he published in German, *Baptism and the Lord's Supper,* afterward translating it into English. He issued a German hymn book in 1810 and an

English version in 1816, some of the hymns being by himself. He also published a catechism in both languages, and was the author of a satirical poem in German.

Moses Henkel, a brother and also a Lutheran minister, was one of the organizers of Pendleton county. A son, Moses M. Henkel, was born in Pendleton in 1798 and died in Richmond in 1864. He was an itinerant Methodist minister in Ohio in 1819, and a missionary to the Wyandot Indians. His tours extended from Pennsylvania to Alabama. He established a religious magazine, and in 1845 was an editor of the *Christian Advocate* at Nashville. From 1847 to 1855 he conducted the *Southern Ladies Companion*. He taught in Philadelphia, Baltimore, and other cities, and was the author of *Masonic Addresses* (1848), *The Primary Platform of Methodism* (1851), *Analysis of Church Government* (1852), *Life of Bishop Bascom* (1853), *Primitive Episcopacy* (1856).

Eli J. Henkle, a brother to Moses M., was born near Baltimore, Md., in 1828, took an academic course, studied medicine, and taught. In 1863 and in 1871-73 he was elected to the Maryland legislature, and in 1864 was a member of the constitutional convention. In 1872 he was a delegate to the Democratic National Convention. He represented Congress in the Baltimore district, 1875-1881, and died in that city in 1893.

John Hepler of the Calfpasture married a Harness. His son John settled in Alleghany, and a grand nephew is J. N. B. Hepler, a famous orator of the Baptist Church and a college president in Missouri.

Captain Jonathan Hicklin, son of Thomas Hicklin, a captain in the Revolution, married Jane Lockridge, and joined the group of pioneers that went from the Pastures to Woodford county, Ky. Jane was a daughter of Robert Lockridge, who went to Woodford also, and a sister to Sarah, who married John Gay, and to Florence McIlvaine. These Hicklins became the first settlers of Lafayette county, Mo. One of these was Sonora Hicklin, who married William M. Boggs. She was the mother of the first American child born in California after the American occupation, and was in some manner a descendant of John Finley, who piloted Daniel Boone to Kentucky.

W. M. Boggs and the father, Governor L. W. Boggs, of Missouri, wrote much on frontier themes. The governor's second wife was a granddaughter of Daniel Boone.

Secretary Herbert Hoover is a descendant of the Hoovers and Younts who went from Virginia to North Carolina. It is believed these Hoovers are connected with those of Pendleton and Rockingham. A brother to the Secretary of Commerce is investigating the matter.

A large genealogy of the Hopkins, a Rockingham family, has been published.

James Hughart of the Cowpasture married Agnes Jordan. His children were James, Thomas, William, Jane, and Nancy. James was one of the original settlers in Williamsburg district in Greenbrier, and descendants are still in that county and Pocahontas. William's descendants are in Kentucky and the West. Thomas, born 1762, married Rebecca Estill, and Agnes, his only daughter, married the Rev. John Montgomery of Washington College. Thomas was a colonel in the Revolution and a justice and sheriff of Augusta.

Jesse Hughes was a famous scout and Indian fighter. It is not positively known where he was born, but in his biography and by a family connection, it is positively stated that he was born on Jackson's River in Alleghany, 1750. Thomas, his father, was killed by Indians on Hacker's Creek, 1778. It is thought that the wife of Thomas was a Baker. Other children of Thomas were Ellis, Thomas, Jr., and Sudna (Sidney?). Ellis was one of the first two settlers of Licking county, Ohio. Thomas was also an Indian fighter. The sister married Colonel William Lowther, delegate from Harrison county, 1788, and "defender and protector of Northwestern Virginia."

In 1750, Peter Thomas Hohl married Susannah Fieffenback in Lancaster county, Pa. She was the mother of his fourteen children, there being none by his first marriage. During the Revolution he changed his surname to Hull. He moved to the Calfpasture, and about 1763 to the Crabbottom.

Peter Hull, Jr., who married Barbara Keith, was a captain in the Revolution and sat in the State Legislature. Other children of the pioneer were Adam, who married Esther Keister and had about ten children; William; George, who went to Greenbrier; David; John. When Hull died in 1776, Peter, Jr., was administrator. Another son called himself Peter Hull, married a Linkenfelter, and lived in Rockbridge. This other Peter had a son John, who settled in Highland county, Ohio, in 1811. A son of this John was Dr. Albert Y. Hull, prominent in Iowa as an editor and abolitionist. While a member of the state legislature, he was the chief instrumentality in moving the capitol to Des Moines, where he and his father owned some land. J. A. T. Hull, a son of Dr. Hull, was a Congressman from Iowa, and for nearly twenty years was chairman of the committee on Military affairs. Colonel John A. Hull, son of this Congressman, received the distinguished service medal in the World War for his work in the judge advocate's department.

Henry, son of the second Peter, was born February 6, 1780, purchased the Matthew Patton farm in Pendleton, and married Hannah Harness. His children were these: William (born 1803) married Irene Scott; John H. (born 1804) married Sally Lackey; Joseph (born 1806), single; Sarah C. (born 1808) married Jacob Palzell; Laban (born 1810) married Martha Tucker and went to Missouri; Eliza A. (born 1811), single; Jemima C. (born 1813), single; Rebecca A. (born 1816), single; Edwin

H. (born 1817), single; Jesse C. (born 1819) married Mahala Grace; Frances H. (born 1821) married Isaac C. Van Meter of Kentucky, member of state legislature.

Peter (son of Henry?) married Eliza Levy and settled in Woodford county, Ky. The following appear to be his children: Sarah (married Capt. Isaac Cunningham of Clark county, Ky.), George (married Rebecca Casey), Joseph (married Rebecca Williams and went to Ohio), Adam (married Elizabeth Baker), Solomon (married Catharine Taps), John (married Hannah Inskeep and moved to Maryland).

Captain William Jameson of the Calfpasture, justice and coroner of Augusta, owned land on Jackson's River in Alleghany. He died about 1753. His sons were George, William, John, and Andrew. George lived in Rockbridge. John, an ensign in the French and Indian war, inherited the farm on Jackson's River and sold it to Archibald Armstrong. William, Jr., who married Rachel McCreery, had these children: John, William, Robert, Margaret, and Phœbe. The first married Martha McClure, and his only daughter, Rachel, married James Dunlap of Mills county, Iowa. William married Mary McKnight and lived in St. Louis county, Missouri. Robert married Margaret McCutchen and settled in Franklin county, Ohio. Margaret married William Armstrong, and Phœbe married Archibald Elliott.

Captain William Kinkead of the Calfpasture married Eleanor Gay, served in the Revolution, and went to Woodford county, Ky. W. B. Kinkead, a grandson, was a leader of the Kentucky bar, and the father of Eleanor T., a novelist, and Elizabeth S., a state historian. A descendant of both William Kinkead and Andrew Hamilton of the Calfpasture is Jennings C. Wise, soldier, author, and lawyer of distinction. David Kinkead went early to Kentucky, returned to the Calfpasture, but in 1784 settled in the Blue Grass state in Jessamine county with Robert Given and his father. He was finally the companion of Daniel Boone, when that pioneer went to Missouri.

Nash Legrand, delegate from Alleghany 1823-24, seems to be identical with an eloquent Presbyterian preacher of Huguenot descent.

Colonel Lockridge, by birth a Kentuckian, figured very prominently in Walker's filibustering expedition to Nicaragua. He recruited some of his men in Texas. Colonel James T. Lockridge, a descendant of Major Andrew, represented Pocahontas in the legislatures of 1859-63.

John McClenahan, merchant, married Agnes McChubit in Scotland, and moved to Ireland. Two of his children were Robert, a pioneer of Augusta, and Elijah, a pioneer of Bath. Elijah married Ann Owen. His children were Margaret, who married John, a son of Robert Crockett of the Calfpasture and went to North Carolina; William, who married Sarah Neeley; Nancy; Thomas, who lived in Augusta; Polly, who married Captain Robert McCreery; Hannah, who married John Green. William appears to be the ancestor of the McClenahans of Botetourt.

Alexander, William, and Robert McClintic, who settled on Jackson's River, 1774, were three of six brothers, and came from near the famous Derry church in Dauphin county, Pennsylvania. William, wounded at Guilford, marrried Alice Mann, and had two children, William and Moses. The former, born 1783, represented Bath in the legislature, 1824-25, 1827-28, 1835-36, 1839. Moses was the father of Archibald, delegate from Alleghany, Bath, and Highland in the '80's. Robert married Jane Mann and settled in Greenbrier. Alexander, of Shanklin, married Sarah Mann and had eleven children, one of whom was William, who married Nancy Shanklin and was a sheriff of Bath. G. W. McClintic, judge of the Federal court of the southern district of West Virginia, is at present the most prominent of the McClintics.

John, son of James McCreery of Ireland, lived a while in Maryland before settling in Bath. His children were Robert, John, Rachel, William, Jane, and perhaps others.

Robert, born 1740, was a captain of militia in the Revolution. He married Polly McClenahan and moved to Kentucky about 1794. His son James, born on the Cowpasture, was the grandfather of James M. McCreary, United States senator from Kentucky and twice governor of that state. Thomas C. McCreery, another United States senator from Kentucky, was also a descendant of Robert.

John, second son of the pioneer, married Martha Feamster and also moved to Kentucky. During the Revolution he was a justice of Augusta and a lieutenant-colonel of militia.

Rachel married William, son of Captain William Jameson, first settler on the site of Goshen. Their son William married Margaret McKnight and lived near St. Louis, Mo. John McKnight Jameson, son of the third William, was born in 1802. He settled in and named Shenandoah Valley in Amador county, California. His daughter Mary married John A. Eagon, a native of Staunton, Virginia, and eminent lawyer of California. He was a member of the California senate and of its constitutional convention. Rachel McCreary McKnight, another daughter, married Tyrie T. Wright, born on the Calfpasture in 1808, and a member of John C. Fremont's famous expedition of 1843. This Wright became a capitalist of Sacramento. J. A. Wright, a brother, settled in St. Louis, Missouri, and became the largest carriage manufacturer in the world. Virginia, a sister, married Colonel John Knapp, owner before the civil war of the *St. Louis Republic,* the oldest newspaper west of the Mississippi.

William, third son of the pioneer, was an ensign in the Revolution.

Jane married Colonel Andrew Donnelly, who built a fort in Greenbrier in 1771. He was a sheriff of that county and three times represented it in the legislature. He moved to Kanawha, of which county he was one of the founders. The late John E. Kenna, United States senator from West Virginia, was a descendant.

Robert McCutchen, one of five brothers who came to Augusta, settled on the Little Calfpasture. He married Margaret Callison. His children were John, Joseph, Jones, Robert, James, Margaret, Samuel, Hannah, Mary, and William. Margaret married David Moore, and Hannah married Joseph Henderson. James went to Tennessee. Robert married Mary McKnight and went to Franklin county, Ohio.

John, born 1750, married Elizabeth Hodge. One of his children was Samuel, also an elder in the Lebanon church. He married Agnes (Nancy) Dunlap, and was the father of John Seabrook McCutchen, minister of the Presbyterian Church in North Carolina. A grandson of John was John McCutchen Travis, D. D., who Presbyterianized a large section of Missouri. Eleanor, a daughter of John, married John McClung of Bath, descendants of whom are now living in Bath and Highland. James, another son of John, was born 1795, and married Ellen Benson of Highland. They were the parents of Colonel J. S. K. McCutchen, member of the Virginia Legislature from Gilmer, Wirt, and Calhoun, and at one time in command of all the Confederate troops in West Virginia.

Jones, son of the pioneer Robert, was born 1774 and lived in Fayette and Nicholas counties, W. Va. He married Rosina Rogers. These were the parents of John R. McCutchen, member of the first constitutional convention of West Virginia, and of Granville McCutchen, a Confederate chaplain of the Methodist Church. A son of John R. was the Rev. John L. McCutchen, president of Broaddus College, W. Va. Dr. Roger P. McCutchen, son of John L., is the head of the English department in Denison University.

Hugh McGary, a native of Ireland, was in Pendleton in 1758, dealing in military supplies. He went to North Carolina, and then to Kentucky, where he was a famous pioneer. He became a major, and it is said his impetuosity caused the loss of the battle of Blue Licks.

William Mann, born 1713 (1731?), married Jane Hamilton 1750 (1760?). The chest he brought from Ireland was in Covington a few years ago. His children were Moses, Alice, Jane, Sarah, Thomas, William, and John.

Major Moses Mann, born 1761, was married first to Jane Kinkead and later to Sarah Lewis. Mary, a daughter by the first wife, married Anthony Bowen of Greenbrier. William, born 1784, was a sheriff of Alleghany. Moses Hamilton Mann,* a second son, born 1787, represented Alleghany in the House of Delegates, also Lewis T.,* a son by the second wife.

Alice, born 1762, married William McClintic, who died 1786. She afterward married William Hunter Cavendish, an Englishman, who was the first clerk of Greenbrier and later the first clerk of Kanawha. He was a delegate from Greenbrier almost continuously from 1790 to 1804. A son was Andrew, a lawyer of Fayette county. A great grandson is R. M. Cavendish, a lawyer of Sutton, W. Va.

Jane, born 1776, married Robert McClintic of Greenbrier.

Sarah, born 1769, married Alexander McClintic of Jackson's River.

Thomas, born 1771, was killed by Indians at Point Pleasant, 1794. He married Elizabeth Armstrong and was the great grandfather of Isaac T. Mann, multimillionaire banker of New York, whose daughter Alice was recently sponsor for the battleship *West Virginia.* The second husband of Elizabeth was James Steele, ancestor of the Steeles of Monroe, W. Va.

William, born 1773, was wounded at Point Pleasant and died on his way home, 1794.

John, born 1775, married Jennie Johnson, also of Monroe county.

Andrew W. Mann, a member of the West Virginia constitutional convention of 1863, sat in the first legislature of that state.

Charles Cary Waddell and his sister, Nancy Mann Waddell (now Mrs. Wilson Woodrow) are novelists and are descendants of an Augusta Mann who went to the Elkhorn River of Kentucky, and was very probably related to the Manns of Alleghany.

Richard Morris of Jackson's River is thought to have been related to Robert Morris of Philadelphia fame. His children married Armstrongs and Elliotts, and moved to Champaign county, Ohio, and Roane county Tennessee.

Andrew Muldrow died about 1758, and his widow Jane moved from near Nimrod Hall to the mouth of the Cowpasture. Their sons were Hugh and John. It may be significant that a member of the Kentucky legislature in 1822 was Andrew Muldrow of Woodford county.

John Oliver, a man of education, was a delegate from Bath, 1792-93, and state senator, 1794-96, from the district comprising Augusta, Bath, Pendleton, Rockbridge, Rockingham, and Shenandoah.

Robert Poage, the first colonel of the Pendleton militia and one of the first justices of that county, was a son of John who lived near Staunton.

John Howe Peyton, a lawyer of Staunton and state senator in 1839-45, owned farms in Alleghany and often visited them. A mass of letters, written between 1740 and 1860 and stored on one of these estates, was burned by Federal soldiers. John Lewis Peyton, a son, wrote a history of Augusta county. A daughter married John N. Henderson, an officer of the Confederacy.

Alexander White Pitzer, son of Bernard and Frances L. (White) Pitzer, born in Roanoke county, 1834, is a noted author and professor of theology. For many years he was pastor of the Central Presbyterian Church of Washington, D. C.

John Jacob Roadcap—spelled Rothgap in German—bought land in Shenandoah county, 1749. His grandson Jacob bought in Bath in 1779 and left descendants in Alleghany.

William P., great grandson of Colonel Ambrose Rucker of the Revolution, practiced medicine in Alleghany, 1855-62, entered the Union army, was captured and indicted for treason against Virginia, but escaped from prison, October 18, 1863. In 1871-73 he was prosecuting attorney of Greenbrier. A son is William P., twenty-four years a Congressman from Missouri.

The Sanduskys were Poles and lived a while on the South Branch. Andrew Sadowski, in 1758, was an appraiser of the estate of William Claypole. He was a soldier, and his sons became prominent in the West, giving their name to a city in Ohio.

Joseph Surber came to the Cowpasture 1781, married Margaret, daughter of Captain James Coursey, and had at least ten sons, two of whom went to Indiana, others settling in Alleghany.

Robert Shanklin of Rockingham lived on the Cowpasture in 1782. Henry Watterson, the famous editor of the *Louisville Courier-Journal,* was a descendant. Other Shanklins went to Monroe.

Hugh Paul Taylor, in the 20's, was a lawyer of Covington and assistant engineer on the James River and Kanawha Canal. He attained some note by writing nine articles for the *Fincastle Mirror* on Augusta border history. He is thought to have written the article on the Clendennin massacre that appeared in the *Lewisburg Palladium* of August 7, 1826. Mr. Taylor, who married a Woltz of Botetourt, was an uncle to William Taylor, the famous evangelist and missionary bishop of the Methodist Church. The mother of the lattter was a Hickman from Back Creek, and of Elliott descent.

William H. Terrill, a lawyer, represented Alleghany in the Legislature, 1829-31. William Rufus Terrill, a son by his first wife, a McCausland, was born at Covington, April 21, 1834, became a brigadier general in the Union army, and was killed in the battle of Perryville, 1862. James Barbour Terrill, another son, born at Warm Springs, February 20, 1838, began the practice of law in 1860. He entered the Confederate service, and was in nearly all the great battles in Virginia until killed at Bethesda Church, May 31, 1864. On that very day the Senate of the Confederate States confirmed him as a brigadier general. The second wife of W. R. Terrill was Rachel Hamilton.

George Teter, a native of Germany, settled first in North Carolina. His son George moved to Pendleton, where George, son of the second George, was born, September 9, 1784. Eter, son of the third George, was born in Pendleton, April 13, 1806, and married Margaret (born in Pendleton September 18, 1813), daughter of Johnson and Catharine (Wimer) Phares. They moved to Hamilton county, Indiana. Their son Eter was one of the noted men of Pendleton descent. He was a vice-president of a General Conference of the Methodist (Protestant?) Church.

H. Jacob Trumbo, a native of Alsace, bought land in Rockingham in 1750. His son John, who married Mary Custer, settled in 1774 on the west side of the Monongahela, and later on Peter's Creek, near Pittsburgh, Pa., where descendants are still to be found. Other sons were George (born 1750); Andrew and Jacob, all of whom lived in Pendleton. This Jacob was twice married; first to Elizabeth Lair and second to Mrs. Hannah Cowger. The children by the first wife were John M., Andrew, Mary, and Dorothy. Mary married a Gray. Dorothy married Charles Beggs, captain of a troop of cavalry in the battle of Tippecanoe, member of the first constitutional convention of Indiana, and member of the Indiana Legislature. The children by the second wife were Jacob and Elizabeth, the latter marrying a Custer. Many of these Trumbos are in Lasalle county, Ill.

Andrew Trumbo bought 600 acres on the South Fork in Pendleton in 1771, but went to Kentucky in 1787. His wife was Kate Harness. His children were George (born 1769), Elizabeth (born 1772), Jacob (born 1774), John (born 1776), Andrew (born 1779), Dorothy (born 1781), Adam, and Isaac. Jacob, son of Andrew, married Kathryn Alkyre of the South Branch, and was the father of Andrew (born 1799), a member of Congress from Kentucky in 1845-47; also of John (born 1803), a member of the Kentucky Legislature from Bath county of that state.

Other notable members of the Trumbo family were Colonel "Ike," a celebrated character of San Francisco, and A. C., a leading banker in Oklahoma.

Dawson Wade, who owned land on the Bullpasture and perhaps lived there a while, moved to Greenbrier, and in 1784 to Kentucky. His son James, born December 10, 1770, claimed to be the first white child born in Greenbrier. The Wades of Bath county, Kentucky, are his descendants.

Martin R. M. Wallace of Illinois was a brother to William H. L. Wallace, and like him was a brevet brigadier general in the Union army. These brothers were of the Wallace family that settled on the Cowpasture a little below Williamsville. General W. H. L. Wallace, who was killed in the battle of Shiloh, also served in the war with Mexico. He married a daughter of T. Lyle Dickey, a justice of the Supreme Court of Illinois, and of Augusta county descent.

Sylvester Ward, of Scotch descent, went from Pendleton to Randolph in 1788, and in 1790 was a trustee of the town of Beverly. He was an ensign in the Revolution. His wife was Mary Cunningham. In Randolph and elsewhere are many descendants of his son Jacob, whose son of the same name married Elizabeth, a daughter of James, son of Roger Dyer, the pioneer at Fort Seybert. Sylvester Ward was buried at a brick church near Huttonsville.

The Westfalls lived on the South Branch below the Pendleton line. Jacob and his son George went to Tygert's Valley in Randolph, and each built a fort. According to John D. Shane, these were the first of the ten or twelve forts in that valley.

Thomas and Peter Wright were sons of Adam Wright, of New England. The first died in 1755 without issue. Peter, who married Jane Hughart, had these children: Sarah, Rebecca, Rachel, Martha, Jane, Nancy, Elizabeth, Thomas, James, William, John, Peter, and a daughter whose name is not known. Sarah married Palsor Kimberlin; Rebecca married a Kinkead; Rachel married Captain James Estill; Martha married William Estill and then a Proctor; Jane married Wallace Estill, Jr.; Nancy married Dr. Christopher Clark, who went to Madison county, Kentucky, 1794; Elizabeth married John Sproule; Thomas, a captain in Greenbrier in the Revolution, married Sarah Henderson; James married Martha, a daughter of Major William Hamilton of Greenbrier, and in 1794 went to Bourbon county, Kentucky, where his son, Colonel William, became a member of the legislature; William, who married Rachel Sawyers and went to Missouri, 1818. The unnamed daughter married a Smith. Peter, Jr., was one of the three justices who organized Boone county, Missouri, in 1830. He was a curator of the University of Missouri, and in 1822-26 a member of the State Legislature. J. M. Wright, son of William, was a Baptist minister of Napa county, California, and in 1849 preached the first sermon at Hangtown, which became the county seat of the county in which gold was first found.

William Youell came from Sterling, Scotland, married Elizabeth Nelson, and in 1773 settled on the Calfpasture, where he was an elder of Lebanon Church. His children were these: 1. Christiana (born 1777) married William Lockridge and afterward an Anderson; 2. Margaret (born 1779) married Benjamin Allen, moving to Shelby county, Ky. 1805, and later to Montgomery county, Ind. 3. Eleanor (born 1781) married William Allen of Shelby county, Ky. 4. Nancy (born 1783) married Joseph McCutchen of the Little Calfpasture; 5. John (born 1787) married Agnes (Nancy) McKnight, and moved to Franklin county, Ohio, in 1809; 6. Elizabeth (born 1790) married John McCutchen and moved to Lewis county, Mo. 7. William N. (born 1793); 8. James G. W. (born 1796) married Nancy Dunlap and settled on Kerr's Creek in Rockbridge.

One of the greatest statesmen of Illinois was James C., son of Benjamin and Margaret (Youell) Allen. In the forties he was a prosecuting attorney in Indiana. He was later a member of the Legislature of Illinois. As a Democrat he was elected to Congress from that state in 1852. He presented his credentials to the Thirty-fourth Congress, but on a contest the seat was declared vacant. He was re-elected, and served from December 1, 1856, to March 3, 1857. For the two years beginning March 4, 1857, he was clerk of the National House of Representatives.

A *History of Southern Illinois* by G. W. Smith and sundry newspaper articles are unquestionable authority for the statement that the Southern delegates to the Charleston convention of 1860 being hostile to Stephen A. Douglas, they urged the Illinois delegation to induce Douglas to withdraw. In the hope of keeping the party together, they would then support the nomination for the presidency of James C. Allen, a man of Southern antecedents and of national popularity. But Douglas would not listen to this, and was able to hold his delegates in line.

Allen became the Democratic candidate for governor of Illinois, but was defeated by Richard Yates. In 1861 he declined the command of the 21st Illinois Infantry on the ground that he had no military training, and asked that the place be given to U. S. Grant. For the same reason he declined in 1862 the offer of President Lincoln to put him in command of a brigade. After serving as a circuit judge in 1861-63, he was Congressman-at-large in 1863-65. In 1870 he was a member of the constitutional convention of Illinois, and during the next six years was a circuit and appellate judge. His wife was a Kitchell, of a family that included several lawyers. Had James C. Allen been nominated for the presidency in 1860, it would have prevented the Democratic split in that campaign, and might have made him president instead of Lincoln.

HIGHLAND FORTS IN THE OLD FRENCH WAR

Major Andrew Lewis wrote from Jackson's River, February 26, 1757, directing Captain William Preston to build a fort on the Bullpasture, should Miller and Wilson remove their families. April 4, 1757, Preston reported that a fort was being erected at Wallace Austin's (Estill's) in obedience to the foregoing order. This was Fort George.

Among the papers of Captain Preston are numerous signed receipts, showing that in 1757-58 many Highland men served as soldiers, and also furnished provisions to him at Forts Lewis and George. These receipts mentioned service at these two posts and at George Wilson's.

Names occurring in these papers as soldiers are Black, Bodkin, Bright, Burnside, Carlile, Day, Droddy, Elliott, Estill, Evans, Gilham, Hamilton, Harper, Hicklin, Hodge, Hughart, Jackson, Johnston, Jordan, Kinkead, Knox, Lewis, McKnight, Martin, Matthews, Miller, Montaney (Delamontony), Phagen, Pryor, Scott, Seeley, Smith, Skillern, Stevenson, Tucker, Wilson, and Wright.

Among those furnishing provisions were Thomas Armstrong, Richard Bodkin, Robert Bratton, John Carlile, Thomas Gilham, Andrew Hamilton, Thomas Hough, and John Hicklin, Samuel Hodge, Mrs. Johnson, George Lewis, Andrew Lockridge, John McCreery, John Miller, Loftus

Pullen, Samuel Tencher, John Vance, William Warwick, and William Wilson.

Preston wrote to Lewis, October 29, 1757, asking for instructions and requesting an interview at Captain James Dunlap's, which place was on Lewis's route to Fort Young. He says two children were taken from Dunlap's house.

The Skillern mentioned was George, a colonel and representative from Botetourt in the Revolution.

Captain Preston was the son of John, who owned land on the Calfpasture, and of whose posterity are the Breckenridges, Browns, Howards, and others. He was the father of James P. Preston, a governor of Virginai, and grandfather of William C. Preston, United States senator from South Carolina. Other descendants were the wives of Governor James McDowell, Thomas H. Benton, senator from Missouri, and John C. Fremont, the Pathfinder. The only partners of Preston in real estate matters were Captain Robert Bratton of the Calfpasture, and one of the Lewis brothers. It was this Preston who patented several tracts on Potts Creek.

It is said that among the descendants of John Preston were ten United States senators.

OFFICERS FROM HIGHLAND IN REVOLUTION

Samuel Black—lieutenant under McCreery.
John Cartmill—captain succeeding McCreery.
Henry Fleisher—second lieutenant under McCoy.
David Green (Gwin?)—captain.
David Gwin—captain.
Joseph Gwin—lieutenant.
Charles Hamilton—captain.
Nicholas Harper—first lieutenant under McCoy.
Thomas Hicklin—captain.
James Hicklin—captain.
Jonathan Hicklin—captain.
Jonathan Humphrey—lieutenant in McCreery's old company.
Andrew Lockridge—captain and major.
John McCoy—captain.
John McCreery—lieutenant-colonel.
John Oliver—captain.
John Peoples—captain.
Nicholas Seybert—first lieutenant under McCoy.
Robert Thompson—lieutenant in McCreerys old company.
Samuel Vance—captain and lieutenant-colonel.

FORTS ON THE SOUTH BRANCH

George Trumbo of Bath county, Ky., interviewed by John D. Shane, made the following statement, which is here given without the abbreviations in the original manuscript:

"Was born Sept. 29, 1769, on South Branch of the Potomac. My grandfather, old Michael Harness, was one of the first settlers there. Used to come seventy-five men from old Virginia to guard him every year. Michael Harness fort was about three miles from Moorefield on the South Branch. Buttermilk Station was between the South Fork and South Branch, but in sight of the South Branch and about a mile from the South Fork. This station was the nearest of any to Harness. Lynch's and Stump's forts (were) on the South (fork) about even with Buttermilk Station. Lynch's was straight across, and Stump's about three miles higher up. Wilson's fort was eight or ten miles higher up, on Mill Creek, which emptied into the South Branch above Harness' Station. Wilson's fort was three miles from the mouth of Mill Creek. Blizzard's fort on the South Fork, about thirty-five miles up from its mouth, was taken before I was born. My father, a young man yet, was on guard there. He obtained a furlough to go home, about thirty miles from there, onto the Shenandoah. I think that was only the day before. Had he not gone, he would have been killed, and I never would have been here. The fort was taken, burnt, and evacuated. George Harness was there then. He went from Pennsylvania in early times. His house stood right on the warpath, where they went from about Fort Pitt to kill the Catawbas in the South, often in parties of fifty or sixty, before the war broke out. They complained (that) the whites were killing off their turkey, deer, etc.; that South Branch was once the garden spot of America. Conrad, Michael, and Adam Harness were killed, and John Harness shot (in) the head. On the South Branch, Fort Cumberland, then called Old Town, was down about the mouth of the South Branch. My father, Andrew Trumbo, did fort up once, one week, after I was of any size, but it was all peace in general after I was grown up. At this time I was about four years old. Broke up at the end of the week, and all went home. Called Brake's fort at the time, though never was known among the forts. It was the time of Dunmore's war and they were "jubous." 'Twas said Indians had been seen."

NOTE:—The fort mentioned as Blizzard's fort was the one commonly known as Fort Seybert.

The following, from the *Williamsburg Gazette* of May 5, 1758, is probably the first newspaper mention of the Pendleton area: "The Indians lately took and burnt two forts, where were stationed one of our ranging companies, forty of whom were killed and scalped, and Lieut. Dunlap and nineteen missing."

BLOODED CATTLE

After settling in Kentucky, Matthew Patton and his sons-in-law, James Gay and Daniel Harrison, returned to Highland and Pendleton and took back some pure-bred cattle that had been raised in the lower Shenandoah Valley. These animals became famous in the cattle industry of Kentucky, and in all histories of shorthorn cattle are mentioned as the first pure-bred cattle in that state.

GINSENG

Walker Kelso, of Mount Sterling, Ky., interviewed by John D. Shane, said in part:

"Major John Gay that lived over the North Mountain in the gap where North Fork comes through—ironworks there now (Goshen Pass)—got 1,000 pounds of ginseng, and refined it, and sent it on to China. Before he had finished the quantity as he had determined, he took in one Walkup. When he got to New York, he was afraid to go on to China in person, as he had intended. The captain to whom he committed it (found) it returned him a handsome profit in silks. This about (the year) 1800. Gay afterwards married and removed to Indiana.

This Gay was father-in-law to James B. Ray, a governor of Indiana.

NOTE:—This is the first attempt on record, by a man of this section, to get into the China trade.

LEGISLATORS

Prior to the war of 1861, the most important citizen in any county of Virginia or Kentucky was its representative in the legislature.

The following is the list belonging to Bath, with the years of service:

Baxter, John—1817-19.

Berry, John—1801-5, 1811-12.

Blackburn, Samuel—1799-1801, 1809-11, 1812-13, 1816-17, 1820-21, 1823-26.

Brown, John—1796-98, 1802-1807, 1818-22, 1829-30.

Byrd, Andrew H.—1836-38, 1840-43, 1846-47.

Cackley, William—1819-20.

Cameron, Andrew W.—1831-32, 1844-45.

Dickenson, John U.—1845-46.

Erving, John S.—1812-13.

Given, Adam—1823-26, 1828-29.

Given, Robert—1805-09, 1810-12, 1814-16.

Hamilton, John D.—1847-48.

Hamilton, Samuel—1822-27.

Jordan, John—1816-17.

Hamilton, Samuel—1822-27.

Lewis, John—1813-15.

Lockridge, William—1839—40.

McClintic, ——1824-25, 1827-28, 1835-36, 1839.

Matthews, Sampson—1809-10.

Mayse (Mayes), George—1822-23, 1830-35, 1841-42.

Oliver, John—1792-93.

Poague, George—1793-99.

Sitlington, Thomas—1826-30.

Van Buren, Henry—1843-45.

Vance, Samuel—1792, 1799-1802.

White, John—1794-99.

BATH AND ALLEGHANY COMBINED

Bryan, Cyrus P.—1863-65.
Carpenter, Samuel—1852, 1855-63.
McGuffin, Andrew G.—1853-54.
Sitlington, Thomas—in convention of 1861.

BATH, ALLEGHANY, AND HIGHLAND

Anderson, George K.—in convention of 1902.
Byrd, John T.—1889-90.
Garrett, Harvey L.—1901-02.
Jones, Charles P.—1883-84.
McAllister, William M.—1859-1900.
McClintic, Archibald M.—1885-88.
Revercomb, William H.—1879-80, 1881-82.
Rinehart, ————1895-96.
Withrow, A. F.—1891-94, 1897-98.

BATH AND HIGHLAND

Brown, James—1849-50.
Byrd, Andrew H.—1848-49.
Glendy, R. J.—1865-67.
Hiner, Harmon—1877-78.
Lightner, Paul—1871-75.
McClintic, Alexander H.—1850-51.
McDonald, C. R.—1875-77.
Popham, John R.—1869-71.
Seig, James M.—1875-76.

BATH, HIGHLAND, ROCKBRIDGE, BUENA VISTA

Stephenson, John W.—1910-18.
Sterrett, Samuel W.—1904-08.

HIGHLAND

Bird, John—1857-58.
Byrd, Andrew H.—1853-56.
Fleming, William W.—1859-65.
Hevener, William—1852.
Hull, George W.—in convention of 1861.

HIGHLAND AND PENDLETON

Hiner, Benjamin—1848-50.
Kee, James B.—1850-51.

PENDLETON

Bird, John—1842-44.
Boggs, James—1861-62.
Conrad, Jacob—1792-93, 1795, 1798-99.

Cunningham, John—1818-19.
Davis, John—1804-07, 1808-10.
Davis, Robert—1793, 1796.
Dice, George W.—1847-48.
Dice, John—1821-28.
Dice, R. B.—1862-63.
Dice, Reuben—1828-29.
Dyer, Roger—1806-07.
Fisher, John—1810-11.
Flanagan, Robert P.—1811-13.
Greiner, Jacob—1825-27.
Henkle, Isaac—1807-08.
Henkle, Jesse—1816-18.
Hiner, Benjamin—1844—46.
Hiner, Harmon—1816-17, 1824-26, 1829-33, 1839-40, 1840-42.
Hopkins, John—1815-16, 1817-19, 1822-23.
Hull, Jacob—1799-1803.
Hall, Peter, Sr.—1789-91, 1794-98, 1803-05, 1811-14.
Hull, Peter, Jr.—1807---, 1812-16.
(NOTE:—It is impossible to tell which of the above Hulls was in the sessions of 1811-15. Peter, Sr., died in 1818.)
Johnson, James—1819-21.
Jones, Thomas—1819-24, 1827-29, 1833-35.
Kee, James B.—1852-61.
McCoy, Benjamin—1829-30.
McCoy, Oliver—1794.
McCoy, William—1798-1804; also in constitutional convention of 1829.
McCoy, William, Jr.—1835-39.
Masters, Henry H.—Convention of 1861.
Newman, Anderson M.—1846-47.
Patton, William—1789-92.
Pendleton, Nathaniel—1805-06, 1813-15.
Reed, James—1797-98.
Saunders, E. T.—1863-65.

SENATE

AUGUSTA, ROCKINGHAM, ROCKBRIDGE, SHENANDOAH, PENDLETON

Alexander, St. Clair—1789.
Sampson, Matthews—1790-91.

AUGUSTA, BATH, ROCKINGHAM, ROCKBRIDGE, SHENANDOAH, PENDLETON

Alexander, St. Clair—1792-93.
John, Oliver—1794-98.
Archibald, Stuart—1798-1800.
Andrew Moore—1800-01.

James Allen—1801-06.
Daniel Smith—1806-10.
Chapman Johnson—1810-18.

AUGUSTA, ROCKBRIDGE, PENDLETON

Chapman, Johnson—1818-26.
David W. Patteson—1826-30.

MONROE, GREENBRIER, BATH, NICHOLAS, BOTETOURT

Andrew Hamilton—1818-21.
George Mayse—Hamilton having accepted a Federal office—1821-22.

MONROE, GREENBRIER, NICHOLAS, ALLEGHANY, POCAHONTAS

John Brown, Jr.—1822—26.
Pere B. Wethered—1826-30.

ROCKINGHAM AND PENDLETON

Charles Beale—1830-31.
Joseph Cravens—1831-33.
William McMahon—1833-37.
Anderson Moffett—1838-45.
George E. Deneale—1845-58.
John D. Pennybacker—1859-63.
Samuel A. Coffman—1863-65.

ALLEGHANY, BATH, POCAHONTAS, BOTETOURT

Charles Beale—1830-34.
John T. Anderson—1835-38.

ALLEGHANY, BATH, POCAHONTAS, BOTETOURT, ROANOKE

John T. Anderson—1839-42.
John McCauley—1843—49.

ALLEGHANY, BATH, POCAHONTAS, BOTETOURT, ROANOKE, HIGHLAND

John McCauley—1849-50.
Douglas R. Layne—1850-51.

BATH, HIGHLAND, ROCKBRIDGE

James H. Paxton—1852-58.
James G. Paxton—1859-61.
William Frazier—1861-65.

ALLEGHANY, BATH, HIGHLAND, BOTETOURT

William W. Boyd and Fleming B. Miller—1865-66.

HIGHLAND AND AUGUSTA

Joseph A. Waddell—1869-71.

ROCKBRIDGE, HIGHLAND, BATH

William A. Anderson—1871-73.
John L. Eubank—1874-77.
Joseph H. Sherrard, Jr.—1877-79.

ALLEGHANY, BATH, BOTETOURT, HIGHLAND, ROCKBRIDGE

Joseph H. Sherrard—1879-80.
William A. Glasgow—1881-84.
Charles P. Jones—1884-96.
S. H. Letcher—1897-98.
C. E. McCorkle—Died 1899.
A. Nash Johnson—1899-1900.
George A. Revercomb—1901-04.

ALLEGHANY, BATH, BOTETOURT, CRAIG

George A. Revercomb—1904.

AUGUSTA, HIGHLAND, STAUNTON

Edward Echols—1906-12.
W. H. Landes—1912-15.
C. T. Jordan—1916-18.

CONSTITUTIONAL CONVENTIONS

ALLEGHANY, BATH, BOTETOURT, GREENBRIER, MONROE, NICHOLAS, POCAHONTAS

Andrew Beirne, William Smith, Fleming B. Miller, John Baxter—1829-30.

AUGUSTA, PENDLETON, ROCKBRIDGE

Briscoe G. Baldwin, Chapman Johnson, William McCoy, Samuel McD. Moore—1829-30.

BATH, HIGHLAND, ROCKBRIDGE

William McLaughlin, Joseph Mayse—1867-68.
George K. Anderson—1901-02.
Samuel Estill, in 1791, was in the Kentucky legislature from Madison county.

ADDENDA

The critical reader will notice in this book a minor deficiency here and there. Some of these appear only because certain letters sent out by the author met with no response. The topics in Chapter XVIII could have been more numerous only by more extended field-work, and this was practically out of the question.

Julius, a slave of Henry Massie, was first charged with the murder of John Gillespie (page 44), and though acquitted, he was ordered flogged for stealing. Jenkins was held for further trial, and we do not know the result.

Chapter X lacks specific mention of the churches in Clifton District. The letters written for this purpose were unanswered.

In 1867, George Peabody, a millionaire banker, gave a very large fund for the advancement of education in the South. Out of this came an allotment, the following year, for a two-months school term in Covington. The feeling against the North was then so bitter that only private schools, maintained by local support, were acceptable. In the face of this opposition, Mrs. Emma Dickson, a well-known lady of this region, opened the first term with seven pupils, and taught the school until 1870. She felt that it was an injustice for children who could not pay tuition to be deprived of schooling. She was succeeded by Mary Farmer. In 1874 a Mr. Osborne took charge, moving his fifteen pupils into a room in the courthouse.

Under the free school system which had become a law of the state, the term was extended in 1877 to eight months, and the school was very successfully taught by a Mrs. Sturgiss until 1881. The citizens now rallied to its support and lengthened the term to nine months. During the next three years the building used was in the rear of the present post-office. In 1885, there was erected on the site of the present grammar school, the first public school building in Covington. It was the first two-roomed school in this county. In 1891 the principal and his two assistants had sixty-two pupils.

(Page 93)—Ogle, not Ogley.

(Chapter XIX)—As superintendent of schools, Mr. Chapman was preceded, in order, by R. L. Parrish—Miller (of Craig county).—Rice (died 1880), A. A. McDonald (died 1886), G. B. McCorkle. Mr. Parrish was the first to hold the office under the statute of 1870.

The two interesting articles which follow were contributed by Mr. R. B. Stephenson.

WAS JESSE HUGHES BORN IN ALLEGHANY COUNTY?

The most noted Indian scout of northwestern Virginia was Jesse Hughes, who spent the most of his life near what is now Buckhannon, West Virginia. Mr. L. V. McWhorter in his book entitled *The Border Settlements of Northwestern Virginia* gives a very full biography of this famous scout. Mr. McWhorter discusses the birthplace of Jesse Hughes at length. It is evident that he was not a native of the section in which he lived the major portion of his life, but that he migrated there during his early manhood, probably from the South Branch of the Potomac River, or from Jackson's River.

In discussing the birthplace of Jesse Hughes, Mr. McWhorter says that one of the descendants of Hughes made the statement that Jesse Hughes was born in Alleghany county, Virginia, on Jackson's River *near the Greenbrier county line* on a farm that had a large river bottom, and that the person who made this statement had frequently passed by the place of his birth in going to and from the Jackson's River section. It happens that there is a place in Alleghany county which exactly fits this description, namely the James R. McAllister farm, which is in the northwestern section of Alleghany county on Jackson's River near the Bath county line. This particular farm lies in the bend of the river and is a large body of bottom land. At this place Jackson's River is near to the Greenbrier county line. It is only four or five miles from the river back to the top of the Alleghany mountains. There is a long narrow valley leading from the river at this point back toward the top of the Alleghany mountains and a road leading across this way, which was no doubt used by the early settlers as a thoroughfare in crossing the mountains. This little valley is called Hughes Draft, and it is entirely probable that Mr. McWhorter's informant traveled right down this draft in crossing from Greenbrier county to Jackson's River. For whom this valley was named we do not know, probably for the famous Jesse Hughes.

Mr. John R. Thomas, a Confederate soldier and aged citizen, now deceased, told the writer in 1918 that he once lived for a long time in Hughes Draft, near the Bath-Alleghany county line. He said that many years ago an old lady by the name of Mrs. Fannie Rucker told him that Jesse Hughes once lived in Hughes Draft. This statement was made by Mrs. Rucker to Mr. Thomas when he was a very young man, which was many years ago, as he was seventy-seven years of age when this statement was made in 1918. Mr. Thomas also stated that there were the ruins of an old house in Hughes Draft where Jesse Hughes is supposed to have lived. Many years ago a curious stone pipe was found near this old house, which has since been lost. The place where this house was located was up in the Hughes Draft about two and one-half miles from Jackson's River. Mr. Thomas further stated that Mrs. Rucker told him a great many things about Jesse Hughes which he could no longer recollect, due to his advanced age. Mrs. Rucker died about 1870 at a very old age, probably one hundred years. Her husband was a veteran of one of the early wars, probably the Mexican war. Her maiden name was Donaldson. She stated that a man by the name of Lovejoy lived in Hughes Draft at the same time Hughes lived there. In Mr. McWhorter's book referred to above the statement is made that Jesse Hughes killed two Indians on one occasion in northwestern Virginia, who were the same Indians who had murdered Benjamin Carpenter and his family on Elk River. The Carpenters were friends and acquaintances of Jesse Hughes and they were born and reared in the big bend of Jackson's River, which is just below Covington. When Jesse Hughes killed these two Indians they had in their possession Carpenter's gun and other property which Hughes knew and identified. He was so enraged because of the murder of Carpenter that he flayed and skinned the Indians, and a shot pouch was made out of one of their skins. This is stated by Mr. McWhorter and seems to be an historical fact.

Now it would seem to be very probable that Jesse Hughes and the Carpenters were acquainted before they moved from Alleghany county, as the big bend of Jackson's River where Carpenter was born and raised is only about eight or nine miles from the place where Jesse Hughes is supposed to have been born. All of these circumstances taken together would seem to indicate that Jesse Hughes was born in Alleghany county, as stated by Mr. McWhorter's informant.

HUNTING REMINISCENCES OF ABNER H. SMITH, NOTED BEAR HUNTER OF OGLE'S CREEK

The following is a statement made March 7, 1918, by Abner H. Smith, who lived on Ogle's Creek in Alleghany county, concerning his hunting exploits:

"I was born in McDowell county, West Virginia, about seventy-two years ago. My father was a great hunter. He killed seventy-six deer, seven bear, and two panthers on Cherry River, West Virginia, in one winter when I was a small boy. The first bear I ever killed was when I was a boy hunting with my father. We tracked a bear in the snow into a hole in a rock. My father told me to git after him and bring him out. I went in the cleft of the rock. It was dark and I couldn't see the bear, but I heard him and he passed by me so close that he slobbered on me. I shot him while in the cave, back of the ear and killed him. The bear didn't attempt to hurt me, *but he slobbered on me.*

"Some time after that I was out hunting with my father and we treed several cub bears up a tree. He put me up the tree to fetch them down. I got out on the limb and the cub bear would fight at me and scratch my hands. Finally I got a strap over his head and choked him down and in that way captured two of the cubs. We raised the cubs until they were grown bear and made pets out of them. That fall my father sold them to a man in Tazewell county and got $40 apiece for them.

"The only black fox I ever saw was while hunting with my father in McDowell county. It was smaller than an ordinary fox and could climb a tree like a squirrel.

"I moved away from McDowell county about forty-one years ago to Alleghany county, Virginia, and have lived in Alleghany county ever since. I first lived in Falling Spring Valley near the W. G. Payne farm, but for the past thirty-three years have been living on Ogle's Creek, where I now live.

"Soon after coming to Alleghany county I was hunting out on Oliver's Mountain in the deep snow. After a while I come to a big tree that had a holler at the ground. There was a big bear curled up in the holler of the tree and I killed him too, at close range, and this bear also slobbered on me, I was so close to him.

"While living in the Falling Spring Valley I killed four bear at the same place and time. This was at Bristow's Gap on Warm Springs Mountain near Healing Springs, and was thirty-six years ago.

"I also killed *nine deer in four days* in McGraw's Gap between Falling Spring Valley and Clifton Forge. These nine deer were loaded on the same wagon and hauled to Clifton Forge, where I sold them. There were lots of bear and deer in the Warm Springs Mountain at that time. Whenever I dreampt about shaking hands with a nigger I always killed a bear. The time I killed four bear at once I had dreampt about shaking hands with a nigger and I told my wife I was going to kill a bear. She said I wouldn't—but I killed the old bear and three cubs.

"I never kept any account of the game I killed until I moved to Ogle's Creek. Since I have lived there I have kept a record of deer killed, and during that time I have killed 220 deer. I had killed a great deal of game before that. I had killed a great many bear, as I hunted bear more than anything else. I know I have killed more than sixty bear in my time, although I don't know the exact number. My brother Isaiah Smith was a pretty good hunter. He killed forty-four bear in ten years.

When I was a boy I first hunted with an old flint-lock gun and then afterwards used a rifle with a percussion cap. During recent years—the last twenty-five or thirty years—I used a Winchester .45-90 calibre part of the time.

"I also killed a great number of small game of various kinds of which I never kept any record."

Mr. Smith was a very reliable and truthful man and his statement will be vouched for by any citizen of Alleghany county who knew him. He was the last of the old time hunters and was known by every one as the greatest bear hunter in this section. His tragic death, by his own hand, occurred on March 10, 1918, only three days after the above statement was made.

His record of 220 deer killed in thirty-six years is no doubt the greatest hunting accomplishment of any man of his time in the Alleghany Mountain section.

An anecdote is told of Mr. Smith and a game warden of West Virginia. In the early days hunters paid very little attention to the hunting laws. The season was never closed until within recent years. Mr. Smith's home was far up on Ogle's Creek only a mile or so from the West Virginia line. After the hunting law was enacted in West Virginia he was suspected by one of the game-wardens of hunting out of season. This warden knew Mr. Smith and came over to his home *presumably* to take a hunt and suggested that they go over into West Virginia. Old man Abner readily assented to this hunting trip, but at the same time strongly suspected that the game warden had a warrant for him for hunting out of season and that he was anxious to get him over the state line and then arrest him. Anyway they went on over into a rather wild section where game was plentiful. Upon arriving at the hunting grounds Mr. Smith said to the game warden, "Well, I've come over to hunt with you, but if you intend to arrest me for huntin' I'll just leave you a-layin' right here now." The game-warden knew the old man meant what he said, and he assured him of his intention to *hunt for game,* while the warrant remained unexecuted in his pocket.

"In 1829, a local antiquary, of Covington, a beautiful little village nestling in a high mountain valley near the head of James River, in Alleghany county, Virginia, gathered from the aged pioneers still lingering on the shores of time, the story of the primitive settlement and border wars of the Virginia Valley. Hugh Paul Taylor, for such was his name, was the precursor, in all that region, of the school of historic gleaners, and published in the nearest village paper, *The Fincastle Mirror,* some twenty miles away, a series of articles, over the signature of a "Son of Cornstalk," extending over a period of some forty stirring years, from about 1740 to the close of the Revolutionary War. These articles formed at least the chief authority for several of the earlier chapters of Mr. Withers's work. Mr. Taylor had scarcely molded his materials into shape, and put them into print, when he was called hence at an early age, without having an opportunity to revise and publish the results of his labors under more favorable auspices."—*From a Memoir of Lyman C. Draper, in Thwaites edition of "Chronicles of Border Warfare." Draper visited Covington in 1845.*

ERRATA

(A few trivial errors are not mentioned)

Page 23, line 4 (down): Read "is," not "in."

Page 35, line 7 (down): Read "same," not "fame."

Page 53, line 3 (up): Read "Stack," not "Stuck."

Page 62, line 5 (up): Probably "Karnes," not "Rarus."

Page 64, line 3 (up): "Jackson's," not "Johnson's."

Page 65, line 3 (down): "Granberry," not "Granbury." See also p. 76, line 14, up.

Page 65, line 15 (down): "1922," not "1902."

Page 65, line 5 (up): Read "Payne," after "Gaston."

Page 76, line 3 (down): "Rosedale," not "Rosemont."

Page 77, line 8 (down): "Collins," not "Alleghany."

Page 83, line 17 (down): "Pythias," not "Phythias."

Page 84, line 9 (down): There is also the Jefferson Hotel.

Page 85, line 8 (up): "Slusser," not "Virginia."